DOLLARS & DICTATORS
A GUIDE TO CENTRAL AMERICA

Tom Barry
Beth Wood
Deb Preusch

Zed Press, 57, Caledonian Road, London N1 9DN

Dollars and Dictators was published in the United Kingdom by Zed Press, 57, Caledonian Road, London N1 9DN in 1983. Originally published in the United States of America in 1982 by The Resource Center, P.O. Box 4726, Albuquerque, New Mexico 87196.

Cover cartoon courtesy of Nuez, *Granma*, Havana
Cover design by Jacque Solomons
Printed by The Pitman Press, Bath, U.K.

British Library Cataloguing in Publication Data
Barry Tom,
   Dollars and dictators.
   1. Central America—Economic conditions
   2. Central America—Politics and government
   I. Title   II. Wood, Beth   III. Preusch, Deb
   330.9728'052   HC141

   ISBN 0-86232-167-0
   ISBN 0-86232-168-9 Pbk

CONTENTS

Part One

Part Two

Methodology, Appendix, and Index

Tables

ACKNOWLEDGEMENTS

Dollars and Dictators would not have been possible without reliable sources of current and background information on Central America. Of the many exceptional news sources we utilized, the following are the most outstanding: *Latin America Regional Reports*, published in London; *Central America Report*, published weekly in Guatemala; *Business Latin America*, a weekly report of business conditions in Latin America; and *Mesoamerica*, a monthly report on Central America published in San Jose, Costa Rica. *The Multinational Monitor*, published by the Corporate Accountability Group in Washington, provided excellent reports on the worldwide activities of the transnational corporations. Special mention goes to the North American Congress on Latin America (NACLA) in New York which has been providing accurate, thorough analysis of Latin American issues for 16 years. Other sources of information were the Center for International Policy and the Institute for Policy Studies, both in Washington, the Data Center in Oakland, and the Institute for Food and Development Policy in San Francisco. A little known but excellent source of information on international finance is *The Political Economics of International Bank Lending* by David Gisselquist, published in 1981 by Praeger Publishers. Another useful source was an unpublished paper by Marc Herold, "Finanzkapital in El Salvador, 1900-1980," from the University of New Hampshire. Valuable books used during the research were *Supplying Repression* by Michael Klare and Cynthia Arnson, *Under the Eagle* by Jenny Pearce and published by the Latin American Bureau of London, and *Acumulacion de Capital y Empresas Transnacionales en Centroamerica* by Donald Castillo Rivas.

Of the many people who helped make *Dollars and Dictators* a reality, we first want to thank the people who have given us continued support through the four years the Resource Center has been in existence — Michael Kelley Carol Bernstein Ferry and W.H. Ferry, and especially Kit Tremaine.

We'd like to thank two diligent researchers, Denise Doughtie and Steve Blake, who carefully and cheerfully compiled the never-ending lists of corporations and whose enthusiasm for the project kept us going through the tough spots. We are grateful to Joani Quinn, Jeffry Finer, and Lou Baldwin for insightful critiques of the manuscript. We are indebted to the many people who provided us with information and interviews. And we want to express gratitude to Ginger Griffin for a fine typesetting job and to Carolyn Kinsman who designed the book with creativity and good humor.

We are thankful to Melissa Anderson and Teri Andre for their good-natured approach to living with this project. And for homemade bread, posole, and unwavering support, warm thanks to Joani Quinn and Lyle Fulks. We are also appreciative of the special encouragement we received from Richard Parker, Steve Goldin of the Institute for Regional Education, and our friends in the Coalition for Human Rights in Latin America and *Las Companeras*, two Central American solidarity organizations in Albuquerque.

And, finally, for their persistence and strength, we thank and dedicate this book to the people of Central America.

PART ONE

Chapter One

Overview: Tremors of Change

El Salvador's "greatest advantage lies in the character of the working people, who are industrious, adapt willingly to new methods, and demand lower wages than those prevailing in the developed world. It is said that if you tell Salvadorans to plant rocks and harvest more rocks, they'll do it . . . . "

> — Rand Corporation, from a study
> commissioned by the U.S.
> Department of Commerce, 1981

"If we only had a little land and our freedom, just think what we Salvadorans could do . . . . "

> — Salvadoran *campesino* in a church
> refugee camp in El Salvador, 1981

Central America is a land of banana companies and coffee plantations, *marimba* bands and *pina coladas*, dirt-poor *campesinos* (peasants), affluent oligarchs, and military dictators. The isthmus, which links the two halves of the Americas, has since 1979 also become the land of Green Berets and Huey helicopters. After a popular uprising overturned the Somoza dictatorship in July 1979, the United States focused its attention on this narrow band of nations that stretch across the center of the hemisphere. The popular victory in Nicaragua was a sign that the old order of oligarchies and dictators in Central America was coming to an end. Not only did mounting social upheaval in the region threaten the interests of the region's economic elite, but it also threatened the continued dominance of the United States in Central America. Seeing the guerilla wars intensifying in Guatemala and El Salvador, the U.S. State Department in 1981 reported that Central America was the area of the world that presented "the main challenge to U.S. interests."

4

Land of Unrest

Tremors of change and revolution have been pulsing through Central America for more than 50 years. Augusto Cesar Sandino led a dedicated army of Nicaraguan rebels against the 1927-33 occupation by the U.S. Marines. A 1932 rebellion led by Farabundo Marti against El Salvador's coffee oligarchy was brutally crushed by military dictator Maximiliano Hernandez. A long period of repression set in, challenged only by occasional peasant protests and a couple of political assassinations. It wasn't until two decades later in 1951 that the pillars of traditional Central American society started to totter. A reformist civilian government in Guatemala dared to redistribute the immense idle landholdings of the nation's oligarchy and of the Boston banana company known then as the United Fruit Company. A 1954 military coup, famous for the backing it received from the United States, restored both the economic elite and the banana company to their traditional place of privilege in Guatemala. Shattered democratic reforms and growing repression by the military gave birth to an armed guerilla movement in Guatemala.

In Nicaragua, the Somoza family had ruled the country with an iron hand after the U.S. Marines in 1933 installed the family patriarch, Anastasio Somoza Garcia, as commander-in-chief of the National Guard. In 1962, a group of women and men, seeing little chance for democratic reforms, took to the hills and formed the National Sandinista Liberation Front (FSLN)*. For over 15 years the Sandinistas fought isolated skirmishes with the National Guard, but in 1979 the popular support for the guerillas broadened to include most sectors of society. Knowing that the end was near, the National Guard, the country's wealthy landowners, and Somoza himself all hastily left Nicaragua.

The Sandinista triumph was the harbinger of the possible fate that awaited the military despots and upper classes of Nicaragua's neighbors if something wasn't done to build up their defenses and stamp out all signs of popular opposition. The long-time rumblings of discontent in El Salvador and Guatemala broke out in open warfare in 1980 and the governments responded with new levels of repression. In Honduras, the most conservative elements of the military ousted the reformist officers in power and soon became accomplices with the United States in the increased militarization of the region. At the southern end of the isthmus, the leadership of Panama's National Guard announced its support for U.S. military intervention in Central America. Costa Rica and Belize haven't shared the Central American traditions of oligarchies, dictatorships, and military rule, but U.S. diplomats have intensified the pressure on these two countries to support U.S. foreign policy in the region. By 1982, the narrow strip of nations had become the center of an explosion of social and political forces that is now shaking the foundations of economic and political power in the region. In a last ditch attempt to stabilize Central

*Abbreviations often represent the original Spanish name of the organization or agency.

America, the U.S. government has tried to shore up old institutions and offer guns and dollars to those governments ready to fight the growing "challenge to U.S. interests."

Guns, dollars, and dictators are a combination with a long history in Central America. Anastasio Somoza Garcia, the prototype of Central American dictators, ruled Nicaragua for a quarter century before handing down power to his two sons. As commander-in-chief of the National Guard, "Somoza conferred upon himself the Cross of Valor, the Medal of Distinction, and the Presidential Medal of Merit. He organized various massacres and grand celebrations for which he dressed his soldiers up in sandals and helmets like Romans." In Guatemala, Jorge Ubico, who gained dictatorial power in 1931, considered himself to be another Napoleon. "He surrounded himself with busts and portraits of the Emperor who, he said, had the same profile. He believed in military discipline: he militarized post office employees, schoolchildren, and the symphony orchestra." Maximiliano Hernandez, a vegetarian and theosophist, became El Salvador's dictator in 1931. Hernandez, who ruled until 1944, said he was protected by "invisible legions" who reported all plots to him and were in direct telepathic communication with the president of the United States. "A pendulum clock showed him if food on a dish placed beneath it was poisoned, or showed places on a map where pirate treasures or political enemies were hidden."[1]

The Role of the United States

The United States hasn't been fussy about its Central American dictators as long as they looked out for U.S. interests; and it hasn't hesitated to send Marines to the shores of Central America if those interests were substantially threatened. Undersecretary of State Robert Olds stated the U.S. foreign policy clearly enough in 1927: "We do control the destinies of Central America and we do so for the simple reason that the national interest absolutely dictates such a course . . . Until now Central America has always understood that governments which we recognize and support stay in power, while those we do not recognize and support fail."[2] The United States, doing what was necessary to protect its national interests in Central America, kept quite a few unpopular governments and dictators in power. In the 1960s, the U.S. government started to modify its heavy-handed approach in Central America. President Kennedy proposed the Alliance for Progress in 1961 as a blend of development assistance programs, U.S. foreign investment, and counterinsurgency training for Central American military. The Alliance was Washington's strategy for counteracting the revolutionary tide that was sweeping Latin America.

Calling for the development of the region through industrialization, the U.S. government proceeded to pave a path into Central America for U.S. transnational corporations. U.S. development planners promised that this increased U.S. investment would foster the expansion of social wealth and democracy in Central America. Instead industrialization brought on the establishment of a new bourgeoisie tied to U.S. corporations' branches and affiliates. By the 1970s, little was left of the early reformist hopes of industrial development. An increasingly brutal collection of U.S.-trained military dictatorships were entrusted with the job of keeping the region safe for U.S. investors. In the mid-1970s, U.S. investment in Central America changed from industrial production for the internal market to export-oriented runaway electronics and textile firms that employed cheap Central American labor to assemble capacitors and clothing for external markets. Also introduced into the region in the 1970s was the production of non-traditional agro-export items like flowers, frozen vegetables, processed fish, and beef. Development trends that have shaped the Central American economy originated outside the region, mainly in the corporate boardrooms of the United States, and as a consequence have not contributed to the development of Central America. Rather, the result of U.S. plans to develop Central America has been regional underdevelopment and increased dependency on the United States.

The Economic Predicament

The industrialization and development of Central America has invariably left the large landholdings intact and the oligarchs in power. The estates in Central America cover vast expanses of the most fertile lands with fields of cotton, sugar cane, and coffee trees. In contrast, 40-70% of the rural population in most Central American nations are landless and those who do have land often live on tracts too small to maintain their own families adequately. This skewed land distribution contributes to inequities in income distribution that give three percent of the Central American population 50% of the income.

Mechanized agriculture has contributed to the expansion of agro-export crop production and has forced more and more *campesinos* off their land and into the cities to search for ways to make a living. Urban population has expanded from 34% of the Central American population in 1960 to 41% in 1980. Many new urban residents set up their cardboard shacks on the outskirts of Central American cities. But the big move to the city solves few *campesinos'* problems, since urban-based industry is providing less and less employment. The many Central Americans who have migrated to the cities cannot scrape up a living for themselves and their families.

While unemployment is on the rise, so is the population, which puts more strain on the already weak economic structure of Central America. But population growth doesn't explain the poverty and desperate conditions in the region. In fact, much of Central America is still underpopulated when contrasted with other parts of the world. El Salvador, roughly the size of Massachusetts, is by far the most densely populated area of Central America, with 575 people per square mile, but it is less densely populated than Massachusetts, which has 733 people per square mile. Nicaragua, with 51 people per square mile, is less densely populated than the United States, which has a population density of 64 per square mile.[3]

The U.S. government generally points to the rates of growth in underdeveloped countries as evidence that these countries are indeed developing. But national income figures refer to the total amount of business activity and tell little about the way the income is distributed or if the income actually ends up in the hands of the country's citizens or in the hands of private foreign investors. Even this standard way of gauging economic development by measuring the rate of growth of the Gross Domestic Product (GDP) shows that Central America is confronting a severe economic crisis. As Table 1A indicates, the GDP has been growing more and more slowly since 1961. The United Nations Economic Commission for Latin America says that Central America is facing the most serious economic crisis in 35 years. While economic growth has slowed down, inflation has skyrocketed, mainly due to the increased costs of imports, like machinery and oil, supplied by the transnational corporations. Never before have the Central American nations been hit by such high rates of inflation. Costa Rica, which experienced little or no inflation in the 1960s, faced a 48% inflation rate in 1981. El Salvador, Guatemala, Honduras, and Nicaragua had inflation rates of one to two percent in 1970, but all the countries endured inflation rates of ten percent or more in 1981.[4]

Table 1A. Annual Variations in GDP

	Annual Average 1961-1970	Annual Average 1971-1975	1980	1981
Costa Rica	6.0%	6.1%	1.9%	-3.6%
El Salvador	5.7%	5.5%	-8.7%	-9.5%
Guatemala	5.5%	5.6%	4.0%	1.0%
Honduras	5.2%	2.1%	2.4%	-0.4%
Nicaragua	7.0%	5.6%	10.4%	8.9%
Panama	8.0%	5.0%	5.5%	3.6%

Source: United Nations Economic Commission for Latin America, 1982.

Foreign Investment

Central America has received an ever increasing infusion of foreign investment and capital without an accompanying redistribution of the wealth. The transnational corporations, with their superior control of capital, technology, and marketing, have relegated the nations of Central America to roles of producers of unprocessed commodities and providers of cheap labor. When President Reagan announced his plans in 1982 for increased economic aid to the Central American nations, he noted that the region was a major trading partner and the focus of substantial U.S. investment. "Nearly half of our trade, two-thirds of our imported oil and over half of our imported strategic minerals pass through the Panama Canal or the Gulf of Mexico," said Reagan. "Make no mistake," he declared, "the well-being and security of our neighbors in this region are in our vital interest."[5]

U.S. lobbyists who favor increased aid to Central America generally are the financial and industrial corporations with investment or trade in the region. They say more financial assistance to Central America will make the region a more stable and profitable area for their operations. The flood of economic and military aid to Central America, as illustrated in Tables 1B and 1C, raises the question of just how large U.S. interests are in the seven Central American countries. Three main forms of private economic interest are common to Central America: 1) direct investment, 2) bank loans, and 3) export and import trade. Each of these forms of economic penetration represents a multi-billion dollar interest in the Central American nations. While many U.S. citizens hardly know where these countries are located, the isthmus has not been ignored by U.S. corporations. Over 1,400 businesses in Central America have some U.S. ownership, and 70 of the 100 largest U.S. corporations conduct operations there. The U.S. Department of Commerce, in an

Table 1B. U.S. Economic Aid to Central America

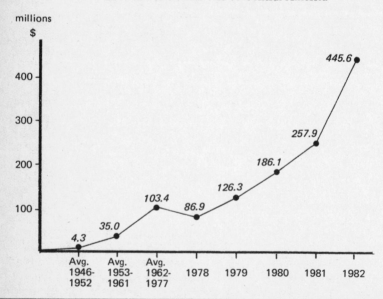

Source: Agency for International Development.

accounting of the direct investments in firms valued at more than $500,000, found that direct investments of U.S. financial and industrial investors in Central America had a book value of $4.2 billion in 1980.[6]

According to the U.S. Department of Commerce, for every dollar that U.S. companies invest in Latin America, an estimated three dollars accrues to the United States in income.[7] In Central America, the rate of return on U.S. investment is higher than Latin America as a whole — one prominent reason why U.S. corporations are so anxious to maintain a stronghold in the region. If the essence of power is money, then U.S. corporations have a great deal of power in Central America. The individual assets of corporations like Exxon, Texaco, IBM, and DuPont all surpass the combined national products of the seven Central American nations. Other corporations like R.J. Reynolds, Dow Chemical, Beatrice Foods, Goodyear, and Philip Morris each have more assets than the national product of any single Central American nation.

Another form of U.S. private economic interest in Central America which has experienced rapid growth over the last ten years is the lending business of U.S. banks. The U.S. transnational banks in 1981 had $3.3 billion in loans outstanding to the private and public sector in Central America.[8] The U.S. banks also pervade the local banking business in Central America, with branches of Citicorp, Bank of America, and Chase Manhattan spread throughout the

Table 1C. U.S. Military Aid to Central America

Sources: Agency for International Development; Department of Defense.

isthmus. Because of all this financial commitment in Central America, the U.S. transnational banks have strongly supported increased U.S. aid to the region and an expanded role for multilateral institutions like the International Monetary Fund (IMF).

The Balance of Trade

The import and export trade is the other main form of U.S. economic interest in Central America. The region represents a $2.6 billion market for U.S. goods, and U.S. suppliers feel that any loss of U.S. influence in the region could mean a trade reduction in this lucrative market.[9] The United States also depends on Central America for $1.1 billion in imports each year. Central America supplies the United States with 69% of its bananas, 15% of its coffee, 14% of its beef, and 17% of its sugar.[10]

The United States has promoted trade and investment as a way to develop Central America. Balance of trade and balance of payments figures show the movement of dollars and trade in and out of the region. These figures also point out the real beneficiaries of international trade and investment. Table 1D shows the state of the balance of trade in Central America (excluding Belize) from 1970 to 1980. Central America had a trade deficit of $369 million in 1970, meaning that it imported goods valued at $369 million more than those it exported. Ten years later, in 1980, the trade deficit expanded over seven times to $2.6 billion.

Table 1D. Total Trade Balance*
(millions $)

	1970	1980	Increase
Costa Rica	- 86	- 565	7x
El Salvador	15	- 256	18x
Guatemala	14	- 78	7x
Honduras	- 42	- 212	5x
Nicaragua	- 19	- 435	23x
Panama	-251	-1106	4x
Central America	*-369*	*-2652*	*7x*

Exports F.O.B. minus imports C.I.F.

Source: United Nations, *Monthly Bulletin of Statistics*

The United States has an especially profitable trade relationship with Central America. In 1981 the United States had a $759 million trade surplus with Central America.[11] The trade balance shows the trade relationship between countries but does not indicate the final destination of trade revenues. Honduras, for example, was the only Central American nation to experience a trade surplus with the United States in 1981, but the U.S. banana companies — not Honduras — received the main benefit of this export trade, and the profits went back to these U.S. fruit companies.

The terms of trade are not set by the underdeveloped nations but by the consuming developed nations and the transnational corporations. The Central American nations depend on the exports of five major products — coffee, bananas, sugar, cotton, and beef — for about 70% of their exports. The United States, which buys the majority of Central American exports, is interested in obtaining these products for the lowest price possible. The result has been that the prices for export commodities from Central America have been rising at a slower rate than the price of goods Central America buys from the United States. Because the region is dependent on its agro-exports, sharp price decreases, like the 20% drop in coffee prices in 1981, have a devastating effect on Central America's economy.[12]

Suffocating Debt

Increasing trade deficits contribute to severe balance of payments problems for Central America. Another factor is the uninhibited flow out of Central America of profits and interest from foreign investment. For many underdeveloped nations, the loss of income from these transfers of profits and interest represents more money than the trade-balance deficit for the entire country. In Costa Rica, for example, the profits and interest payments leaving the country in 1981 were three times higher than the country's trade deficit. In recent years, Central America's external public debt, which is the amount of money that one nation owes the rest of the world, has swelled to unmanageable proportions. This debt has become the modern symbol of the region's increasing dependency on the developed industrial world. In 1960, the external public debt was only 3% of the region's national product, but by 1970 it had risen to eight percent, and by 1980 to 46%. In 1981, the external public debt of Central America totalled almost $11 billion, more than the value of the region's annual exports.[13]

The underdeveloped nations of Central America initially had hoped that loans from multilateral banks like the World Bank, and bilateral sources like the U.S. Agency for International Development (AID), would give them the boost they needed to become part of the developed world. But instead of fostering self-reliance, international financing has fostered greater dependence by encouraging increased imports, mainly from the United States, and by covering the costs of expensive infrastructure projects, like road and dam construction, that are the prerequisites for profitable investment. In the last 20 years, the banking institutions of the developed world, particularly the United States, have pushed financing on the governments of Central America like drug dealers pushing heroin. The result is the region's deep indebtedness and addiction to the continued flow of external financing to cover the servicing costs of old debts.

The Central American governments that contracted all this indebtedness to the developed world represent the interests of the consuming classes who form the economic and military elite of Central America, rather than those of the people as a whole. The international loans provide outside support for unpopular regimes that surely would be shaken without the quick fixes offered by foreign financing and aid. These funds flow to governments willing to open up their economies to international trade and investment and to governments willing to ignore or repress the interests of the poor in order to collect the revenues necessary to keep up their country's debt payments.

The present debt crisis in Central America has been a long time coming, but the region's inability to meet its debt payments and import bills has dramatically worsened in the last few years due to three factors: 1) steep increases in petroleum import bills and other imports from the developed world, 2) sudden decreases in the prices for its commodities, and 3) rising interest rates in the United States. From 1973 to 1980, the cost of petroleum imports to Central America rose sixfold.[14] Recessionary trends in the developed world has meant shrinking markets for Central American commodities and resulted in severe balance of payments problems. The capital necessary to alleviate these problems continually has come from the transnational banks at interest rates that increased 300% from 1972 to 1981.[15] In Central America, this borrowing habit is reaching desperate levels as the debt rises to impossible heights. If each person in Costa Rica were to take a share of the country's external public debt, it would mean a $1,200 bill for each Costa Rican – more than the average Costa Rican makes in an entire year. Growing warfare and deteriorating trade conditions make it unlikely that the Central American nations will be able to keep up their debt payments to banks and governments of the developed world.

The countries of Central America have been forced to work to exhaustion to produce coffee, bananas, and sugar for the United States and other developed nations. But they are falling even further behind in their ability to pay for necessary imports and even deeper into debt. All the development schemes for Central America have fit the changing needs of international trade and production rather than meeting the independent development needs of Central America. Per capita income in Central America is as little as one tenth the U.S. average, as shown in Table 1E, and each year it is falling further behind the United States.

A more appropriate model of development of the Central American nations includes the following measures:

- higher commodity prices set by the producing countries,

- limitations on foreign investment that would encourage the growth of locally-owned industries,

- restrictions on the importation of non-essential goods,

- a thorough agrarian reform program.

Measures such as these run contrary to the narrowly-defined economic interests of the United States. Continuing recessionary trends in the United States combined with the expansion of European and Japanese trade have caused the U.S. government to adopt a yet more aggressive foreign policy to protect the foreign economic interests of the transnational corporations in Central America and throughout the world. The political and economic interests of the United States have dominated Central America since the early part of this century, and the current U.S. government sees the broadening of the popular opposition in the region as a threat to its continued hegemony over the area. President Reagan reacted to the eruption of social discontent in Central America by pouring unprecedented quantities of arms into the region. While each country by itself represents only a small economic interest, the U.S. government is concerned that if it loses its economic and political influence in one country, the entire region may fall from its sphere of influence. Referring to the opposition movement in El Salvador, former U.S. Ambassador Robert White said: "The heart of the problem grew out of intolerable poverty and constant terror; it is authentic and homegrown. Our policymakers refuse to recognize this fact; that is why their policies don't work."

President Reagan's policies and practices support political leaders and military despots like Guatemala's Rios Montt, a fanatical evangelist who says

Table 1E. Per Capita Income 1980

United States $9,511

Panama $1,918

Costa Rica $1,527

Guatemala $1,198

Nicaragua $ 897

Belize $ 755

El Salvador $ 681

Honduras $ 639

```
   0  | 1000 | 2000 | 3000 | 4000 | 5000 | 6000 | 7000 | 8000 | 9000 |
     500   1500  2500  3500  4500  5500  6500  7500  8500  9500
```

Source: Inter-American Development Bank, *Economic and Social Progress in Latin America 1980-81 Report.*

14

he is waging a "holy war" against his country's own population; Roberto D'Aubuisson, a right-wing extremist who has been labelled a "pathological killer"; and such rabid anti-communists as General Gustavo Alvarez of Honduras. As a part of their plan to stabilize the region, President Reagan and the State Department are pressuring the nations of Central America to adopt tax and trade incentives that give still greater advantages to U.S. investors. Now, as in the past, the United States has refused to recognize that the conditions which make Central America so advantageous to U.S. investors — low wages, a large unemployed labor force, and the lack of strong independent popular organizations — are the seeds of revolutionary movements that seek to change the conditions of underdevelopment.

REFERENCE NOTES

1. Eduardo Galeano, *Open Veins of Latin America*, (New York: Monthly Review Press, 1973), p. 126.
2. Jenny Pearce, *Under the Eagle*, (London: Latin American Bureau, 1982), p. 19.
3. U.S. Statistical Abstract, 1981.
4. "La Evolucion Economica de America Latina en 1981," CEPAL, January 1982, p. 4.
5. Speech by President Reagan, February 24, 1982, U.S. State Department, Policy 370.
6. *Survey of Current Business*, (Washington: Dept. of Commerce, August 1981), p. 31.
7. Penny Lernoux, *Cry of the People*, (New York: Doubleday, 1980), p. 58.
8. "Cross-Border and Non-Local Currency Claims on Foreigners by Country of Guarantors," *Joint News Release*, Comptroller of the Currency, Federal Deposit Insurance Corporation, and Federal Reserve Board, June 1981.
9. *Vocero Comercial*, November-December 1981.
10. Foreign Agricultural Trade of the United States (FATUS), U.S. Dept. of Agriculture, January-February 1981.
11. *Business Latin America*, March 8, 1982, p. 19.
12. CEPAL, p. 6.
13. *Annual Report 1982*, World Bank.
14. *Economic and Social Progress in Latin America*, (Washington: Inter-American Development Bank, 1980-1981), p. 34.
15. CEPAL, p. 1.

Chapter Two

Agriculture:
Beyond Banana Boats

The Fruit Company, Inc.
reserved for itself the most succulent,
the central coast of my own land,
the delicate waist of America.
It rechristened its territories
as the "Banana Republics"
and over the sleeping dead,
over the restless heroes
who brought about the greatness,
the liberty and the flags,
it established the comic opera

— Pablo Neruda
"The United Fruit Co."

The image of Banana Republics as enclaves of U.S. corporations is still not far from the economic and political reality of Central America. What has changed is that there are more than bananas in the fertile coastal lands of Central America — there are pineapples, cattle, palm oil, vegetables, and flowers being farmed by U.S. corporations.

One can see the changing nature of the U.S. agricultural domain on the drive from hot and sticky San Pedro Sula through the agricultural heartland of Honduras. Banana trees line the road, stretching endlessly across the coastal lowlands. In one-room shacks, unemployed farmworkers wait out the heat of the day and also wait for the next harvest season to begin. The road heads to Tela, the main port of United Brands. Tela is the namesake of the Tela Railroad Company, which is the banana-producing subsidiary of United Brands in Honduras. A railroad and an ocean port are the two main ingredients of the banana trade in Central America, where cheap labor and cheap governments are easy pickings.

After leaving Tela, the road winds along the coast to La Ceiba, the center of Castle & Cooke's operations in Honduras. Twenty-five years ago the banana enclaves of the two companies were still operated like feudal estates and had little contact with the rest of the country. The companies have sold most of their land to the government or to local producers in the last two decades. Through contracts, however, the companies still maintain control of production. The bananas may not grow on company land these days, but they end up with Chiquita (United Brands) and Dole (Castle & Cooke) labels just the same. Another change is that the carefully-planted forests of lush African palm trees now form an important part of the company operations. United Brands and Castle & Cooke's Standard Fruit process the red fruit of the African palm into margarine and salad oil. A worker at one African palm farm said his company's name was La Compania Ceibena. "But there are two *sombreros* here," he added with a smirk. "One *sombrero*, the smaller one, is called La Ceibena; but the other one, the larger one, is Standard Fruit." What he didn't know was that Standard is covered by a yet larger *sombrero* by the name of Castle & Cooke.[1]

Nearer to La Ceiba, the landscape opens up into the coastal lowlands, where hundreds of farmworkers bend over to pick pineapples which will carry the Dole label back to supermarkets in the United States, or will be crushed and canned at Standard Fruit's processing complex in La Ceiba. La Ceiba is a company town that grew up around Standard's warehouse and dock. The company's fruit arrives at La Ceiba on the company train and leaves to foreign markets on one of Castle & Cooke's fleet of cargo ships.

Life in La Ceiba revolves around Standard Fruit, which sponsors the community's fiestas and offers three brands of company beer to its employees to drink. Retired Standard workers line up at the company headquarters on the central plaza to collect their pension payments. They remember with a sense of pride the benefits and higher wages they won in the hard-fought strike of 1954. It's a pride tinged with sadness, however, because although so much was gained, the younger workers still have to fight to gain decent wages and working conditions. Banana workers labor in the humid orchards from sunrise to sunset harvesting the ripe bananas. They often suffer from extreme fatigue from the monotonous, wearing work. One study in Costa Rica found that each worker swings the machete as many as 5,000 times a day, frequently in close proximity to co-workers. There is an average of one occupational accident per worker each year at a Standard plantation in Costa Rica. A nearly universal complaint of the workers is that they are unable to sleep well because of a burning sensation on their skin caused by the heavy use of pesticides by the banana companies.

The forerunners of United Fruit Company and Standard Fruit and Steamship Company carved out the first banana enclaves in the 1880s. U.S. investors financed construction of several railroads in Central America and had undertaken the financing of public debts of several countries, but banana production was the first substantial U.S. agricultural investment in the region. By 1914, 60% of the direct foreign investment in Central America came from the United States and was concentrated mainly in the banana enclaves in Honduras, Costa Rica, Nicaragua, Guatemala, and Panama.[2] The first phase of diversification by the banana companies in Central America occurred in the 1920s when they expanded their investment into banking, utilities, transportation, and communication facilities.

Industrialization came to Central America with the establishment of the Central American Common Market (CACM). Initially, United Brands and Standard Fruit regarded new investment coming into the region as competition and opposed the CACM. Later they recognized the advantages of an integrated Central American market and expanded their investments to include food processing and manufacturing companies that produce for the regional market. This deepened the already extensive involvement of the banana companies in the life, politics, and economy of Central America. The people of the region commonly refer to the banana corporations as *pulpos* (octopuses).

The banana companies have also altered their investment patterns to reduce their risk and to maintain their profit margins. The Overseas Private Investment Corporation (OPIC) says that due to "expropriation, revolution, or insurrection," plantations are a poor risk.[3] The three top banana corporations have been divesting their landholdings and contracting with local producers, but these producers are hardly independent. In their book *Empresas Transnacionales y Agricultura*, authors Daniel Slutzky and Esther Alonzo describe contract arrangements in Honduras: "The associate producers are under the administrative control of the superintendent of Tela and they act according to the advice of the company; the infrastructure and the development expenses of production all are handled by the company, and they depend totally on the companies for the sale of their fruit."[4]

The corporation usually provides its "associate producers" with credit, technical advice, seeds, fertilizer, farm machinery, chemicals, aerial spraying of pesticides, irrigation equipment, plastic wrapping, and cardboard packing boxes. While the grower is guaranteed in advance a certain percentage of the purchase price, it is usually less than 25%. From that must come labor costs, taxes and other expenses so that the associate producers frequently come up short on the corporate record books. In many cases, the companies advance the guaranteed percentage in the form of loans, which pushes the associate producers further into debt.[5] Concerning a similar system of contract production in Asia, the *Far Eastern Economic Review* noted in 1980 that the associate producers are often left "perpetually in bondage."[6] Workers on the associate producer plantations often get less pay and endure worse living conditions than workers on company plantations. In the associate producer system, the producers bear the brunt of banana diseases and hurricanes that can ruin a year's harvest; and if the market is low, the companies can simply reduce the quotas of production from their associates. It's a system that keeps the banana land under company control without the expense and political difficulties of direct ownership.[7] An overriding effect of the associate producer system is the creation of a local economic sector that is dependent upon the banana companies and likely to side with the interests of the companies on political questions. Thomas Sunderland, president of United Fruit, stated this goal in 1962: "Upon stimulating the citizens of the country to enter the banana industry. . . we gain associates that will be valuable allies for the promotion of our interests."[8]

The banana companies also involve international development banks and the government in new projects. What the companies want is a three-way deal shared by 1) an independent producer or agricultural cooperative, 2) the state, and 3) themselves as the contractor and marketer. This strategy has worked well for the banana companies in Honduras, where the government has received funds from the Inter-American Development Bank to develop African palm projects for its agrarian reform program. The companies simply buy the African palm harvests from the farm projects, without having to bear any of the initial investment in the project or deal with the manifold problems of direct production.

The banana companies have always been able to count on the national oligarchies of Central America. Both groups have had a common interest in maintaining repressive military governments and upholding strict class divisions. There was hope at first among other social and economic sectors, particularly elements of the small Central American bourgeoisie, that the advancement of the banana corporations in the region would spur on the development of the entire economy. The banana companies, however, have managed to grab for themselves any additional opportunities for profit, whether it be breweries, banking institutions, or providing their own companies with cardboard shipping boxes and plastic. Until the 1950s, there was never much in the way of interchange between the companies and the rest of the country. They had their own, self-sufficient and profitable enclaves and didn't contribute their fair share of the national tax burden. In Honduras, the banana tax was two percent in 1950, while the tax on coffee was 20 percent.[9]

BUSINESS, BANANAS, AND BLACKMAIL

In 1974, five Central American banana exporting nations joined together to form the Union of Banana Exporting Countries (UPEB), which tried to establish a uniform tax increase of $1.00 a box. Del Monte, Castle & Cooke, and United Brands handle 90% of the bananas shipped by UPEB member nations. UPEB hoped to gain the leverage they needed to increase taxes in a common front against the companies. The companies fought the increase through economic pressure and through bribery. Fernando Manfredo, one of UPEB's founders, charged that the companies had used "threats and blackmail" to weaken UPEB and lower the banana taxes.[10] Panama, typical of the other countries, backed down from the $1.00 tax and imposed a tax of only 20 cents a box.

In 1977, the banana producing nations, excluding Guatemala and Equador, formed Comunbana as the marketing arm of UPEB. This marked the beginning of a new stage in what has come to be known as the "banana wars."

United Fruit refused to load its bananas onto Comunbana ships, and the Panamanian government threatened to nationalize company holdings. Although Comunbana has secured contracts in Greece, Yugoslavia, Italy, and Hungary, the monopolization of the world banana market by the big three banana companies has hindered the growth of UPEB and Comunbana. Also contributing to the weakness of the associations has been their failure to include all the banana exporting countries. The success of the banana producing and marketing union has been limited. It wasn't until 1981, seven years after the formation of UPEB, that the banana export tax in one country (Costa Rica) actually reached the $1.00 tax originally proposed by UPEB.

Despite the stated goals to raise the taxes of the banana companies and to break their monopoly over marketing, the producing countries have not yet addressed some of the basic concessions under which the companies still operate. In all the Central American nations, the banana companies operate under very favorable conditions with respect to monetary and exchange regulations. For example, in Honduras, Panama, and Guatemala, there are no stipulations as to the amount of the value of exports that must be converted into local currency. Therefore these countries have no control over how much of the income from the sales of bananas come back to the country. Only Costa Rica has this type of regulation, which requires that 50% of all export sales return to the Central Bank, but banana companies are exempt from this obligation.[11]

U.S. corporations control the production of virtually all Central American bananas and United States consumers eat 56% of the bananas produced in Central America. Little of the retail value of bananas ever returns to the producing nations. A United Nations study found that only 17 cents of each retail dollar spent on bananas goes back to the producing country in any form, even taxes.[12] While in developed countries the per capita income has more than doubled since World War Two, the real price the developed countries are paying for bananas dropped 44% from 1950 to 1974.[13]

United Brands, Castle & Cooke, and R.J. Reynolds dwarf the Central American nations with the immensity of their operations and financial power. The value of the entirety of Honduran export trade in 1981 only amounted to 20% of the 1981 annual sales of United Brands. The combined annual sales of the three corporations is three times as large as the combined export sales of the seven countries of Central America. This imbalance of economic power helps keep the banana companies growing richer and the countries poorer. Using this power, the companies maintain operations that shamelessly exploit the people and resources of Central America while regularly violating the sovereignty of the nations where they do business.

United Brands

United Fruit became United Brands in a 1970 merger with AMK Corporation.

The company's Chiquita Banana is the top-selling banana in the world. United Fruit formed in 1888 when Boston Fruit merged with three banana companies controlled by Minor C. Keith, the founder of International Railways of Central America. The new company solidified its hold on the international banana market in 1930 when it bought out its main competitor, the Cuyamel Fruit Company, from Samuel Zemurray. For the next 20 years, Sam "the Banana Man" Zemurray ran United Fruit; and when he stepped down in 1950, United Fruit owned more than three million acres throughout Latin America. In Cuba, Angel Castro and his sons, Raul and Fidel, worked on a United Fruit sugar plantation.[14]

In 1954, after Guatemala threatened to nationalize the company's uncultivated landholdings, United Fruit helped to engineer a coup against the progressive Arbenz government. Five years later when the Cuban Revolution nationalized company holdings in 1959, the company decided to sell most of its other plantations in Latin America. In the 1960s, the company also began diversifying; in 1965, it acquired Numar, a Costa Rican margarine plant, and soon after purchased 12 Central American firms from Polymer International.[15] Through its subsidiary John Morrell & Company, United Brands has become one of the largest meat marketers in the United States and it has also expanded its cattle business on lands it owns or leases in Central America.

Table 2A. United Brands

Production	Processing	Industrial	Miscellaneous
Chiriqui Land Company	Numar	Productos Plásticos	Unimar
Tela Railroad	Compañía Procesadora de Frutas	Polymer	TRT Telecommunications Corporation
Compañía Bananera de Costa Rica	Compañía Agrícola de Rio Tinto	Empresa Hondureña de Vapores	Compañía Mundimar
United Fruit	Fábrica de Aceites de Palma	Frigorífica Hondureña	Electronic Data Systems and Management Sciences Company
Compañía Agricola de Guatemala	Aceitera Corona	Fábrica de Cajas de Cartón	Balboa Shipping Company
Productos Acuáticos y Terrestres	Projecto Agro-Industrial de Sixaola	PATSA	Caribbean Enterprises
Compañía Bananera Atlantica			Caronas
			SIATSA

In the United Brands *1968 Annual Report*, company executive Herbert Cornuelle summed up the company's approach to doing business in Central America. He said the multinationals' role "in the development process becomes more urgently clear every day, as we witness the limitations and handicaps of local governments . . . even if local governments were strong and assistance to them plentiful, the fact is that the enormous complexities of the development process require abilities and attributes which are as natural to the multinational corporation as they are unnatural to government."

Castle & Cooke

This Hawaii-based company now sells more bananas in the United States than any other corporation. Founded by two missionaries in 1894, Castle & Cooke is one of the largest landholders in Hawaii. A common Hawaiian saying is "when the missionaries came, the Hawaiians had all the land and the missionaries had all the Bibles. Now the Hawaiians have the Bibles and the missionaries have all the land."[16]

In 1964, Castle & Cooke gained control of Standard Fruit when it purchased 55% of Standard stock and then in 1968 it bought the remaining 45%. In Honduras and Costa Rica, the company has been selling its landholdings to private producers. More than half of its bananas are now grown under contract arrangements with associate producers. According to one company official, Castle & Cooke is "becoming more of a marketing than a farming company." In 1981, *Multinational Monitor* reported that the company controlled 8,800 acres of banana land in Honduras and 15-17,000 acres in Costa Rica through associate producer arrangements.[17]

Table 2B. Castle & Cooke

Production	Processing	Industrial	Miscellaneous
Standard Fruit	Industria Aceitera Hondureña	Envases Industriales	Financiera de Costa Rica
Bananera Antillana	Compañia Agrícola Industrial Ceibena	Cementos de Honduras	Standard Fruit & Steamship Company
Dole Pineapple		Manufacturera de Carton	
Servicios Agrícolas	Cervecería Tegucigalpa	Fábrica de Manteca y Jabon Atlántida	Banco del Comercio
	Cervecería Hondureña	Plásticos	Nacional Inmobiliaria
	Belize Brewing Company	Aceros Industriales	Servicios de Investigaciones Areas
	Enlatadora del Campo	Semillas Mejoradas	
	Frutera Hondureña		

Standard Fruit has often allied itself with the military governments in Central America to crush unionization and worker organizing. Standard Fruit President Don Kirchoff is responsible for a widely-quoted statement in which he urged corporate leaders to "take the offensive" in a "guerilla war against opponents of business."

R.J. Reynolds

First a cigarette company and still the leader of the nation in cigarette sales, R.J. Reynolds is a conglomerate. Through its subsidiary Chun King, it sells more packaged Oriental food than any other company. It also operates Sealand, the largest container shipping firm in the world. In 1969, R.J. Reynolds bought Del Monte, the largest vegetable and fruit packer in the United States. In Central America, Del Monte has agricultural production companies in Costa Rica, Guatemala, and Honduras. Del Monte is also one of the largest food processing firms in Central America, operating Conservas Panamenas in Panama, Conservas del Campo in Costa Rica and Honduras, and Monte Libano in Costa Rica.

Table 2C. R.J. Reynolds

Production	Processing	Miscellaneous
Bandegua	Conservas Panameñas	Federal Transport
Compañía de Desarrollo Bananero de Guatemala	South American Development	Sealand Service
Productores Unidos de Banano	Del Monte Foreign Sales	
Bananera del Carmen	Del Campo	
Banana Development Corporation of Costa Rica	Monte Libano	

Alfred Eames, chairperson of Del Monte, said in 1970, "Bananas are like money trees. I wish we had more of them." At that time, Del Monte had owned bananas for only two years, acquiring the banana company in 1968 to stop a possible takeover by United Fruit, which could not legally acquire another banana company. In a 1972 acquisition of Guatemalan banana plantations, Del Monte paid a half-million dollars to a "consultant" who persuaded the Guatemalan government to approve the purchase.[18] Del Monte owns 57,000 acres in Guatemala but produces on only 9,000 acres.

"Our business isn't just canning, it's feeding people," said Eames in a Del Monte annual report. But, as Frances Moore Lappe and Joseph Collins asked in their book, Food First, "Which people? Del Monte is operating Philippine plantations to feed the banana-starved Japanese; contracting with Mexican growers to feed asparagus-cravers in France, Denmark, and Switzerland; and opening a new plantation in Kenya so that no Britisher need go without his or her ration of jet-fresh pineapple."[19]

OUTSIDE THE BANANA ENCLAVE

Bananas symbolize the exploited condition of Central America, but it was coffee, the region's first important export crop that began the regional tradition of dependence on the world agricultural market. It was also the expansion of coffee production that concentrated wealth in the hands of a small group of families that became the national oligarchies. Unlike banana production, the cultivation of coffee has historically been a local affair. Though the production of coffee in Central America has been more widely shared among local farmers than other agro-export crops, the coffee industry has become increasingly controlled by oligarchies. Smaller producers, unable to withstand sudden drops in the coffee market and unable to afford new farm technology, sold their land to large growers. In Guatemala, a United States Department of Agriculture (USDA) study found that large coffee estates accounted for 75% of the total production area. These estates, reported the USDA, are among the largest private agricultural estates in the world. In El Salvador, 4% of the 40,000 growers control 67% of coffee production.[20]

Coffee, like other world-trade commodities, is controlled by a small number of processors and distributors. Just 23 firms, including Procter & Gamble (Folger's) and General Foods (Maxwell House) control 82% of the world coffee trade, which, in terms of value, is the world's most heavily traded commodity after oil.[21] Central American coffee goes to Europe and U.S. markets. In the U.S. in 1980, U.S. residents drank 27.8 gallons per person. Foreign capital provides most of the financing for Central American coffee growers. In Guatemala, for example, 70% of the national production of coffee has been financed by loans secured from abroad by the large coffee exporting companies. While such loans are easily obtained, annual interest rates are as high as 28%.[22]

Like coffee, transnational firms are only rarely involved in the direct production of cotton and sugar cane. Instead, they exert their control by providing credit, influencing world commodity prices, and distributing and marketing. An advertisement by Citibank circulated in major U.S. magazines boasted that the "cloud-soft cotton of El Salvador [is] brought from boll to bale with the help of worldwide Citibank." The ad continued: "Cotton is El Salvador's number two crop (second to coffee), and Citibank's customer, a 10,500 member cooperative, includes every grower in the country. . . . About 80% of [El Salvador's cotton] is exported, and a substantial portion of it is financed through a direct line of credit from Citibank, amounting this year to some $16 million."[23]

Eight of the world's ten largest cotton trading companies are U.S. corporations. Cotton production, which rapidly developed in Central America after World War Two, represents the switch of the region's agricultural economy from semi-feudal practices to a system of modern capitalist agribusiness. The magic of the "Green Revolution" — heavy doses of fertilizer and pesticides combined with large capital inputs of farm technology — has fostered the expansion of agribusiness for new export crops. But this magic has driven hundreds of thousands of peasants off their lands and forced them to work 12-hour shifts for one to three dollars a day.

One half of Central America's agricultural land is now devoted to agro-export crops,[24] a trend that has decreased the available food for internal consumption and increased the region's food import bill. USDA figures show that the value of U.S. farm product exports to Central America jumped 54% in 1980.[25] A basic part of the Central American diet is roots and tubers, but the USDA reported that per capita consumption of even these most staple items has declined because of decreasing production in the last few years.[26] Overall, the production of staple foods is growing more slowly than that of total agricultural output. More agricultural production doesn't necessarily mean less hunger. Rather, in Central America, increased agricultural production usually means more production for export and less land for food in Central America. The Institute for Food Policy and Development in San Francisco, addressing these worldwide issues, said that "the cause of hunger and rural poverty is not overpopulation, not a scarcity of agricultural resources, nor a lack of modern technology. Rather, the root cause of hunger is a tight concentration of control over food producing resources."[27]

El Big Mac

Millions of U.S. residents regularly gobble up a hamburger or two at their favorite fast food restaurant. Most are unaware that they are at the end of a food chain that is eradicating the Central American tropical forests. The rapid expansion of the cattle industry in Central America to meet the booming beef market in the United States has contributed to the destruction of two-thirds of the region's tropical forests in the last several decades. If this trend continues for another ten years, little will remain of these lush forest areas.[28] Since 1961, Costa Rica, Guatemala, Honduras, and Nicaragua have more than doubled their beef production and tripled their beef exports. Ninety percent of these beef exports go to the United States, accounting for 14.5% of all U.S. beef imports.[29]

Cattle ranching is responsible for the conversion of 20,000 square kilometers of land every year in Latin America, wrote Dr. Norman Myers in *The Sinking Ark*.[30] After twenty years of grazing on converted tropical forests, the soil is expended and eroded, leaving what soil conservationists call a "red desert." A dramatic example of this conversion is the Panama Canal Zone, where the United States permitted cattle ranchers to cut down the tropical forests for pastures. The U.S. Agency for International Development (AID) funded a project to reforest the area and to re-establish the watershed along the Canal since water levels in the Canal have dropped to dangerous lows in recent years. In Costa Rica, 150,000 acres are deforested every year, while only 12,500 acres are reforested. Within ten years, Costa Rica will have to import a billion cubic meters of wood each year.[31]

Cattle production isn't the only threat to Central America's forests. Over 80% of U.S. hardwood imports come from the tropical areas of the world, including Central America, where over 50 U.S. corporations busily harvest wood. Land is then turned over to grazing. The demand for hardwood is expected to increase 75% in the United States by the year 2000.[32] To clear forests for pastures, some companies employ local *campesinos* to go into the woods with their machetes and chain-saws. An increasingly popular practice is to use two DC-8 tractors with a heavy chain between them to drag down the forest. Also fashionable is the use of defoliants like 2,4,5-T, the basic ingredient in Agent Orange, that has been banned for most uses in the United States. Companies like Monsanto, Dow, and Hercules continue to produce the poison and export it to foreign markets.

In the 1960s, the Alliance for Progress funded the construction of roads and bridges that prepared isolated tropical areas for exploitation. Currently, the U.S. Eximbank and the Overseas Private Development Corporation (OPIC) support U.S. businesses that play a large part in the rampant deforestation of Central America. An example is the OPIC support of the Alberti Foods cattle operation in Catacamas, Honduras — an area now largely deforested.[32]

One problem with cattle production in Central America is the destruction of tropical forests. Another problem is one that the U.S. Foreign Agriculture Service recognized as early as 1969 when it said that "the considerable growth of meat exports in recent years has been at the expense of domestic beef consumption." Between 1960 and 1974, per capita beef consumption fell 41.2% in Costa Rica and 37.5% in El Salvador.[34] In Guatemala, beef consumption dropped a staggering 50% in the same ten year period when exports rose from zero to 30 million pounds per year. While U.S. beef consumption has been on the steady increase to 123 pounds per capita by 1978, the average Costa Rican was eating only 35 pounds a year by 1978, the Guatemalan 23 pounds, the Salvadoran 15 pounds, and the Honduran 13 pounds. The emphasis on production for the export market has made beef scarce and high-priced in Central America.[35]

While Central Americans are finding beef more and more expensive, U.S. companies have found that raising beef on the cheap tropical forest land in Central America lowers their costs. A report done for the U.S. State Department called it "a quick and dirty business," where the investor extracts as much profit as possible from the converted forests before the land becomes eroded and worthless.[36] Unlike most U.S. cattle, Central American beef is grass-fed rather than grain-fed. As such, it isn't as lean as American beef, but the U.S. fast food chains, which buy most of the Central American meat, don't mind. Fast food outlets are spreading their neon signs and hamburger dining style throughout the world at a quickening pace, having increased their numbers by 81% in four years. McDonald's sells *El Big Mac* in every Central American capital. In Panama, McDonald's serves local beef and decorates its restaurants with the traditional artwork of the Kuna Indians to complement its own Golden Arches motif.[37]

Flowers Fresh from Central America

A new plan for U.S. investors is non-traditional export crops like ornamental flowers, sesame seeds, and vegetables from Central America for U.S. markets. The Bank of America pulled together 15 companies in 1970 to form the Latin American Agribusiness Development Corporation (LAAD) for development of non-traditional exports in Latin America. (See Table 2D.) By 1981, LAAD had

Table 2D. 1981 Shareholders of LAAD

Castle & Cooke	Borden
BankAmerica International Financial Corporation	Chase Manhattan Overseas Banking Corporation
Caterpillar Tractor Company	Ralston Purina Company
Gerber Products Company	Cargill
Adela Investment Company	CPC International
Monsanto Company	Centrale Rabonbank Curacao N.V.
Girard International Bank	Deere & Company
Southeast First National Bank of Miami	The Goodyear Tire and Rubber Company

Source: LAAD, 1981 Annual Report.

a stake in 173 companies in Latin America, 70% of which are in Central America.[38] LAAD furthers the non-traditional export business by financing companies that contract local producers, cattle ranchers, and fishermen. LAAD has also helped establish ornamental flower companies in Guatemala, Panama, and Costa Rica.

LAAD promotes private enterprise through government subsidies. Without the $29 million in concessional loans from AID, there would be no LAAD. Two AID loans financed the founding of LAAD de Centroamerica, one of the three branches of the organization. AID justifies its financial aid to LAAD on the corporation's stated goal to "open up new markets for small farmers and to provide employment" in Latin America. In 1981, AID authorized a loan of six million dollars to further LAAD's investment activities. The goal of this loan was to "improve the standard of living of Central American rural poor."

LAAD has 20 years to repay the loan, including a grace period of five years. The interest on the loan is only four percent. LAAD estimates that it will be able to circulate the six million dollar loan several times before it has to pay back the principal to AID.[39]

Typical of LAAD projects in Central America are cattle companies, vegetable processing operations, and firms that provide over 100 varieties of ornamental flowers to foreign markets. In Guatemala, LAAD backs several nursery and flower export companies that are partially responsible for $3.3 million worth of nursery and greenhouse stock for export.[40]

LAAD no longer publishes the names of its client corporations in its annual report as it had previously. "A number of our clients considered the publication a hit list," explained LAAD President Robert Ross. According to Ross, firms associated with LAAD have been targets of violence from political groups objecting to LAAD's presence in Central America.[41] Appendix III lists companies in Central America that have received or will receive LAAD financing.

In Guatemala, LAAD has close ties with the Bank of America and the American Chamber of Commerce, organizations that support the military government in Guatemala. Through at least one of its managers, Bank of America has representation in the right-wing lobbying organization, Amigos del Pais.

Tom Mooney, president of the American Chamber of Commerce in Guatemala, also serves as president of LAAD de Centroamerica. Describing his and the Chamber's attitude about the escalating social/political situation in Guatemala, Mooney said: "The only way to stop Communism is to destroy it quickly. Argentina and Chile are . . . nations which used this approach with considerable effectiveness and have gone on to become among Latin America's most stable and successful economies."[42]

One of LAAD's investments in Guatemala is Alimentos Congelados Monte Bello (ALCOSA) that, according to LAAD's 1977 Annual Report, is "a Guatemalan frozen foods company" that supplies U.S. supermarkets with broccoli, cauliflower, and okra "grown by Indian communities." But ALCOSA is hardly a "Guatemalan" company. LAAD helped the company get started in 1971; and in 1975 ALCOSA was acquired by Hanover Brands, a large U.S. frozen food company.

In a 1980 study, AID attempted to "discover and describe the social impact — intended and unintended — of this agribusiness firm on the farmer and the worker who have been affected by its growth."[43] The study revealed that "more than 1,300 farmers, most of them new to ALCOSA, were convinced to commit significant portions of their available land and labor resources to produce a crop which few had even seen before, and which — as several of them said — 'we can't even pronounce'."[44]

In 17 mountain villages, ALCOSA had contracting and buying stations, where company field employees contracted Indian peasants to convert their farming operations into vegetable production for ALCOSA. At a factory near Guatemala City, the company employed about 400 women to process and freeze the vegetables for marketing in the United States. Along with the contract, the company offered the Indian farmers seeds, transplanted seedlings, fertilizer, and insecticides in interest-free loans against harvested deliveries. For most of the peasant farmers, this association with Hanover Brands' ALCOSA was the first time that they had received any form of agricultural credit, and the program brought the farmers more income than their previous operations. Another result of the ALCOSA contracts, according to the AID study, was that "cultivation shifted from a pattern of diversified vegetable and corn production to a concentration upon cauliflower; displaced crops were primarily corn, beans, and cabbage."[45]

From 1975 to 1980, ALCOSA gradually raised its quality standards and lowered prices, so that farmers could no longer cover production costs of the labor intensive crops. The farmers also reported that company field employees were defrauding them. In 1980, however, differences between ALCOSA and its contracting producers sharpened. On July 21, 1980, as the cauliflower plants were ready to harvest, ALCOSA abruptly suspended its purchases of cauliflower, "an action that immediately plunged most of its cauliflower growers into panic and financial crisis . . . . As farmers discovered for the first time . . . , the contract contains no clause binding ALCOSA to purchase as unambiguous as the clause that binds the farmer to sell."[46]

ALCOSA over-contracted for both broccoli and cauliflower and didn't have the plant capacity to process all the deliveries. Management said it was forced to divert the flow of raw materials or go bankrupt. ALCOSA decided that it was better to let the growers suffer than suffer itself, and it told the farmers that it wouldn't be paying them for the harvest that year. Because ALCOSA had urged them to grow cauliflower instead of corn, there was neither corn nor the money to pay for food. The Indians said that because of the crisis their children had to quit school and leave home for work as farm laborers or domestic servants. The AID study reported that "aggravating the situation was their fear that the most logical response, collective action to convince the company to resume buying (either through negotiations or legal proceedings), would be dangerous in Guatemala's political climate."

Despite the AID findings, the agency has continued to finance LAAD, which in turn has continued to finance ALCOSA. In 1981, ALCOSA received another boost when it received financial backing from the Overseas Private Investment Corporation (OPIC). Two companies that supply broccoli to ALCOSA also have received LAAD loans. While there is some question that LAAD has improved the lot of Central America's poor, there is no doubt that it is a profitable business. In 1981, LAAD received $5.4 million in principal payments on its loans and chalked up a 50% increase in net earnings, to just over one million dollars. At the year's end, it had assets of $36.9 million. As of October 1981, LAAD had 131 projects in Central America, 52 of these in Guatemala.[47]

LAAD plays a groundbreaking role for U.S. corporations. It first establishes the control of U.S. capital through financing arrangements, and then encourages the company to depend on U.S. technology, markets, and capital. The U.S. government has considered LAAD so successful that it has promoted its extension in the Caribbean and throughout South America. AID is also considering financing a similar organization for Africa.

Pesticides: For Export Only

In a 1977 midnight raid on a small landing strip in La Flora, Guatemala, the Guerilla Army of the Poor (EGP) destroyed 22 planes, not military planes that drop bombs and napalm, but crop dusters that drop inordinate amounts of pesticides on the cotton fields and the Indian farmworkers below. "We treat 30 or 40 people a day for pesticide poisoning," said a nurse at a clinic in Guatemala's cotton region. "The farmers often tell the peasants to give another reason for their sickness, but you can smell the pesticide in their clothing."[48]

The biting smell of pesticides seems ever-present in the Pacific plains of Guatemala. While pesticides kill the insects that bother the country's agroexport crops, they also are killing the Guatemalan people. According to the Central American Research Institute for Industry, the average DDT content in human blood in Guatemala's cotton areas is 520.6 parts per billion contrasted with 46.4 in Dade County, Florida. A study by the Central American Nutritional Institute found that the amounts of DDT in mothers' milk in Guatemala were the highest in the Western world and over 185 times higher than the safety limit.[49] Other Central American countries also face the dangers of pesticides. In the Danli area of Honduras, large-scale pesticide sprayings on cotton crops caused mosquitos to develop a resistance to DDT. After three years, one fourth of the 32,000 Danli inhabitants had contracted malaria.[50]

Pesticides for the agro-export industry in Central America are a booming business for U.S. chemical manufacturers. Major corporations active in the trade include Monsanto, Chevron (Ortho), Du Pont, Hercules, and Dow, all of which also have factories in Central America. Common pesticides in the region are DDT, toxaphene, and parathion, all banned or severely restricted in the United States. A report by the Central American Institute of Industrial Technology listed more than 14,000 poisonings and 40 deaths from pesticides between 1972 and 1975 in the cotton growing regions of Central America. According to the World Health Organization, someone in the underdeveloped world is poisoned by pesticides every minute.[51] Dizziness, vomiting, and general weakness are the common symptoms of pesticide poisoning, symptoms that farmworkers have learned to endure to keep their jobs. Those that suffer from pesticides rarely make it to a doctor; many die in the fields and are buried on the farms where they work.

David Weir and Mark Schapiro, authors of *Circle of Poison*, reported that parathion, developed by the Nazis and 60 times more toxic than DDT, causes 80% of Central America's poisonings. Cotton production in tiny El Salvador absorbs one-fifth of all the parathion used in the world.[52] Pesticides in the United States often read "For Export Only," but frequently do not carry any warnings. Weir and Schapiro found that at least 20% of the U.S. pesticide exports are banned or have never been registered for use in the United States. Concerning this situation of the unregulated sale and use of pesticides in Third World countries, Dr. Harold Hubbard of the Pan American Health Organization said "that there is absolutely no control over the manufacture, the transportation, the storage, the record keeping — the entire distribution of this stuff. These very toxic pesticides are being thrown all over the world, and there's no control over any of it."[53]

In May 1982, the Pesticide Action Network (PAN) formed to call "a halt to the indiscriminate sale and misuse of hazardous chemical pesticides throughout the world." PAN blamed the transnational agro-chemical corporations for their "irresponsible and abusive marketing practices," and demanded that the World Bank and regional development banks like the Inter-American Development Bank stop funding agricultural projects that involve the overuse and abuse of dangerous pesticides.[54]

Pesticide poisoning is a problem that is coming back to the United States from Central America. DDT applied to cotton in Nicaragua showed up in beef carcasses imported through Miami.[55] Although banned in the United States, the pesticides are used on crops produced in the region, but eaten in the U.S.

A chemical fog hangs over the rich farmland of Central America. Crop dusters, chemical plants owned by Chevron and Monsanto, and the ever-present John Deere farm machinery are all signs that Central American agriculture is an outpost of U.S. agriculture. Known in the past as Banana Republics, the countries now export much more: cotton, coffee, sugar, beef, vegetables, and flowers — headed to the United States. Meanwhile, there's less and less to eat in Central America, more and more pesticide poisoning, and at least as much government repression. Whether traditional or non-traditional crops, U.S. agribusiness corporations continue doing business in Central America the traditional Banana Republic way.

REFERENCES

1. Interview by Tom Barry, April 1982.
2. "El Financiamiento Exterior de America Latina," CEPAL (E/CN. 121649 Rev. 1) p. 16.
3. Cited in Frances Moore Lappe and Joseph Collins, *Food First: Beyond the Myth of Scarcity* (New York: Ballantine, 1980), p. 299.
4. Daniel Slutzky and Esther Alonso, *Empresas Transnacionales y Agricultura: El Caso del Enclave Bananero en Honduras* (Tegucigalpa: Editorial Universitaria, 1982), p. 43.
5. "The Other Banana Company," *Multinational Monitor*, July 1981, p. 16.
6. *Ibid.*
7. *Ibid.*
8. Cited in "Que es La United Fruit," by David Tobis, Editorial Periferia, Buenos Aires, 1962.
9. Slutzky and Alonso, p. 23.
10. "Transnationals Stand Accused," *Latin America Commodities Report*, October 8, 1982, p. 8.
11. Slutzky and Alonso, p. 97.
12. "Trouble in Honduras," *Food Monitor*, September-October 1979, p. 11.
13. Cheryl Payer, *Trade of the Third World* (New York: John Wiley and Son, 1975), p. 135.
14. Milton Moskowitz, Michael Katz, and Robert Levering, *Everybody's Business, An Almanac: The Irreverent Guide to Corporate America* (San Francisco: Harper & Row, 1980), pp. 78, 79.
15. *Moody's Industrial Manual*, 1981.
16. Moskowitz, Katz, and Levering, pp. 13, 14.
17. *Multinational Monitor*, July 1981.
18. "Guatemala: Del Monte's Banana Republic," *North American Congress on Latin America* (referred to as *NACLA* in all references that follow), September 1976, p. 25.
19. Lappe and Collins, p. 279.
20. "Landowners Attack Official Wage Policy," *Latin America Regional Report* (referred to as *LARR* in all references that follow), April 4, 1980, p. 7.
21. *Latin America Commodities Report*, June 6, 1980.
22. "A Coffee Crisis Without Precedent," *Central America Report*, July 1982, p. 216.
23. Marc Herold, "From Riches to 'Rags': Finanzkapital in El Salvador, 1900-1980," (unpublished manuscript, University of New Hampshire, 1980), p. 1.
24. American Friends Service Committee, "Roots of the Crisis," which cites figures from *Tenecia de la Tierra y Desarollo Rural en Centroamerica*, CIDA, 1975.
25. "U.S. Farm Exports Gain in Central America," *Foreign Agriculture*, October 1981, p. 20.
26. "USDA Examines Food Prospects in Latin America," *Business Latin America*, October 14, 1981.

27. "Reflections: Aid as an Obstacle," *Food Monitor*, January-February, 1980, p. 22.
28. Statement by Hon. Donald Bonker, "Tropical Deforestation," Subcommittee on International Organizations, House Committee on Foreign Affairs, May 7, June 19, September 18, 1980.
29. Foreign Agricultural Service, USDA, February 1977, February 1978, December 1979, February 1980.
30. Dr. Norman Myers, *The Sinking Ark* (Peramon Press, 1979).
31. *La Nacion* (Costa Rica), April 4, 1982.
32. "Tropical Deforestation," Committee hearings.
33. Douglas R. Shane, "Hoofprints on the Forest: An Inquiry into the Beef Cattle Industry in the Tropical Forest Areas of Latin America," prepared for the Office of Environmental Affairs, U.S. Department of State, March 1980.
34. Valdes and Nores, "Growth Potential of the Beef Sector in Latin America — A Survey of Issues and Policies," p. 26; Inter-American Development Bank, *Economic and Social Progress in Latin America*, p. 143, See Appendix 5.
35. "Central America is Growing More Beef and Eating Less," *Multinational Monitor*, October 1981, p. 17.
36. Shane, p. 27.
37. Shane, p. 68.
38. "LAAD Finances, Aids Agribusiness Development in Latin America," *Business Latin America*, June 2, 1982, p. 175.
39. "Agribusiness Employment/Investment Promotion, Project Number: 596-0097."
40. USDA Agricultural Imports, 1981.
41. Robert Stickler, "Coral Gables Firm Develops Agribusiness in Latin America," *Miami Herald*, October 27, 1980.
42. Jenny Pearce, *Under the Eagle* (London: Latin America Bureau, 1981), p. 176.
43. "The Social Impact of Agribusiness: A Case Study of ALCOSA in Guatemala," Agency for International Development, July 1981.
44. David Kinley, "A Case Study Questions the Value of Reagan's Caribbean Basin Initiative," *Multinational Monitor*, May 1982, p. 17.
45. Agency for International Development, July 1981.
46. *Ibid.*
47. LAAD's *1981 Annual Report.*
48. Alan Riding, "Free Use of Pesticides in Guatemala Takes a Deadly Toll," *New York Times*, November 9, 1977.
49. *Ibid.*
50. Lappe and Collins, p. 20.
51. David Weir and Mark Schapiro, *Circle of Poison: Pesticides and People in a Hungry World*, (San Francisco: Institute for Food and Development Policy, 1981), p. 3.
52. *Ibid.*, pp. 12, 32.
53. "Circles of Poison: Pesticides and the Third World," *Multinational Monitor*, July 1980, p. 19.
54. Matthew Rothschild, "New Coalition Forms to Combat Pesticide Abuse," *Multinational Monitor*, July 1982, p. 22.
55. Lappe and Collins, p. 67.

Chapter Three

Industry: Backyard Business

"We cannot meet the competition of the Japanese in Europe with supplies from the United States. The U.S. cost of production is higher than the selling price in Europe. But we can compete from Central America . . . . and our experience shows that you can operate in a disturbed climate."

— AVX Ceramics executive
El Salvador, 1981

Twenty years ago Central America started on the road toward industrialization, hoping that local manufacturing would deliver the region from economic dependence on developed countries like the United States. But industrialization only increased the region's vulnerability to exploitation by foreign capital. After two decades of industrialization, the Central American nations have discovered that if they are ever to obtain their economic independence they will have to take another road.

OPEN DOOR TO CENTRAL AMERICA

South America had taken its first steps toward the local manufacture of items previously imported (import-substitution) in the 1930s. During the war years, when the United States and the European countries were otherwise occupied, the South American nations took long strides toward industrialization. But in Central America, the banana companies and the national oligarchies kept the economic structure under their control, leaving little room outside the coffee plantations and banana enclaves for new financial activity.

In the 1950s, business and government leaders in Central America started to chart a path away from the region's longtime dependence on a few agricultural exports and toward industrialization. The immediate obstacle was the limited national market in each of the countries. Not only did the nations have relatively small populations, but the market for consumer goods was also limited by the concentration of the national wealth among a small minority.

One possible solution was to widen the national markets through agrarian reform and increased wage levels. But the national oligarchies and business elites would have none of that. Instead, they were attracted by a proposal by the United Nations Economic Commission for Latin America (ECLA) to boost import-substitution in Central America through an integrated, regional market. Local industries, then, would be able to market their goods throughout the whole of Central America rather than being constrained to their own national markets.

In 1958, the five countries of Guatemala, Honduras, Nicaragua, Costa Rica, and El Salvador signed the first regional market treaty based on the ECLA plan. The treaty called for the gradual loosening of all trade barriers within the region and the creation of "integration industries" that would produce for the entire market. Under this plan, the economic development would be balanced by preventing the concentration of the new industries in one or two countries. At the time, Honduras, Nicaragua, and Costa Rica feared that an uncontrolled common market could favor the more developed countries of Guatemala and El Salvador.

The United States also wanted a common market for the region but ECLA's program of planned growth for locally-controlled industries was an anathema to the U.S. principles of free trade and free enterprise. The United States didn't want any barriers to U.S. investment, but rather an open door into the region. U.S. diplomats met with government representatives of El Salvador and Guatemala to discuss a proposal for a total and immediate liberalization of Central American regional trade. The United States lured the Central American nations with the promise of a $100,000 grant to establish a common market system. The General Treaty on Central American Economic Integration that established the Central American Common Market (CACM) was signed in 1961, superseding the ECLA-sponsored treaty. By promoting free trade and allowing foreign investment, the new treaty cleared the way for an invasion of U.S. capital into the region.

In 1962, the Agency for International Development (AID) opened a regional office to further U.S. goals in the region. AID's mission was to channel U.S. technical and financial assistance to the region, to improve private investment opportunities in Central America, and to make certain that integration of U.S. foreign investment proceeded smoothly.[1] The director of AID's program to build U.S. investment in Central America was Tom Mooney, who came to AID from the World Bank.

Mooney later became the head of the Latin American Agribusiness Development Corporation (LAAD) in Central America and the president of the American Chamber of Commerce in Guatemala.[2]

Wanting to guarantee that the CACM would benefit U.S. interests, the U.S. government contributed the bulk of funding for the planning, research, and financial agencies of the CACM. In 1965 and 1966, the United States contributed 54% of the budget for the nine CACM agencies while 33% came from other countries outside the region and only 13% of the annual budget came from the Central American nations themselves.[3]

During this formative period, the United States provided the initial loan to establish the Central American Bank for Economic Integration (Banco Centroamericana de Integracion Economica, BCIE). Subsequent U.S. financing required that loan money from BCIE be used only to purchase U.S. goods and services which were to be shipped on U.S. vessels. One study of BCIE found that by 1969, 86% of the bank's resources originated from foreign money, mostly from the United States.[4] BCIE was established to finance regional development projects and most of BCIE's loans go to large infrastructure projects, although some go directly to private enterprise, including U.S. companies.

Before the creation of the Central American Common Market, U.S. non-agricultural investment was limited to a few corporations like Coca-Cola and Sears, but CACM created a regional market large enough to interest an array of transnational corporations. U.S. direct investment increased from $389 million in 1959 to $677 million in 1977 for the five CACM nations. In 1961, only 4.8% of U.S. total investment in Central America was in manufacturing, but by 1968 that figure had increased to over 15%.[5] Table 3A demonstrates the growth of U.S. investment in Central America.[6]

Table 3A. U.S. Direct Investment in Central America
(excluding Panama & Belize)

1887	1914	1929	1940	1950	1959	1967	1977
12	77	206	149	254	389	501	677

Figures in millions $.
Source: CEPAL

One immediate result of the CACM was to change the composition of intra-regional trade from mostly unprocessed agricultural products to consumer goods, processed food, and chemicals. The introduction of the CACM successfully increased intra-regional imports from $32 million in 1960 to $297 million in 1970, a tenfold increase. Another sign that CACM was working well was that the percentage of intra-regional imports rose as a percentage of total imports from 6% in 1960 to 24% in 1970.[7] The CACM achieved its purpose of expanding the regional market and fostering industrialization in Central America, but there were several underlying problems with the system. One major weakness was that it did not protect the market from the investment of outside capital. Corporations that had previously been exporting to Central America moved to the region to avoid high external tariffs and to take advantage of the low internal tariffs on goods manufactured within the region. Many of the new industries that located in Central America were only finishing operations (sometimes called screwdriver or wrap and pack industries) for semi-manufactured goods. The factories in Central America put only the last touches on products such as cosmetics, pharmaceuticals, and home products. The product on the store shelf may have an *Hecho en Centroamerica* label, but often the only elements genuinely Central American are the air or water added during packaging.

Another major and related problem for Central America was that although the region's import bill for consumer goods decreased, its bill for machinery, spare parts, and semi-processed goods increased dramatically. A study by Marc Herold of the University of New Hampshire found that the bulk of the new industrial ventures in El Salvador processed imported materials: ALCOA's joint venture (1963) produced aluminum sheets from imported industrial molds; Pillsbury (1959) milled imported wheat grain; Lenox (1964) manufactured plastic products from imported plastic powder and resin; Crown Zellerbach (1965) produced corrugated cardboard boxes from imported paper.[8] This trend toward import-intensive manufacturing drove up the import bill for the Central American countries, resulting in ever greater trade deficits.

Although foreign capital dominated the new industrialization in Central America, the expansion of regional trade did diversify the economy and produce a new economic sector that stood apart from the traditional agrarian structure. Most of the rewards of industrialization, however, fell to a new bourgeoisie allied with the transnational corporations.

The lack of central planning for the industrialization resulted in the majority of the new investment flowing to El Salvador and Guatemala, leaving Nicaragua and particularly Honduras to suffer from this uneven development. The lesser developed countries in the market were damaged by a shift in their imports from the lower-priced goods of the foreign industrial countries toward high-cost Guatemalan and Salvadoran products. This reduced national tax revenues because of the switch to un-taxed CACM trade away from taxed foreign imports.[9] The circumstances of uneven development added to existing tension between El Salvador and Honduras, culminating in the so-called Soccer War of 1969. Honduras began boycotting Salvadoran products and turned its anger on the Salvadoran immigrants within Honduras. An attack by the Salvadoran army on Honduras initiated the six-day war. Honduras broke off all trade with El Salvador and withdrew from the CACM, signalling the end to the CACM as an open market for all five countries.

The growth of regional trade, however, continued through the decade despite this and other trade disputes. The economies of the CACM nations weakened in the late 1970s; and in 1980, regional trade dropped 23%. Each nation began fending for itself, resorting to import taxes on products from their neighbors in a frantic effort to protect their own economies. The continuing guerilla warfare in Guatemala and El Salvador, the regional tensions over Nicaragua, and the deteriorating economic situation all make another regional economic agreement unlikely. A government representative of Nicaragua said that Nicaragua is in favor of a new treaty but one that satisfies "the needs of the people, and not the interests of the manufacturers, most of which are transnationals."

Buying Out Local Business

Rather than starting from scratch, U.S. corporations frequently acquire, partially or wholly, the assets of local companies. In Guatemala, 20 of the 44 largest U.S. corporations operating in the country in 1970 started their operations by acquiring Guatemala firms.[10] Table 3B lists a selection of the companies that U.S. corporations have acquired in Central America. The U.S. corporations often leave their names behind when they go to Central America and assume the name of the local company they purchase.

Table 3B. Examples of Central American Firms Acquired by U.S. Companies

Acquired Firm	Product	Country	U.S. Company
Chiricana de Leche	dairy products	Panama	Borden
Cervecería Tegucigalpa	drinks	Honduras	Castle & Cooke
Industria Aceitera	cottonseed oils	Honduras	Castle & Cooke
Alimentos Mariscol	feed mill	Guatemala	Central Soya
Productos Alimentos Sharp	canned foods	Guatemala	Coca-Cola
Industria de Café	coffee	Guatemala	Coca-Cola
Alimentos Kern	ketchup, baby foods	Guatemala	Colgate Palmolive
Alimentos de Istmo	corn starch	Honduras	CPC International
Del Campo	fruit, vegetables	Costa Rica	Del Monte (R.J. Reynolds)
Industria del Maíz	flour, cereals	Guatemala	General Mills
Famosa	ice cream, milk	Honduras	Foremost-McKesson
Corp Bonima	drugs	El Salvador	Foremost-McKesson
Empresas Lácteas	dairy products	El Salvador	Foremost-McKesson
Felipe Pozuelo e Hijos	biscuits, candy	Costa Rica	W.R. Grace
Industria Cristal	crackers	Nicaragua	Nabisco
Incubadores Centro-americanos	poultry	Guatemala	Ralston Purina
Golden	margarine	Costa Rica	Standard Brands
Dely	margarine	Guatemala	Standard Brands
Aceitera Corona	edible oils	Nicaragua	United Brands
Numar	margarine	Costa Rica	United Brands
Tabacalera Centroamericana	cigarettes	Guatemala	Philip Morris
Tabacalera Costarricense	cigarettes	Costa Rica	Philip Morris
Aluminios de Centroamérica	aluminum shapes	El Salvador	ALCOA

Sources: *Moody's Industrial* 1981; Marc Herold, *From Riches to 'Rags'*; NACLA, *Agribusiness in the Americas*.

Another common form of corporate investment in Central America is a joint venture with local owners. In El Salvador 41 of the 55 foreign investments since 1960 were joint ventures.[11] U.S. firms, by associating with local firms, gain the important knowledge and local market experience necessary to make businesses run profitably. A joint venture is an excellent way for a U.S. corporation to gradually absorb local wealth. It also has the effect of creating a dependent class of capitalists who are allied with U.S. political and business interests.

The influx of foreign capital also has the effect of driving out of business local company owners not tied to the transnationals. Access of the transnationals to credit and higher technology, as well as the ability to withstand temporary losses all contribute to the ascendancy of foreign capital and the disintegration of local capital formation.

IMPORT SUBSTITUTION TO LABOR SUBSTITUTION

Economic development through import-substitution is a fading dream for Central America. The postwar experiment with industrialization ended in failure. Industrialization came to mean the growth of U.S. industry in Central America, not the development of Central American industry. Two decades of industrialization deepened the region's dependency on international capitalism and worsened its trade balance.

In the 1970s, industrialization through import-substitution degenerated to a system of industrialization that substituted cheap Central American labor for U.S. labor. The Central American nations, rather than creating barriers to protect their fragile economies against incursions of foreign investment, welcomed a new penetration of foreign corporations through the establishment of free-trade zones as havens for runaway shops. Corporations, especially in the electronics and textile industries, set up labor-intensive assembly operations in Central America called offshore industries or *maquiladoras*. Rather than producing for the Central American market, the *maquiladoras* merely assemble basic materials produced in the United States. The assembled electronics parts or clothing are then shipped back to the United States for further manufacture or distribution. The *maquiladora* arrangement is ideal for transnational companies worried about possible nationalization and the political instability of Central America. Having little or no investment in plant or equipment, a company can close up shop almost overnight and move on to a more secure and possibly cheaper part of the world.

There are two types of *maquiladoras*. One transfers part of the production process to Central America. Such is the case of electronic companies like Texas Instruments, AVX Ceramics, and Dataram. The second type involves sub-contracting a Central American business. This arrangement is common to the textile industry, where a U.S. corporation contracts a firm in Central America to sew together pieces for pants, blouses, or brassieres. Though the U.S. firms have no direct investment in the country, they control the sub-contractor through financing, marketing, and technology. A 1978 study of seven companies in Costa Rica's textile industry found that 96% of the production immediately left the region for marketing.[12] The *Multinational Monitor*, in an article on the international textile industry, described the process: "Multinationals are fragmenting output and trade into a chain of partial operations, spaced along a planetary assembly line according to cost consideration and marketing strategems."[13]

It's no small savings for a U.S. company to run away to Central America. Latin American *maquiladoras* were first established in Mexico, but when the Mexican government raised the minimum wage in the mid-1970s, many companies packed up and moved to Central America to take advantage of the cheapest labor supply in Latin America. A Department of Commerce report showed that average wage rates in Central America (excluding Panama) in 1977 were eight times lower than the average wage rates for parent companies in the United States. The average hourly rate in manufacturing in the United States in 1980 was $8.76, while the average rate in Central America for employees of U.S. affiliates was $1.08.[14]

In all the countries, the *maquiladoras* prefer to employ women. At the free-trade zone in Puerto Cortes in Honduras, hundreds of women park their bicycles in front of a complex of unidentified buildings where they make baseballs, bras, and men's underwear for U.S. consumers. "The concentration of capital and resources affects everybody," commented Saralee Hamilton, coordinator of the Women's Network on Global Corporations, "but it affects women in particularly damaging ways, for it increases the subordination of women in the international division of labor. . . . Multinationals see women as a super-exploitable work force, and institute deliberate policies of preferential female hiring."[15]

Because El Salvador's bourgeoisie has traditionally been tied to U.S. capitalism, it was El Salvador that initiated the regional campaign to attract *maquiladoras*. During the mid-1970s, the government of El Salvador advertised that Salvadorans had the "will to work" and that their country had an "outstanding labor force of two million close to North American markets."[16] Competition is heavy among the Central American countries vying for the *maquiladoras*. The countries try to outdo each other in their offers of cheap labor. With the exception of the Colon Free-Trade Zone in Panama, the zones have not attracted the expected numbers of companies. A U.S. Embassy spokesperson said that "Honduras is losing its shirt on the Puerto Cortes Zone since it hasn't been able to attract enough industry to pay for the costs of establishing and building the zone."[17] The governments try to justify the incentives they offer to *maquiladoras* by saying that the new industries provide jobs for the urban unemployed and raise the value of national exports. These justifications for the runaway plants are remarkably similar to the justifications for the concessions given to the banana companies in the early 1900s.

U.S. INVESTMENT

U.S. investors from the very largest transnationals to small farming and retail operations are doing business in Central America. The Resource Center has identified 1,458 businesses with U.S. ownership in the seven Central American

Table 3C. Largest U.S. Corporations

Top 10 Paper Companies*	No. of Central American Countries
1. Georgia-Pacific	1
2. International Paper	1
3. Weyerhaeuser	2
4. Champion International	1
5. Boise Cascade	3
6. Crown Zellerbach	3
7. Mead	-
8. St. Regis Paper	3
9. Kimberly-Clark	3
10. Scott Paper	1

Top 10 Chemical Producers*	No. of Central American Countries
1. Du Pont	3
2. Dow Chemical	3
3. Union Carbide	3
4. Exxon	6
5. Monsanto	5
6. W.R. Grace	2
7. Allied Chemical	2
8. Shell Oil	1
9. American Cyanamid	3
10. Celanese	1

Top 14 Drug Companies*	No. of Central American Countries
1. Johnson & Johnson	4
2. American Home Products	4
3. Warner-Lambert	2
4. Bristol-Myers	5
5. Pfizer	3
6. Merck	3
7. Eli Lilly	1
8. Abbott Laboratories	4
9. Upjohn	2
10. Sterling Drug	5
11. Schering-Plough	3
12. Squibb	2
13. SmithKline	-
14. Richardson-Merrell	2

*by sales

Top 25 Food Processors*	No. of Central American Countries
1. Dart & Kraft	2
2. Beatrice Foods	4
3. General Foods	-
4. Coca-Cola	5
5. Esmark	1
6. Ralston Purina	3
7. United Brands	5
8. Consolidated Foods	2
9. CPC International	2
10. Iowa Beef	-
11. PepsiCo	3
12. Greyhound	3
13. Anheuser-Busch	-
14. H.J. Heinz	1
15. Seagrams	1
16. Standard Brands (Nabisco)	5
17. Campbell Soup	-
18. LTV	-
19. Carnation	1
20. Philip Morris	3
21. Borden	4
22. Procter & Gamble	-
23. General Mills	4
24. Archer-Daniels-Midland	-
25. R.J. Reynolds	4

Top 11 Oil Companies*	No. of Central American Countries
1. Exxon	6
2. Mobil	3
3. Texaco	7
4. Standard Oil of California	6
5. Gulf	3
6. Standard Oil of Indiana	1
7. Atlantic Richfield	1
8. Shell Oil	1
9. Conoco	2
10. Phillips Petroleum	2
11. Standard Oil of Ohio	1

Sources: *Food Processing*, December 1979; *Everybody's Business*, 1980; *Business Week*, October 29, 1979; various Annual Reports; *Chemical Week*, April 23, 1980; The Resource Center, 1982.

The Resource Center has found evidence of 1,458 businesses with U.S. investment in Central America. Many of these companies are subsidiaries, affiliates, and branches of the largest U.S. corporations. This table lists the largest U.S. oil, chemical, paper, drug, and food processing corporations and the number of Central American countries in which they are currently operating.

countries. (See Methodology) Seventy of the 100 largest U.S. corporations (according to the *Fortune* 1982 rankings) do business in Central America. As listed in Table 3C, the nation's top 11 energy companies from Exxon to Standard Oil of Ohio are in Central America, as are 13 of the 14 leading drug companies in the United States, nine of the top ten paper companies, 18 of the top 25 food processors, and all ten of the largest chemical producers.[18]

The U.S. Department of Commerce reported that in 1977 direct U.S. investment in Central America amounted to $3.1 billion; in 1980, U.S. direct investment rose to $4.2 billion, an increase of 34%.[19] (See Table 3D.) Panama is the location of the most U.S. direct investment, attributable to the presence of the International Finance Center, the Colon Free-Trade Zone, and its oil transshipment and pipeline complex. Figures from the Department of Commerce show that 210 U.S. transnational corporations had at least one affiliate in Central America in 1977.[20]* The Department of Commerce reported that in 1979 the rate of return on U.S. direct investment in Latin America was 19.6% while the average international rate of return for U.S. direct investment was 7.6%.[21]

Table 3D. U.S. Direct Investment in Central America by Country 1977 & 1980
(millions $)

	1977	1980	% Change
Belize	21	24	15%
Costa Rica	178	303	70%
El Salvador	79	103	30%
Guatemala	155	226	46%
Honduras	157	288	83%
Nicaragua	108	89	18%
Panama	2,442	3,190	31%
Central America	*3,140*	*4,223*	*34%*

Sources: U.S. Department of Commerce, *U.S. Direct Investment Abroad 1977*, April 1981; U.S. Department of Commerce, International Investment Division, Obie Whichard.

Central America is not only fertile ground for direct U.S. investment but also an annual market for $2.6 billion in sales of U.S. products. The United States provides 56% of the imported manufactured products to Central America (not including Belize), followed by Japan with 16%. The leading U.S. exports to Central America in 1981 were food products, fertilizer, pesticides, and synthetic resins.[22]

*The Department of Commerce surveyed foreign affiliates with ten percent or more U.S. direct investment and which had over $500,000 in assets, sales, or income.

The Corporate Power Bloc

The United States is going all out to stop what it sees as the growing radicalization of Central America and the Caribbean region. When President Reagan announced his proposed Caribbean Basin Initiative (CBI), the Caribbean Basin Initiative Coalition formed to lobby for Reagan's CBI program. Directors of the new coalition included David Rockefeller and Frank Borman, Chairperson of Eastern Airlines. Other corporate advocacy groups with a Central American focus are the Council of the Americas, the Americas Society, the Association of American Chambers of Commerce in Latin America (AACCLA), and Caribbean/Central American Action (C/CAA).

In 1980, the Agency for International Development launched C/CAA with a $250,000 grant. The new organization is at the forefront of a new assault on the region by U.S. corporations. Members of C/CAA's board of directors include representatives from United Brands, Gulf+Western, and Exxon.[23] The organization has rallied the support of many corporations doing business in the region as listed in Table 3E. One of the purposes of C/CAA is to promote new U.S. investment in nontraditional exports from the area, by having the U.S. government pave the way through pre-investment surveys and easy

Table 3E. Corporate Supporters of C/CAA

Aluminum Company of America	IBM World Trade Americas/
Amerada Hess	Far East Corporation
Amoco Foundation	Inter-Continental Hotels
Amoco International Oil	InterNorth
Arnold and Porter	Litwin Engineers & Constructors
Arthur D. Little International	Maidenform
Ashland Oil	Miami Herald Publishing
Atlantic Richfield	Mobil Oil
Bali Company, Division of Hanes	Occidental Exploration and
Bank of America National Trust	Production
and Savings Association	Pan American World Airways
Caribbean Holidays	Peoples Energy
The Charter Company	PepsiCo
The Chase Manhattan Bank	Pet
Citibank	Procter & Gamble
Coca-Cola	Reynolds Metals
Continental Telephone	Rosario Dominicana
Control Data	Santa Fe International
E.F. Hutton & Company	Sealand Industries
Eastern Airlines	Shrimp Culture
Esso Inter-America	Southeast First National Bank of Miami
General Electric	Tenneco
General Foods	Tesoro Petroleum
Grace Foundation	Texaco
Gulf+Western Industries	Touche Ross & Company
H.B. Fuller	Tropical Shipping and Construction
Hvide Shipping	United Brands

Source: C/CAA Fact Sheet, 1981.

financing schemes. One focus is to attract new investors from the Sunbelt in the United States. Chairperson of C/CAA is Governor Bob Graham of Florida, the state with the most financial and trade links with Central America and the Caribbean. C/CAA is working to establish twin chambers of commerce in Central America and in the southwestern United States. C/CAA organized a "Conference of Cooperation between the United States and the Central American Chambers of Commerce," in Guatemala, which gave strong backing to Reagan's Caribbean Basin Initiative.[24]

Close cooperation with AID is a key to C/CAA's strategy to increase U.S. investment in Central America. Executive Director of C/CAA Peter Johnson, who is on leave from the State Department, said that "C/CAA is working with Central American private-sector leaders to create a region-wide vehicle for business leadership in development, and for channeling funds from AID and other donors directly into the private sector." C/CAA not only has the government's money, but also seems to share its view of foreign affairs. As Johnson commented: "I'd like to see some military hardware going into Guatemala. Not lethal stuff, but I'd like to see some of the basic little things, like helicopters. Things that would enable the U.S. government to have better access to the current Guatemalan government."[25]

The Association of American Chambers of Commerce in Latin America (AACCLA) has offices in each of the Central American countries, except Belize. In Guatemala, the Chamber of Commerce has stood steadfastly behind the military governments and has supported continued military aid. Tom Mooney, president of the Chamber in Guatemala, said, "The government of Guatemala, despite its numerous faults, is better than most governments of the world in terms of the very human rights grounds on which it is so severely attacked. . . ."[26] Regional president of AACCLA is R. Bruce Cuthbertson, also the representative of the Nicaragua-based Inter-American Builders Associates. Cuthbertson said that the entire future of Central America depends on "neutralizing and eliminating terrorists" and on the "removal of the Sandinistas in Nicaragua."[27]

The most well-connected corporate power bloc for Latin America is the Council of the Americas. The Council represents over 200 of the largest U.S. corporations and 85% of the U.S. investment in Central and Latin America. Founded in 1958 as the U.S. Inter-American Council, the goal of the organization is "further understanding and acceptance of the role of private enterprise as a positive force for the development of the Americas."[28] Its most influential member is David Rockefeller, former president of the Chase Manhattan Bank and a founder of the Trilateral Commission. The Council encouraged the establishment of Panama's International Finance Center in 1970 and later lobbied in support of the ratification of the new Canal treaties.

In 1981, David Rockefeller founded another Latin American organization, called the Americas Society. "It is the intention of the Americas Society to make clear the splendid relationship among the countries of the Western Hemisphere and to emphasize once again that this relationship is not exclusively economic, but rather is based firmly in similar political aspirations. . . ," said

Rockefeller. Supporting the formation of the new corporate group, U.S. Assistant Secretary of State for Inter-American Affairs Thomas Enders said, "As you know the administration believes the private sector has a vital role to play in the hemisphere. So we are pleased that the Americas Society has been formed and we heartily endorse its objectives." Rockefeller said the organization will devote itself to cultural, public, and business affairs.[29]

AFTERMATH OF "DEVELOPMENT"

Development economist Milton Friedman of the University of Chicago once said: "Look for the sources of American influence on foreign attitudes and cultures and where will one find them? Not in the literature disseminated by USIS [U.S. Information Service], useful though that may be, but in the activities of International Harvester, Caterpillar Tractor, Singer Sewing Machines, Coca-Cola, Hollywood, and so on. Channels of trade are by all odds the most effective means of disseminating understanding and knowledge of the United States."

Friedman has been right on some counts. The invasion of U.S. transnational corporations into Central America has certainly created an understanding of the United States. U.S. corporations are everywhere in Central America. Just about everything seems either to have been made in the United States or made by a U.S. company doing business in Central America. Culture in Central America has become a product of Hollywood and Madison Avenue.

Central American government and business leaders regularly visit Washington to talk money and policy. Despite occasional nationalistic rhetoric to please the folks at home, they know all too well that their politics and economic programs must come within the boundaries set by the United States for Central America.

The United Nations Economic Commission for Latin America (ECLA) in 1981 published a development plan for the 1980s which said that a major reason for the continued underdevelopment of Latin America was that it had developed an unhealthy dependence on the industrialized world. ECLA challenged the notion espoused by Friedman and other advocates of imperialist development. Transnationals, said ECLA, have channeled significant levels of imports, foreign financing, and technology to the area but have done little to augment exports, thereby keeping the region dependent on outside resources.

This economic exploitation by the world capitalist market has been accompanied by a more subtle type of integration. The U.S. corporations have achieved great success in integrating many Central Americans into the American Way through its consumer culture, music, and movies. But this, for the most part, has only been an affectation. Years of economic development by Coca-Cola, Texas Instruments, and United Brands, accompanied by an ever-increasing poverty, have given Central Americans a deeper understanding of the United States. It's a knowledge that the American Way of corporate development is ultimately reponsible for the underdevelopment that affects the great

44

majority in Central America. This understanding has produced a rising chorus of "Yankee Go Home" throughout Central America. The lesson learned from the pervasive presence of foreign corporations in Central America is that economic development for the corporations doesn't mean economic development for Central America.

REFERENCE NOTES

1. Suzanne Jonas and David Tobis, Editors, *Guatemala*, (Berkeley and New York: *North American Congress on Latin America*, referred to as *NACLA* in all references that follow, 1974), p. 89.
2. *Ibid.*, p. 148.
3. Donald Castillo Rivas, *Acumulacion de Capital y Empresas Transnacionales en Centroamerica* (Mexico City: Siglo Veintiuno Editores, 1980), Information from *El Proceso de Industrializacion* by Rene Poitevin (Costa Rica: EDUCA, 1977).
4. Isaac Cohen, *Regional Integration in Central America* (Lexington, MA: Heath, 1972), p. 60, cited in Jonas and Tobis.
5. David Tobis, "CACM: The Integration of Underdevelopment," *NACLA*, June 1970.
6. "El Financiamiento Exterior de America Latina," (CEPAL, 1964); Gert Rosenthal, "Algunos Apuntes sobre el Grado de Participacion de la Inversion Extranjera," La Integracion Economica Centroamerica, (Mexico: Fondo de Cultura Economica, 1975); *U.S. Direct Investment Position Abroad* (Washington: Dept. of Commerce, 1977).
7. SIECA, 1982.
8. Marc Herold, "From Riches to 'Rags': Finanzkapital in El Salvador, 1900-1980," (unpublished manuscript, University of New Hampshire, 1980), p. 22.
9. *Ibid.*, p. 21.
10. Jonas and Tobis, p. 132.
11. Herold, p. 22.
12. Juan J. Munoz, "La Participacion del Capital Extranjero en la Economica Costarricense, 1978, cited in Donald Castillo Rivas, *Acumulacion de Capital y Empresas Transnacionales en Centroamerica,* (Mexico City: Siglo Veintiuno Editores, 1980).
13. John Cavanagh, "Fibers and Textiles," *Multinational Monitor*, August 1981, p. 16.
14. *Survey of Current Business*, (Washington: Dept. of Commerce, February 1982), p. 48.
15. "Ten People Who Aim to Tame the Multinationals," *Multinational Monitor*, January 1982.
16. El Salvador Tourist Commission, Promotional Material, 1979.
17. Interview by Tom Barry, April 1982.
18. The Resource Center, Summer 1982.
19. *U.S. Direct Investment Abroad 1977*, (Washington: Dept. of Commerce, April 1981), p. 6; Obie Whichard, U.S. Dept. of Commerce, International Investment Division, interview May 1982.
20. *Survey of Current Business*, (Washington: Dept. of Commerce, October 1981), p. 50.
21. *Survey of Current Business*, (Washington: Dept. of Commerce, August 1981), p. 27.
22. *Vocero Comercial*, November-December 1981, p. 7.
23. "Chambers of Commerce Rally 'Round Reagan," *Central America Report*, April 1982.
24. "Caribbean Investment: Following the Flag?" *Multinational Monitor*, November 1981.
25. *Ibid.*
26. Bulletin of the American Chamber of Commerce in Guatemala, May 23, 1980, cited in Interfaith Center on Corporate Responsibility Brief, November 1980.
27. Robert H. Holden, "Corporate Officers Embrace Latin Dictators," *Multinational Monitor*, June 1982, p. 12.
28. "Multinationals, Development, and Democracy: An Interview with Henry Geyelin," *Multinational Monitor*, March 1980, p. 12.
29. "Rockefeller Launches Another Businessmen's Club," *Multinational Monitor*, September 1981, p. 3.

Chapter Four

Finance: Lending a Hand

> *If you see a starving man,*
> *Don't give him a fish.*
> *Rather, give him a fishing pole.*

> — Old Chinese Proverb

World conditions have changed dramatically since the days of the Chinese philosophers, but hunger and poverty still persist. The developed nations of the modern world have recognized these problems, but they have given too little of either fish or fishing poles to the people of the underdeveloped world. Today's wisdom is not to give away fishing poles, but to sell them. To deal with the obvious fact that people can't buy fishing poles without any money, the developed nations make use of financing and development assistance. As shown in Table 4A, three methods are used to facilitate the financing of the underdeveloped world: 1) multilateral financing, 2) bilateral financing, and 3) private transnational banking.

Table 4A. International Channels of Money to Underdeveloped Countries

		Source of Capital			
Type/Example	Sector	No. of Countries	Use of Capital	Capital Recipient
1. Multilateral/ World Bank	Public and Private	Two or more	Loans	Mostly Public, Some Private
2. Bilateral/ U.S. AID	Public	One	Loans	Public and Private
3. Multinational Financial Firms/ Chase Manhattan Bank	Private	One or more	Loans Portfolio Investment Direct Investment	Mostly Private, Some Public

Since the Second World War, bilateral and multilateral institutions have poured over $7.5 billion in loans into Central America. In addition, commercial banks have invested many billions of dollars in Central America. Multilateral and U.S. bilateral lending in the region is detailed in Table 4B.

Table 4B. Cumulative Multilateral and Bilateral Loans to Central America, 1946-1981

(millions $)

	Financing
Multilateral *	
International Bank for Reconstruction and Development	1,850
International Development Association	173
International Finance Corporation	53
Inter-American Development Bank	2,450
Central American Bank (BCIE)	1,060**
Sub-total	*5,586*
U.S. Bilateral	
Military	71
Agency for International Development	1,335
PL 480, Food for Peace Program	58
Export/Import Bank	358
Other	134
Sub-total	*1,956*
Total	*7,542*

*International Monetary Fund not included
**Through 1978

Source: Agency for International Development, *U.S. Overseas Loans and Grants.*

Another way to gauge the extent of financing in Central America is to measure the growth of the region's indebtedness. In 1960, the external public debt of the Central American nations amounted to $262 million. By 1981, the indebtedness of the Central American governments had increased 42 times to over $11 billion. External public debt by country is listed in Table 4C.

Table 4C.   External Public Debt 1960, 1970, 1981
(millions $)

	1960	1970	1981	Increase 1960 - 81
Costa Rica	55	227	2,700	49 x
El Salvador	33	126	800	24 x
Guatemala	51	176	700	14 x
Honduras	23	144	1,500	65 x
Nicaragua	41	222	2,400	59 x
Panama	59	290	2,900	49 x
Central America	*262*	*1,185*	*11,000*	*42 x*

Sources: Inter-American Development Bank, Economic and Social Progress in Latin America 1980-81 Report; Latin America Regional Report.

EARLY INROADS

Central America's indebtedness to the industrial world is hardly a recent phenomenon. Banks and other financial investors from the United States have been managing the external debt of Central American nations since the turn of the century. Earlier, in the 19th century, the British controlled Central America's banking and public finance. When there was a railroad to build or a government short of cash, the British bankers were always on hand. By 1930, however, an aggressive campaign by U.S. government-backed financial institutions broke the financial hegemony of Great Britain in Central America. A common method used by U.S. financial investors to gain inroads into a country was to offer to pay the nation's entire European debt with one large U.S. loan. As a guarantee of repayment, the United States would place the country under a customs receivership, which would mean the U.S. would control a country's trade revenues. Such a situation occurred in Nicaragua after the United States backed a coup in 1909 against the Liberal Party government of Jose Zelaya Santos. Zelaya had angered the United States by negotiating a hefty loan with London banks. In 1911, the United States installed a Collector General of Nicaraguan customs to insure that a new $1.5 million loan from Brown Brothers and J.W. Seligman Company would be paid back; Nicaragua remained under a customs receivership until 1949. U.S. loans to El Salvador included a provision for a similar customs receivership. U.S. bankers not only serviced the debts of Central American nations but also provided the capital for new roads, electric plants, and communications systems — infrastructure projects that facilitated mineral exploitation and export crop production.

Before the Great Depression, private banks managed all U.S. international loans through bond sales and short-term lending. The United States had become an exporter of private capital, with the U.S. government backing up this role with gunboat diplomacy. The slowdown in the domestic economy of the 1930s, however, put a crimp in U.S. international lending. Though U.S. bankers weren't suffering, they were concerned that the U.S. government no longer had the power or inclination to take up the Big Stick against delinquent debtors. The power of the lending country was always necessary in order to guarantee repayment of international loans. The largest foreign lenders hailed from nations with substantial military clout. If a debtor country felt it could default on an international loan without repercussions, it usually did so. A notable example of this "law" of international finance was the failure of the United States to honor British railroad loans in the 19th century. The United States, as a growing imperialist power, rightly concluded that the British could not force it to pay up.

After World War Two, the United States again began to export its capital to international markets. But, this time instead of private banks, the U.S. government itself, along with the new multilateral banks, handled most of the international lending.

MULTILATERAL FINANCING

The Second World War marked the end of the old colonial world order where imperialist powers lorded over their own colonies and trade blocs. It opened up the world for a new economic order dominated by the United States, which had emerged from the war as the strongest capitalist power on the globe. The United States and England created two institutions in 1944 for the purposes of guiding the postwar recovery of international trade, insuring the stability and convertibility of major currencies, and pooling resources. The new institutions, the World Bank and the International Monetary Fund (IMF), were loosely associated with the United Nations. However, they were structured more like a plutocrat's United Nations since the amount of financial commitment determined a member's voting power.

The World Bank and the IMF are called multilateral institutions because they receive financial subscriptions from over 140 nations to finance projects and governments throughout the world. After financing the reconstruction of postwar Europe, the multilateral institutions turned to the underdeveloped world. Their objectives were to integrate the underdeveloped nations into the orderly expansion of the international capitalist market and to prevent these nations from falling into the socialist orbit. The direct colonialism of earlier eras was dead, but it was replaced by a system of indirect colonialism ruled by finance capital and foreign investment. This multilateral approach suited the United States which never had much of a worldwide colonial empire to rely on, but did have an expansive economy ready for new frontiers. The theory propagated by the United States was that all nations were interdependent and that tariffs, currency exchange regulations, and other trade restrictions should be broken down to allow the free rein and flow of capital. The multilaterals' role was to foster a climate favorable to investment by guaranteeing free trade and by financing projects that would open up the underdeveloped world to foreign capital.

The multilaterals perform an important function in presenting to the underdeveloped world a united front composed of the industrial nations and investors. When the developed countries are all working cooperatively, the underdeveloped countries find it hard to blame a particular imperialist nation for their exploitation. The multilateral front is also an advantage to private financial investors, who loan their money to the multilateral banks, which in turn loan the money to the "developing nations." In this way, the combined power of the world's governments guarantees their loans. The concern of the multilateral institutions has never been to promote independent and economically strong Third World nations but to encourage a kind of development that services the already developed world through cheap exports and reliance on imports. In this way, the multilaterals have operated as the grand coordinators of the underdevelopment process, and the result has been further dependency rather than self-reliance. A February 1982 report by the U.S. Treasury summarized the reasons why the United States should continue to support the multilateral institutions. It said that the multilaterals make "capital markets work efficiently" and that the "promotion of private investment" is the principal purpose of these institutions.[1]

World Bank

Although the World Bank enjoys the image of a charitable foundation with the task of distributing the largess of the industrial world, the reality is that the World Bank is first and foremost a banking institution. Like any bank, it is interested in getting a return on its loans. The World Bank has three divisions: the International Bank for Reconstruction and Development (IBRD), the International Development Association (IDA), and the International Finance Corporation (IFC). The president of the United States appoints the president of the World Bank. In 1981, after 12 years as president, Robert McNamara resigned to become a director of Royal Dutch Shell. Before joining the World Bank, McNamara served as Secretary of Defense during the Vietnam War and prior to that post was the president of Ford Motor Company. Known as a liberal, McNamara vastly expanded the operations of the bank and stressed the development assistance aspects of the World Bank. President Reagan's appointment of A.W. Clausen, the former president of Bank of America, as the new president of the World Bank reflects a more conservative, self-interested approach to multilateral financing by the U.S. government. Clausen has promised to put his supply-side economic principles and his belief in private enterprise as a development tool to work at the World Bank. Concerning the role of transnational corporations, Clausen said, "No other entity is better equipped to bring together resources, expertise, capital and markets on a global basis in such an efficient manner."[2]

The World Bank and regional multilateral institutions require that the "developing" nations guarantee the loans and carry the responsibility of the multilateral debts. The projects sponsored by the World Bank are ostensibly intended to develop the debtor nations so that some day they can join the developed group of nations. Development, however, has been defined as what's good for the industrial world. Since the developed nations need a steady supply of minerals and agricultural products, the World Bank funds projects to increase the productivity of the agro-export sector. Because the developed nations need good roads and communications systems to make foreign private investment more profitable, the World Bank finances these infrastructure projects. The World Bank and other multilateral institutions search for programs that minimize risks and provide interest on their investment. As one World Bank report frankly noted, "Failures of credit payments have been reduced when the payments have been coordinated with the search for a market for harvests that are processed centrally, as for example tobacco, cotton, cocoa, tea, and coffee"[3] — products destined not for local consumption but for export markets.

Most active of the World Bank's divisions is the IBRD, known as its hard-loan window because its interest rates are not "soft" or concessionary. Between 1945 and 1981, of the more than $2.1 billion in Central American projects financed by the three divisions of the World Bank, 86% have come through this hard-loan window. IBRD loans are repayable over a 15-20 year period, with an interest rate (in 1982) of 12% a year plus several small service fees. The soft-loan window of the World Bank, the IDA, gives credit for 50-year periods, including ten-year grace periods. The IDA loans carry no interest, just a small annual service charge.

The World Bank puts most of its financing in infrastructure projects that facilitate new private investment by constructing a base of production. In 1982, over 20% of the Bank's funds went to transportation projects. These infrastructure projects create a foreign market for road machinery, construction materials, and technical consultants. This import-heavy development increases trade deficits and severely reduces foreign exchange reserves.

In 1981, the IBRD put 0.1% of its financing into "Population, Health and Nutrition," the only category for direct services. About 14% of World Bank (IBRD and IDA) financing goes to development finance companies, which are intermediate institutions designed to channel multilateral and bilateral financing to industrial and agricultural projects in the underdeveloped world. In 1982, the World Bank lent $30 million to a development finance corporation that will provide credit for various industrial projects in Honduras. Precious little World Bank money goes to projects that directly alleviate the desperate conditions of the people of the underdeveloped world.

The IDA, the World Bank's soft-loan window, directs its financing to the poorest nations of the world. The Reagan Administration wants to slow down the programs of IDA in favor of more projects that are co-financed with commercial banks and that carry higher interest rates.

The third component of the World Bank is the International Finance Corporation (IFC), which lends exclusively to the private sector in under-developed nations. President Reagan wants to expand the IFC and has commissioned the U.S. Agency for International Development (AID) to co-finance projects with this division of the World Bank. IFC literature contains no elevated talk about helping the world's poor, but just straight talk about helping private enterprise in underdeveloped countries through multilateral lending and by attracting commercial co-financing. Since the IFC is primarily interested in profits, it is not inclined to loan money to or invest in small businesses producing for the internal market. Instead, it has a propensity for financing export businesses and finance companies, many of which involve U.S. private investment. Tourism is one major IFC emphasis in Central America and the rest of the world. In 1981, the IFC reported that it was financially involved in the following firms in Central America.[4]

Costa Rica: Maricultura (U.S. ownership), shrimp processing; Scott Paper Company (U.S. ownership), paper products.

El Salvador: Hoteles de Centro America, tourism.

Guatemala: Cementos Progreso, cement; Eximbal (U.S. ownership), mining (currently not in operation).

Honduras: Textiles Rio Lindo (U.S. ownership), textiles.

Nicaragua: Nicaragua Sugar Estates (U.S. ownership), food processing; Posada del Sol, tourism; Textiles Fabricato, textiles.

Panama: Banco Latinoamericano de Exportaciones, financing; Corporacion de Desarrollo Hotelero, tourism; Vidrios Panamenos, glass containers.

Inter-American Development Bank

In the 1950s and 1960s, a new network of multilateral banks, formed at the regional level to complement the operations of the World Bank. The regional multilateral bank for Latin America, the Inter-American Development Bank

(IDB), was often called the "Alliance for Progress Bank" because of the close correlation between its lending programs and U.S. development assistance in Latin America. The IDB still follows the outlines of U.S. foreign policy; and, like the U.S. government, it favors increased financing of infrastructure projects over financing of social development programming. Since its founding in 1959, the IDB has loaned over $20 billion in Latin America with only 16% of this total funding devoted to projects in public health, urban development, or education. The emphasis on productive and physical infrastructure projects is demonstrated in the following breakdown of 1981 IDB lending: 32% for productive sectors like agriculture and mining; 53.3% for physical infrastructure projects in energy, transportation, and communications; 11.3% for projects with some social service orientation; and 3.4% for export financing and pre-investment surveys.

More than any other multilateral bank, the IDB considers political as well as economic conditions in its lending decisions. IDB loans in Chile dried up during the progressive Allende government but resumed after a U.S.-backed military faction took state power. In Central America, Guatemala and El Salvador — the two worst human rights violators in Latin America — received increased funding from the IDB in 1981, while the Sandinista government of Nicaragua received the least amount of IDB money in Central America the same year.[5] El Salvador in 1980 received a $45.4 million loan for U.S.-sponsored agrarian reform projects despite objections of IDB members West Germany, Denmark, Canada, and Mexico. In 1981, the IDB loaned El Salvador $30 million to build 200 kilometers of rural roads to promote integration of the country's rural northwest — a loan with obvious military implications. The IDB also approved a controversial $70 million loan for the Chixoy hydroelectric plant in the Quiche province of Guatemala.

In line with Washington policy, the IDB in 1981 voted to further reduce the already small amount of loans for public sector projects and to increase loans to the private sector that will impede what the IDB refers to as the "socialization of states."[6] A major area of interest for the IDB has been the promotion of development banks that finance private enterprises. In its over two decades of lending, the IDB has helped create or strengthen more than 80 of these development banks, commonly called *financieras*.[7] U.S. government and business have also heavily supported these development banks, which among other things make local and multilateral capital available for U.S. investors.

Central American Bank

The Central American Bank for Economic Integration (Banco Centroamericana de Integracion Economica, BCIE) promotes the industrialization of Central America through international financing. The United States, the major financial backer of this regional development bank at its inception in 1961, continues to control the institution. Through June 1981, the bank had received loans in the amount of $981 million from the following sources:

Agency for International Development (AID)	$195 million
Transnational bank syndicates	424 million
U.S. transnational banks (individual)	172 million
Inter-American Development Bank	190 million

The BCIE has served the needs of U.S. transnational corporations with investments in Central America through both the financing of infrastructure projects and the direct financing of corporate operations. Corporations that have received loans from the BCIE include Colgate Palmolive, U.S. Steel, United Brands, Castle & Cooke, Hercules, Pennwalt, and Phelps Dodge. In 1981, the BCIE joined with the Inter-American Development Bank and the World Bank's IBRD to form the Central American Consultative Group to coordinate financing activities in Central America. A key objective of the group is to increase assistance to the private sector. The group says new financing will be conditioned by agreements for "needed structural adjustment measures to be taken by the recipient countries." The group's 1982 plan included a $2 billion package of loans for Central American countries.[8]

International Monetary Fund

Unlike the other multilateral institutions, the International Monetary Fund (IMF) doesn't fund specific projects, but rather steps in with general expense loans when a country can't pay its debts. The United States together with the European nations established the IMF in 1944 to guide postwar economic growth. Like the other multilateral institutions, voting power corresponds to each country's financial commitments to the IMF, resulting in the dominance of the United States, and other industrial countries. The IMF's power has increased with the growing indebtedness of the underdeveloped world. It has become the financial sheriff of the "Free World" with the job of patrolling the globe to insure that the underdeveloped nations meet their public debt obligations to the multilateral and commercial banks. If a country falls short of the foreign exchange it needs to meet its debt burden, the IMF provides quick debt relief and balance of payments support.

The IMF offers carrot-and-stick arrangements to underdeveloped countries. The emergency funding is the carrot, while the stick is the IMF austerity plan. A country receiving the standby funding is required to sign a letter of intent, binding the country to IMF measures to stabilize the nation's economy. The arrangement lasts from one to three years but the IMF can withhold undisbursed loan money if at any time it concludes that the country is not abiding by the agreed-upon stabilization measures. The emergency measures are designed to increase the foreign exchange revenue available to each country so that it can pay off the IMF loan and other external debts. These "stabilization" measures typically include the following:

- severe cuts in public spending,
- freeze on wages,
- liberalization of exchange rates,
- unrestricted currency convertibility to allow easy flow of capital,
- elimination of price ceilings on commodities,
- incentives for new foreign investment,
- promotion of export-led growth.

Business Latin America said that the IMF proposes "the kinds of austerity strategy that [multinational corporations] would like to see governments adopt."9 Under the IMF agreements, more capital is made available to corporations producing exports, business becomes more profitable because of new government incentives, and the foreign investors can freely return all their profits to their home countries. The austerity refers to the effects on the poor and working people of the indebted nations. Criticizing the Costa Rican government's agreement with the IMF, the Unity Federation of Workers in Costa Rica stated: "The new government is bowing to the demands of the IMF in order to obtain new and more weighty debts. The IMF measures mean school closings, hospital closings, the firing of employees and the freezing of salaries."

The IMF plays a political as well as an economic role, as illustrated by its emergency loan to Nicaragua only two months before the victory of the Sandinistas. The IMF gave Somoza a $22.3 million loan when Nicaragua's problems were more political than economic. The Sandinistas asked the IMF to withhold its loan on the grounds that the money would be used to prolong the war. When the Sandinistas later came to power, the IMF cancelled the standby loan arrangement with Nicaragua, depriving the new government of possible reconstruction funding. As in Nicaragua, the IMF provided the governments of El Salvador and Guatemala with loans to stabilize their economies at a time when the largest threat was growing civil war. Because the loans go to a recipient nation's central bank for general purposes, the funds can be readily used for military expenditures. Recent IMF lending to Central America, from July 1981 through July 1982, was as follows: El Salvador, $124.6 million; Honduras, $15 million; Guatemala, $112.7 million; and Panama, $60.7 million.10

The IMF is the acknowledged leader and protector of the world's international lending market. Multilateral, bilateral, and private commercial lenders all take their cues from the IMF, and they won't initiate new lending unless the country is in good standing with the IMF. The IMF's stamp of approval on a country's trade, monetary, and investment policies is the green light for international lending. The U.S. government and the commercial banks want the IMF to increase its financing capabilities and to expand its role as the overseer of the budgets of underdeveloped nations. As Julius Nyerere of Tanzania once said, the IMF has become the "International Ministry of Finance" whose tremendous power is used to promote stability and free trade to the detriment of the internal growth and development of Third World nations. Nyerere said that his country was "not prepared to surrender its right to restrict imports by measures designed to insure that we import quinine rather than cosmetics or buses rather than cars for the elite."[11]

U.S. Participation in Multilaterals

The United States holds the most voting power in multilateral institutions, because it is their leading financial contributor. As shown in Table 4D, the United States controls 20-35% of the voting power while the Central American nations generally hold less than one percent.

The large U.S. financial contribution to these institutions is not charity. The United States has a "very practical commercial reason for participation" in the multilateral institutions, noted Treasury Secretary Donald Regan. The Department of the Treasury estimates that for every dollar the United States puts into the World Bank, at least two dollars are returned to the United States through export sales. In 1980, U.S. firms received over $960 million in export sales generated by multilateral lending.[12] In a 1982 report on U.S. participation in the multilateral institutions, the Department of the Treasury concluded that the multilateral development banks "have been most effective in contributing to the achievement of our global economic and financial objectives and thereby also helping us in our long-term political/strategic interests."[13] President Reagan has cut back some U.S. commitments to the concessionary programs of the multilateral banks and encouraged the banks to put more funds directly into private sector investments. Reagan also has demanded stricter conditions for multilateral loans. Beryl Sprinkel, a Treasury Depart-

Table 4D. Multilateral Voting Power

	U.S.	Central America
IMF	20.0 %	0.8 %
IBRD	20.8 %	0.6 %
IDA	21.4 %	1.2 %
IFC	28.4 %	0.6 %
IDB	34.6 %	3.1 %

Source: 1981 Annual Reports, IMF, World Bank, IDB.

ment official, said that "the United States will not vote for loans" unless the recipient country has provided incentives for production, a guarantee of free and open markets, and minimized government interference in the economy.[14]

BILATERAL FINANCING

U.S. bilateral loans to Central America come mainly from the State Department and the Defense Department. The food aid program and the U.S. Eximbank's export-credit financing program are other sources of bilateral financing. A detailed discussion of bilateral funding follows in Chapter Six. Cumulative U.S. bilateral financing to Central America from 1946-1981 comes to almost two billion dollars. In March 1982, the Central American nations still owed the U.S. government $1.1 billion from all postwar bilateral lending, as shown in Table 4E.

Bilateral financing supports the special foreign policy and economic interests of the industrial countries. The United States has stepped up its bilateral programs in Central America since 1980 in an attempt to stabilize tottering governments and to stave off revolutionary movements. A prime advocate of increased bilateral assistance and decreased multilateral assistance is the conservative Heritage Foundation, founded in 1974 through contributions of Joseph Coors and Richard Mellon Scaife, heir to the Mellon fortune. The Heritage Foundation's publications serve as a forum for communication between the right-wing establishment and the Reagan Administration. The foundation says the rationale for all foreign aid is inherently political. It reasons that since the United States has more control over bilateral aid, such aid can better serve this country's political and corporate objectives.[15]

Table 4E. Outstanding Indebtedness of Central American Countries on U.S. Government Credits as of March 31, 1982
(millions $)

	Total	Eximbank	AID & Military	PL 480	Other
Belize	*	n/a	n/a	n/a	n/a
Costa Rica	112.0	18.8	93.1	-0-	0.1
El Salvador	222.9	6.0	189.7	5.6	-0-
Guatemala	139.9	20.9	118.8	27.2	0.2
Honduras	168.1	10.8	146.0	11.2	0.1
Nicaragua	261.8	18.3	226.1	17.5	-0-
Panama	188.0	26.1	161.9	-0-	-0-
Central America	*1,092.7*	*100.9*	*935.6*	*61.5*	*0.4*

*Under $500,000

Source: U.S. Treasury Department

PRIVATE FINANCING

In the early 1970s, U.S. banks started expanding foreign lending activities. Relaxed government regulations allowed banks to establish overseas operations that service U.S. industrial corporations. The government also encouraged private banks to give government-backed credits to foreign purchasers of U.S. exports in an effort to make U.S. goods more attractive than European and Japanese products. In the last decade, the worldwide sales of U.S. owned foreign affiliates tripled and profits from foreign investments increased six-fold. U.S. direct investment in Central America (excluding Panama) increased over 300% from 1960 to 1980.[16] The U.S. banks, not about to let foreign banks get the business of U.S. transnational corporations, hurriedly set up their own foreign branches. In 1960, only eight U.S. banks had international branches, but by 1980 over 135 U.S. banks had international operations. Most of these U.S. banks have located in banking centers like the International Finance Center in Panama City and have little to do with local commercial banking. Rather the U.S. banks concentrate on serving the transnational corporations and financing international trade.

Most transnational banks operating overseas only serve the financing and banking needs of U.S. corporations and don't involve themselves in local deposit and lending business in Central America. The exceptions are the largest U.S. banks — Bank of America, Citicorp, and Chase Manhattan — which have branches throughout the region that enable them to tap a new source of capital in the form of local deposits. These banks, however, generally discriminate against small businesses involved in the local market in favor of large corporations (usually U.S.) and those businesses that produce for the export market. Large private sector projects in Central America are generally financed by U.S. banks. The 1976 expansion of a cement factory in El Salvador, for example, was jointly financed by Marine Midland Bank, the U.S. Export-Import Bank, the Private Export Funding Corporation, Chase Manhattan, Morgan & Company, and the Banco de Comercio de El Salvador.[17] This type of financing scheme is common in Central America and represents an indirect form of economic control by U.S. transnationals.

In the 1970s, the U.S. banks found that they had more money than they could lend to U.S. business. This curious state of affairs was partly the result of a tremendous influx of OPEC money into the U.S. banks. The OPEC nations couldn't spend all their oil royalties and neither could they find enough places to profitably and securely invest their money. These oil-rich countries decided to rely on U.S. financial institutions to find places to invest their money and trust that the U.S. government would back up those investments with its economic and military might. The U.S. energy corporations were also putting more money in the bank than ever before as a result of their windfall oil and gas profits during the 1970s. By the late 1970s, the underdeveloped nations of Central America were experiencing balance of payments problems due to the high cost of petroleum imports from the U.S. oil companies and weakening markets for their principal exports. The U.S. transnational banks stepped in with their extra money to service Central America's external public debt. Unlike most lending, this new private lending went to pay debts, not to development or infrastructure projects. These loans provided short-term relief for Central American countries, but complicated the long-term debt picture. Bank loan interest rates were as much as double the multilateral and bilateral rates, and commercial bank loans were often one-year or medium-term agreements. The result was that the Central American nations had to borrow money the next year to pay off the previous year's loan at ever increasing interest rates. Walter Wriston of Citicorp credited banks for carrying out "the greatest transfer of wealth in the shortest time frame and with the least casualties in history." But the banks were hardly giving away their money. The profits of the transnational banks outstripped those of U.S. industrial corporations. While bank profits were rising, the Central American public debt skyrocketed. In 1972, $271 million of Central America's external public debt was owed to foreign private financial institutions. In 1980, this public debt to private financial institutions had increased 15 times to over four billion dollars.[18]

The U.S. transnational banks loaned money to underdeveloped nations at a dizzying pace. In the case of Nicaragua, the private banks poured loans into pre-Sandinista Nicaragua "long after arrears had begun to accumulate when there was no reasonable prospect of improvement in the balance of payments in the medium term."[19] The U.S. banks, besides stepping up their lending to the public sector, have also increased financing for the private sector in Central America. The main exports of Central America — bananas, coffee, sugar, meat, and cotton — are sold to foreign markets by growers' associations and transnational corporations in conjunction with financing from the large money center banks. These U.S. banks provide credit for planting prerequisites like seeds, fertilizers, and pesticides and then get reimbursed plus interest after harvesting.

U.S. bankers, however, have become more reluctant to supply the private sector in Central America with credit because of the region's political and economic turmoil. The Chamber of Commerce in Guatemala in 1982 estimated that the line of credit from commercial banks and commodity traders shrunk by more than $760 million since 1979. In Guatemala, about 70% of the financing for major export crops is provided by foreign banks and creditors. With U.S. banks shying away from financing the private sector in Central America, the economic downturn has worsened and Central American governments have gone begging to multilateral and bilateral sources for substitute financing.

Another important part of U.S. private financing in Central America is the system of supplier credit for imports from the United States, but that too is less available to Central American business. Suppliers are less willing to ship goods out without immediate payment. One business owner in Guatemala said that his suppliers no longer ship on a full-credit account. "They say, 'Sure your business is still good, but if you get your ass shot off, who is going to respond?' "[20] After a decade of wild lending activity in the underdeveloped world, the transnational bankers are becoming concerned that they may not see their money again.

The transnational banks have called for increased multilateral funding to the IMF. The additional financial power of the IMF would allow it to provide more debt relief to nations unable to meet debt payments to the private banks. The private bankers are also pressuring the IMF to stiffen its conditions for lending in a push to wring more loan payments out of the underdeveloped world.

Underlying the rampage of private international lending in the 1970s by the U.S. transnational banks was the assumption that if things got rough the U.S. government would bail them out. A leading European banking specialist, Pierre Latour, told a congressional hearing in 1976, "Though it was never articulated in so many words, many bankers must . . . have assumed that loans to [Third World] governments would be underwritten by the official aid programs of the developed world."[21] Part of this bailout has occurred in the form of Economic Support Fund (ESF) assistance to the Central American nations.

The transnational banks often support the governments which they think can guarantee the best security for their loans and investment. In the underdeveloped world, such governments are usually among the most repressive. Stephen O. Martin, a vice-president of the Bank of America, expressed his support for the conservative trend in Panama's politics and the increasing power of Panama's National Guard. Martin said that because of the need to promote private investment, the National Guard will play a bigger role in the civil government in Panama.[22] Keith Parker, manager for Bank of America operations in Guatemala, said, "What they should do is declare martial law. There you catch somebody; they go to a military court. The colonels are sitting there; you're guilty, you're shot. It works very well."[23] There is some question whether military rule is working well in Central America, but it is becoming increasingly clear to U.S. transnational bankers that something drastic has to be done to guarantee that they will get their loan money back from this destitute region of the world.

The Private Banks

Three transnational banks dominate private banking in Central America: Bank of America, Citicorp, and Chase Manhattan. Other important U.S. banks in the region include: First Boston Corporation, First Pennsylvania National Bank, Wells Fargo Bank, Marine Midland Bank, and First National Bank of Chicago. The local, hometown bank for most Central Americans is one of these U.S. transnationals. In Honduras, Chase Manhattan owns the major commercial bank, Banco Atlantida, whose business slogan is *"Amigo a Amigo."* If Hondurans don't want to bank with Chase Manhattan, they can walk across the plaza in Tegucigalpa to Banco de Honduras, which is owned by Citicorp. The U.S. banks have three kinds of banking operations in Central America: branches, which are wholly-owned by a parent company; subsidiaries, which are majority-owned; and affiliates, which are minority-owned. Table 4F shows the breakdown of U.S. banking in Central America by type of operation. In 1979, U.S. banks had investment in 29 of the 41 transnational banks in Central America (excluding Panama).

Table 4F. Transnational Banks in Central America

	Total Transnational Banks	Total U.S. TNBs	U.S. Branches	U.S. Subsidiaries	U.S. Affiliates
Belize	4	1	0	1	0
Costa Rica	13	11	1	6	4
El Salvador	5	2	1	0	1
Guatemala	3	2	1	0	1
Honduras	9	8	4	2	2
Nicaragua	7	5	1	0	4
Total	*41*	*29*	*8*	*9*	*12*

Source: P. Thorn, J. Lack and M. Elstob, *Who Owns What in World Banking, 1977-78*, London: Banker Research Unit, 1979.

Transnational banks also invest in non-financial firms in Central America. A survey of U.S. international banking investments submitted in 1976 to the House Committee on Banking found that U.S. banks had invested in breweries, country clubs, sugar mills, textile mills, local finance companies, and other banks in Central America. Chase Manhattan, for example, was part owner of the following businesses in Costa Rica: Costa Rica Tennis Club, Textilera Tres Rios, Costa Rican Farms, Intropica (poultry), and Desarrollo Agropecuario (rice farming).[24]

The United Nations Centre on Transnational Corporations in 1981 reported that one out of four transnational banks in the world was a U.S. bank.[25] Published data for certain U.S. transnational banks show the return on assets in Latin America and other developing regions to be substantially higher than on assets in western Europe or the United States.[26] One reason for this higher profit margin is that the transnational banks can obtain capital on world markets and then re-lend the money in internal Central American markets at interest rates which are often much higher than the international rate. Six U.S. banks are ranked among the top ten banks in the syndicated loan market in Latin America. These banks and their rank in Latin America are the following:[27]

Bank	*Latin American Rank*
Bank of America	1
Citicorp	2
Midland Bank/Crocker	5
Chase Manhattan	7
Wells Fargo	8
Manufacturers Hanover	9

ADELA

Private foreign financing also comes in the form of investment consortiums. Two such consortiums, Latin American Agribusiness Development Corporation (LAAD) and INRECORP are discussed elsewhere in this book. The earliest investment consortium was the ADELA Investment Company whose 222 shareholders are among the largest transnational firms and banks in the world. This elite but obscure investment company was formed in 1964 "to promote economic and social progress in Latin America by encouraging the development of a dynamic private enterprise sector capable of better employing the Continent's rich resources."[28] Former Senator Jacob Javits persuaded the Ford Foundation to finance the study that later led to the creation of ADELA. Henry Ford II, George Moore, former chairperson of Citicorp, and Emilio Collado, vice-president of Exxon, were among the founders of ADELA. The concept of ADELA was to establish a conduit for development investment into Latin America either through stock ownership or through loans to new companies.[29]

This international company had its origins in the United States, and is dominated by U.S. ownership, with 49 corporate shareholders, followed by Switzerland with 20. U.S. corporations with interests in ADELA include: Citicorp, Caterpillar Tractor, Bank of America, Coca-Cola, IBM, and Castle & Cooke. Bertram H. Witham, retired treasurer of IBM, is the president of ADELA.[30] Its 1981 *Annual Report* states: "ADELA has employed over two billion dollars to implement its objectives and it has been involved in creating and developing over 190 ventures, mainly in the agro-industrial and general manufacturing sectors." In 1981, ADELA had stock ownership in 22 companies in Central America and loan agreements with 23 others. In Latin America, ADELA has worked frequently with multilateral agencies and other investment companies. The 1968 *Annual Report* described ADELA's "close relationship with the Inter-American Development Bank (IDB) and the International Finance Corporation," both of which made parallel loans to ADELA projects. In Honduras, ADELA was the capital organizer and technical advisor during the initial stages of COPINA, a project to exploit three million acres of the Honduran Olancho Forest. ADELA also has investments in Agrodinamica, a company reported to be the largest beef exporter in Central America.

Despite its impressive backing, in the past few years ADELA has been forced to divest some holdings and to cut back its investment plans for Latin America. To counteract hard financial times, the company has reorganized and sought new capital to sustain the losses it attributes in part to the "political conditions" in Latin America.

The Bottom Line

The bottom line, financially speaking, is that the $7.5 billion in multilateral and bilateral loans and the many billions more in private commercial financing of the public sector in Central America haven't succeeded in developing the region. The sad fact is that there are at least as many hungry people now and that they would have preferred to have been given the fish rather than the shaft of financing. One problem is that the financing hasn't been evenly distributed. Instead of giving credit to the least privileged, the lending institutions have given to the most privileged sectors. The criteria for financing is not need, but "credit-worthiness." The economic principle behind this pattern of lending is self-evident from the point of view of the international financiers: If credit is used to buy fishing poles that catch fish which are sold in the foreign market, then a profit is made and the lenders can get their money back plus interest. However, if the fishing pole is used first to catch fish for a hungry family and only secondarily for the export market, there is less return on the investment. Fish that are eaten in Central America don't make much of a profit, fish that are sold to the U.S. market do.

Another problem with this system of investment is its dependence on a high percentage of imports from the industrial countries. Development plans for Central America have been tailored to the development of the U.S. export market through purchases of U.S. technology, farm machinery, and consultant services. In other words, in this financing fish story, the bait, the pole, and probably the latest model in fishing boats are purchased from the United States.

From the point of view of the international lenders, the record of development financing in Central America hasn't been all that bad. Indeed, the World Bank points to all of Latin America as its success story. The Gross Domestic Product has grown steadily in Central America until the last two years, and all the countries are importing and exporting more than before. The development economists said that this development would "trickle down" to the poor and hungry, but even they are hard put to find evidence of this trickle of benefits. Financing undeniably has contributed to increased production in Central America, but when there is not enough food to eat at home the production of cotton is a far cry from true development. The financing for development has gone to governments and businesses, not to people and certainly not to the poor people who so desperately need to change the conditions of underdevelopment. Like the financing, the development the financiers so proudly point to has been unevenly distributed.

Financing for development has slowed down in recent years under the weight of heavy external debts. In 1981, the external public debt for all Central American nations was close to $11 billion — more than twice the value of annual exports. Table 4G lists the external public debt by source and country. This public debt means that every woman, man, and child in Central America owes about $500 apiece to the international money lenders. No longer is there much banker talk about leading the poor nations of Central America along the rosy path of development or of eradicating poverty; instead there is anxious discussion on how to keep the indebted nations from defaulting. The International Monetary Fund calls the debt collection process the "stabilization" of the debtor nations. As debt collector, the IMF doesn't come knocking on the door but steps inside to direct the financial management of the debt-ridden underdeveloped countries. The effects of "stabilization" are more widely distributed than the effects of development. Since a government can't declare bankruptcy as readily as a business, the poor have to suffer through wage freezes, increased utility bills, and cutbacks in social services.

Table 4G. External Public Debt, December 1980*
(millions $)

	Total (includes undisbursed)	Bilateral	Multilateral	Suppliers	Financial Institutions	Other
Costa Rica	2,415	397	940	509	1,766	110
El Salvador	936	311	603	-0-	22	-0-
Guatemala	864	259	605	**	-0-	-0-
Honduras	1,609	398	1,018	21	171	-0-
Nicaragua	2,122	661	689	20	751	-0-
Panama	2,727	325	640	36	1,374	353
Central America	*10,673*	*2,351*	*4,495*	*586*	*4,084*	*463*

*lists medium and long term debts only; does not include debt of Central America's private sector.
**under $500,000

Source: Annual Report 1982, World Bank.

"Stabilization" is a political/economic process that gives the multilaterals, the United States, and the private lenders yet more influence over the underdeveloped, now indebted nations. To enforce the process, the lenders tend to support the most authoritative regimes as the only governments capable of enforcing their harsh debt-repayment schemes. But the IMF and the other world lenders haven't figured out how to impose "stabilization" and their

64

austerity measures without causing a storm of social unrest that may ultimately destabilize their increasingly fragile system of development and international finance.

REFERENCE NOTES

1. *United States Participation in the Multilateral Development Banks in the 1980s* (Washington: Dept. of the Treasury, 1982), p. 27.
2. "World Bank's Clausen Lauds Multinationals," *Multinational Monitor*, October 1981, p. 3.
3. *Assault on World Poverty* (New York: The World Bank, 1975), p. 143.
4. Hearings before the Subcommittee on Foreign Operations and Related Agencies of the Committee on Appropriations, House of Representatives, *Foreign Assistance and Related Programs Appropriations for 1983, Part 6* (Washington: Government Printing Office, 1982), pp. 55-58.
5. Inter-American Development Bank Press Releases and Newsletters, 1980 and 1981.
6. *Central America Report*, April 2, 1982, p. 100.
7. *Inter-American Development Bank News*, February 1982.
8. *AID Congressional Presentation, FY 1983, Annex III, Latin America and the Caribbean* (Washington: AID, 1982), p. 42.
9. "IMF Prescribes Austerity," *Business Latin America*, September 8, 1982, p. 287.
10. *IMF Survey*, various issues 1981 and 1982.
11. Hearings before the Subcommittee on International Finance of the Senate Committee on Banking, Housing and Urban Affairs, *International Monetary Fund and Related Information* (Washington: Government Printing Office, 1980), p. 119.
12. Hearings before the Subcommittee of the Committee on Appropriations, House of Representatives, *Foreign Assistance and Related Programs for 1982, Part 4* (Washington: Government Printing Office, 1982), p. 169.
13. *United States Participation in the Multilateral Development Banks in the 1980s*, p. 4.
14. *The Banker*, March 8, 1982, p. 7.
15. *Agenda for Progress*, The Heritage Foundation, 1981.
16. *Selected Data on U.S. Direct Investment Abroad 1950-76* (Washington: U.S. Dept. of Commerce, 1982); Obie Whichard, U.S. Dept. of Commerce, International Investment Division, interview May 1982.
17. Advertisement in *Wall Street Journal*, June 16, 1976, p. 63.
18. *The World Debt Tables 1979*, World Bank, 1981.
19. *The Banker*, July 1981, p. 37.
20. *Forbes*, May 10, 1982, p. 111.
21. *Multinational Monitor*, April 1980, p. 13.
22. Robert H. Holden, "Corporate Officials Embrace Latin Dictators," *Multinational Monitor*, June 1982, p. 14.
23. Alan Nairn, "Bank of America Subsidizing Terror in Guatemala," *Washington Report on the Hemisphere*, Council on Hemispheric Affairs, February 23, 1982, p. 4.
24. Staff Report of the House Committee on Banking Currency and Housing, *International Banking* (Washington: Government Printing Office, May 1976), pp. 231-270.
25. *Transnational Banks: Operations, Strategies and their Effects in Developing Countries* (New York: United Nations Center on Transnational Corporations, 1981), p. 3.
26. *Ibid.*, p. 69.
27. "Latin American Survey," *Euromoney*, April 1982, p. 5.
28. *Annual Report 1981*, ADELA.
29. Tim Anderson, "ADELA: The Violator of the Bond Market," *Euromoney*, September 1981, p. 10.
30. *Annual Report 1981*, ADELA.

Chapter Five

Military: Partners in Repression

We're going to lose Latin America.
We're losing it right now.

— Rear Admiral M. Briggs, 1961

U.S. military leaders knew something was seriously wrong when a poorly-armed band of Cuban guerillas defeated the well-equipped army of dictator Fulgencio Batista. The United States lost a favorite gambling hotspot as well as lucrative sugar cane plantations, but it was determined never to lose again. By 1961, the U.S. military high command had decided to switch its Latin American strategy from defense against external attack to defense against internal subversion. Guerilla insurgency would be met with U.S.-sponsored counterinsurgency.

With the Alliance for Progress, President Kennedy promised to give a helping hand to the "developing" nations of Latin America through infusions of U.S. private investment and development assistance. An important ingredient in this recipe for progress was the modernization of armed forces in the hemisphere. Stressing that economic development needed a framework of law and order, the Defense Department said that Latin American governments "must have the effective force to cope with subversion, prevent terrorism, and deal with outbreaks of violence before they reach unmanageable proportions."[1] The military build-up in Latin America took three forms: 1) training of police and military; 2) transfers of military and police hardware; and 3) civic action, intelligence work, and close coordination of U.S. programs.

In 1961, Kennedy transferred the Office of Public Safety (OPS) to the Agency for International Development (AID) to provide equipment and training to the police forces of underdeveloped nations. In Latin America, the police and military often perform similar security functions and the U.S. recognized the important role the national police could play in controlling civil unrest and popular opposition. The OPS program trained Central American police at the International Police Academy in Washington, and sent Public Safety Advisors to the countries for on-site training work. Table 5A shows the OPS expenditures and the Central American police students trained through 1973, when Congressional outcry that OPS was "making repressive regimes even more repressive" forced the termination of the program.

Table 5A. U.S. Assistance to Foreign Police Forces under the Public Safety Program, Fiscal Years 1961 - 1973

(thousands $)

	Students Trained in the U.S.	U.S. Public Safety Advisors	Total Expenditures
Costa Rica	160	4	$ 1,921
El Salvador	168	1	2,092
Guatemala	377	7	4,855
Honduras	105	3	1,741
Nicaragua	81	2	315
Panama	202	3	2,148
Total	*1,093*	*20*	*$13,072*

Source: Michael Klare and Cynthia Arnson, *Supplying Repression.*

Currently the United States trains foreign military personnel through the International Military Education and Training program (IMET), which the Pentagon says fosters "military-to-military relationships of enduring value." It proudly notes that "many of those trained now occupy positions from which they are able to influence favorably the receptivity of their armed forces and their government to U.S. ideals, methods, and standards."[2] Training Latin American military personnel not only improves their combat capabilities but also contributes to heightened U.S. influence in the internal affairs of the countries. The *Army Digest* said this preparation in "skills, leadership techniques, and doctrine paves the way for cooperation and support of U.S. military missions, *attaches*, military assistance advisory groups, and commissions operating in Latin America."[3]

In addition to training, the U.S. has regularly supplied Central America with military weapons and equipment. According to the Defense Department, there are five purposes of weapons brokering: to help deter aggression, to strengthen mutual security arrangements, to keep friends and allies competitive militarily, to foster regional and internal stability, and to help enhance the U.S. defense production business.* The United States has been the largest supplier of arms to some of the world's most repressive dictatorships including Somoza's Nicaragua, El Salvador, the Philippines, South Korea, Indonesia, and

*Unless otherwise noted, current military aid figures and statements from the Department of Defense are from Hearings before the Subcommittee on Foreign Operations and Related Agencies of the Committee on Appropriations, House of Representatives, *Foreign Assistance and Related Programs Appropriations for 1983*, Part 6, (Washington: Government Printing Office, 1982)

Thailand. The largest contemporary recipient of U.S. Foreign Military Sales (FMS) is Israel, which in 1982 received $1.4 billion in FMS transfers, or 34% of the entire annual FMS authorization. Israel is a generous supplier of arms to repressive regimes and is currently sending military equipment to Guatemala and El Salvador.

Civic action and intelligence work were integrated into counterinsurgency coordination in 1962 with the formation of "Country Teams," composed of the chief representatives of the embassy, the military *attaches*, the United States Information Agency, AID, the CIA, and the military missions or Military Assistance Groups in each country.[4] Even non-military personnel began receiving counterinsurgency training before taking assignments in Latin America. A Pentagon official explained: "Civic action is primarily coordinated with the AID program and very closely coordinated. In some areas the Peace Corps people are in a position to enter into some of the civic action in which we engage."[5] The United States has found that "military-to-military" relationships are the easiest to manage and control in Latin America.

The U.S. training of the foreign military in techniques and political philosophy has increased the power and the effectiveness of military institutions in Central America, and the United States has consistently advocated that the military play a role in political affairs. "Governments of the civil-military type of El Salvador are the most effective in containing communist penetration in Latin America," said President Kennedy,[6] referring to a short-lived Salvadoran junta in 1962. The U.S. State Department continues to espouse civilian-military governments, even though, as in the present case of El Salvador, it's the military that actually calls the shots.

After the Cuban revolution of 1959, the United States was able to prevent other revolutions in the hemisphere; but in 1979, the successful uprising of the Nicaraguan people broke the 20-year winning streak of the United States. Although the U.S. government pumped $30.6 million in military aid into the Somoza dictatorship from 1962-1979, in 1979 the United States suddenly found that it had lost another Latin American nation. It also realized that if something wasn't done quickly it would face the possibility of more than one revolutionary state in Central America.

Military strategists identified Central America as a world trouble spot and the United States began pouring yet more military aid into the region. From 1950-1979, the United States had spent an average of $7.5 million to equip and train the Central American military. In 1980, U.S. military aid increased to $8.8 million, in 1981 to $44.8 million, and in 1982 to $109.1 million. The top five recipients of U.S. military aid to Latin America in 1982 were (in order of amount received): El Salvador, Honduras, Colombia, Dominican Republic, and Panama. In 1981, El Salvador received 75% of all military aid sent to Latin America and the Caribbean. As in Vietnam, the crisis in Central America is testing the resolve of the United States as an imperialist power to obstruct revolutions in the underdeveloped world. Gone is the liberalism of the Alliance for Progress. What is important to the Reagan Administration is holding the line against revolution in Central America, even if it means cuddling up with repressive governments.

The United States is counting on the ability of U.S.-trained and supplied client governments to put out the brush fires of guerilla resistance, but always available as a last resort is direct U.S. military intervention. The U.S. Marines went to Central America several times in the early 1900s, and more recently, in 1965, the United States sent troops to the Dominican Republic. The United States has already committed Green Berets as advisors to Central America and is building three military bases in Honduras. If the flames of resistance spread any farther through the isthmus, the United States may again decide to call out the Marines. Assistant Secretary of State Thomas Enders warned: "The United States is not going to allow military triumph of the guerillas [in El Salvador]. It has the means and the desire to do so, irrespective of the political cost."[7]

The Defense Department's 1983 proposed budget is directed "toward maintaining stability in the region by helping deter aggression or subversion by the Soviet Union and its allies, especially in the areas of particular security interest to the United States, such as the Caribbean Basin." Reagan has brought Cold War politics to the Caribbean Basin, refusing to recognize that the roots of revolution are sustained by the desire of people for a better life and reach deep into the history of injustice in Central America. But a victory for the opposition forces in Central America would, in the eyes of the State Department, signal another loss for the United States.

MILITARY ALLIANCES

The main strength of U.S. foreign policy, said Salvadoran poet Roque Dalton, is its ability to use local governments and armies for the protection of its own interests. In the early 1960s, the coordination of the armies of Central America was part of the strategy to prevent another Cuba in the hemisphere. Upon the urging of the United States, the Defense Ministers of Guatemala, Honduras, El Salvador, and Nicaragua signed an agreement in 1964 to establish CONDECA (Central American Council for Defense) as a joint defense organization for the region. The council's goal was to create a coordinated attack on "internal subversion" and to "centralize all information on subversives."[8]

Through CONDECA, the United States had a role in determining the organizational structure of the Central American armies. Several countries like Panama and Honduras adopted U.S. ranking and command structures. CONDECA also standardized military training in Central America through joint military maneuvers that instilled a sense of a common enemy, namely communist insurgency. Nicaragua's dictator Somoza had been the strong man for the United States in Central America; and when the Sandinistas triumphed in 1979, CONDECA crumbled.

Later that year, the three military governments of Honduras, Guatemala, and El Salvador formed a new organization called the Northern Triangle, which they created "to prevent the arrival of communism to Nicaragua and to coordinate efforts to insure that democratic values prevail."[9] The Northern Triangle never got off the ground, but three years later, the Reagan Administration was successful in establishing a united front in Central America. On January 19, 1982, Costa Rica, Honduras, and El Salvador formed the Central American Democratic Community (CDC). Soon after, Guatemala joined the alliance which has two stated objectives: 1) to stimulate the development of the private sector, and 2) to provide mutual aid and solidarity in the case of external aggression. At CDC's founding meeting, attended by U.S. advisors, the country representatives discussed the failure of the Central American Common Market (CACM) and the possibility of forming another regional union to supersede CACM. The founding statement referred to granting privileged access to this new economic union to what was discreetly called "powers of greater resources." The CDC said it will seek to negotiate better trade arrangements with such powers.[10]

Belize and Panama, disapproving of CDC's anti-Sandinista focus, refused to join the organization. President Royo of Panama called the alliance a "dart aimed at the heart of Nicaragua." Royo's resignation in 1982 and the mounting influence of the National Guard make it more likely that Panama will join the CDC. Nicaragua, which had not been invited to join CDC, denounced it as an "instrument of imperialism."[11]

TYPES OF SECURITY ASSISTANCE

The Military Assistance Program (MAP), Foreign Military Sales (FMS), and International Military Education and Training (IMET) are the major forms of foreign security assistance. Also part of U.S. support for the military in Central America are Direct Commercial Sales and Commerce Department Sales. Economic Support Fund (ESF) is yet another vehicle for security assistance from the United States.

IMET

The United States has trained over a half million foreign military personnel throughout the world under the International Military Education and Training (IMET). From 1962-1982, the United States has spent over $42 million in training over 22,500 soldiers and officers from Central America, not including the 1,600 Salvadoran troops trained in 1982 with emergency funds from the

Department of Defense. Nicaragua, under the Somoza family dictatorship, received the largest part of IMET funding for Central America. Military students receive training at the School of the Americas in Panama or in the United States at military schools like those in Fort Bragg, North Carolina, and Fort Benning, Georgia. The training includes courses in Counterinsurgency Operations, Urban Counterinsurgency, Military Intelligence Interrogation, and Military Explosives and Detonators. The United States also provides in-country training through Mobile Training Teams, composed of members from the U.S. Special Forces and technical experts. Summarizing the effectiveness of the IMET program, the Defense Department in 1982 told the House Committee on Appropriations: "IMET provides soldiers with a better understanding of U.S. society, institutions, and goals .... Never before in history have so many governments voluntarily and continually entrusted so many personnel, in such sensitive positions, and over such an extended period of time to training by another government."

Coordinating these training activities and the defense of Latin America is the U.S. Southern Command (SOUTHCOM) based in the Panama Canal Zone. SOUTHCOM has jurisdiction over 14 military bases and over 9,000 troops. Ft. Gulick in the Canal Zone houses the Eighth Special Forces (Green Berets) and the School of the Americas. The Inter-American Air Force Academy is also located in the Canal Zone which, since its formation in 1943, has trained over 14,000 Latin American air force personnel. The repressive function of the military forces trained by the United States is often masked by misleading

Table 5B. Number of Trainees under IMET
1950-1982

	FY 1950 FY 1980	FY 1981	FY 1982	FY 1950 FY 1982	Initially Proposed FY 1983
Belize	-0-	-0-	25	25	62
Costa Rica	711	37	56	804	103
El Salvador	2,113	145	289*	2,547 *	293
Guatemala	3,360	-0-	-0-	3,360	190
Honduras	3,609	262	282	4,153	340
Nicaragua	5,740	-0-	-0-	5,470	-0-
Panama	5,161	306	315	5,782	334
Central America	*20,694*	*750*	*967* *	*22,411* *	*1,322*

*Doesn't include 1,600 Salvadoran troops and officers trained in the United States from January-May 1982.

Sources: Department of Defense, *Foreign Military Sales, Foreign Military Assistance Facts as of September 1981;* House of Representatives Hearings, *Foreign Assistance and Related Programs Appropriations for 1983, Part 6.*

military language. The 250 Salvadorans brought to the United States for training during the Carter Administration supposedly studied "Human Rights Aspects in International Defense and Development."[12] Former Secretary of Defense Robert McNamara, describing the effects of IMET, said: "Probably the greatest return on our military assistance program investment comes from the training of selected officers and key specialists at our military schools — leaders, the men who will have the know-how and impart it to their forces. I need not dwell upon the value of having in positions of leadership men who have the first-hand knowledge of how Americans do things and how they think. It is beyond price to us to make friends of such men."[13]

MAP

The U.S. government provides direct grants of military aid through the Military Assistance Program (MAP). In the post-World War Two era, MAP grants consisted of standard military combat equipment, but after the Cuban Revolution MAP grants more frequently provided counterinsurgency equipment, such as armored cars, jeeps, and helicopter gunships. Over $141 million in MAP grants have poured into Central America from 1950-1982 — 70% of which was granted in 1981 and 1982. The Defense Department is requesting a worldwide 1983 MAP budget of $112 million, of which $20 million will

Table 5C. Military Assistance Program
1950-1982

(thousands $)

	FY 1950 FY 1980	FY 1981	FY 1982	FY 1950 FY 1982
Belize	-0-	-0-	-0-	-0-
Costa Rica	930	-0-	2,000	2,930
El Salvador	4,832	25,003	63,500	93,335
Guatemala	16,250	-0-	1	16,251
Honduras	5,617	-0-	11,001	16,618
Nicaragua	7,633	-0-	-0-	7,633
Panama	4,495	-0-	1	4,496
Central America	*39,757*	*25,003*	*76,503*	*141,263*

Sources: Department of Defense, *Foreign Military Sales, Foreign Military Assistance Facts as of September 1981;* House of Representatives Hearings, *Foreign Assistance and Related Programs Appropriations for 1983, Part 6.*

reimburse the department for emergency assistance sent to El Salvador in 1981. The proposed 1983 budget includes a $50 million fund to "enable us to provide grant military assistance in response to unforeseen circumstances." MAP grants worldwide, however, are being cut back in favor of FMS cash and credit agreements.

FMS

The Arms and Export Act authorizes the sale of defense items and services to "friendly countries" under the Foreign Military Sales program (FMS). These military sales come under three categories: 1) credit sales, 2) loan guarantees, and 3) cash sales. The sales involve standard military hardware like tanks as well as counterinsurgency equipment, and many FMS agreements cover the services of U.S. technical consultants. The United States is the broker in FMS agreements, buying from arms manufacturers and then selling them to developing countries. The number of FMS contracts has shot up in recent years. Central American contracts during 1981 and 1982 amounted to 43% of the total number of FMS contracts from 1950-1980. An increasing number of FMS contracts are under the form of direct credit sales, which give the purchasing countries extremely attractive financial terms from the United States. FMS loan guarantees allow a country to purchase arms from the

Table 5D. Foreign Military Sales
1950-1982
(thousands $)

	FY 1950 FY 1980	FY 1981	FY 1982	FY 1950 FY 1982	Initially Proposed FY 1983
Belize	-0-	-0-	-0-	-0-	-0-
Costa Rica	1,480	-0-	-0-	1,480	-0-
El Salvador	5,912	10,000	16,500	32,412	60,000
Guatemala	31,998	-0-	-0-	31,998	-0-
Honduras	14,701	8,400	9,000	32,101	14,500
Nicaragua	5,303	-0-	-0-	5,303	-0-
Panama	5,402	-0-	5,000	10,402	5,000
Central America	*64,796*	*18,400*	*30,500*	*113,696*	*79,500*

Sources: Department of Defense, *Foreign Military Sales, Foreign Military Assistance Facts as of September 1981;* House of Representatives Hearings, *Foreign Assistance and Related Programs Appropriations for 1983, Part 6.*

United States with U.S. bank loans that are guaranteed by the Pentagon. Cash sales are direct government to government sales of U.S. military hardware with the purchasing country making direct payments for its purchases. Most arms transfers to Guatemala since 1977 have been cash sales since these don't come under congressional review when sales amount to less than $25 million. The United States has arranged FMS agreements with Israel that waive payments. In 1982, an estimated $550 million in FMS payments were waived for Israel, a major supplier of arms to Guatemala and El Salvador. The Defense Department has proposed that $500 million in FMS transfers to Israel in 1983 also be waived.

Direct Commercial Sales

Direct Commercial Sales cover the sale of U.S.-manufactured light arms and combat-support equipment that are negotiated directly with the foreign purchaser. Of the 1982 Direct Commercial Sales, $2.8 million flowed to the Central American nations. Among the items which normally fall into this category are police weapons and related equipment such as tear-gas grenades and MACE.[14] In 1982, Guatemala purchased $750,000 worth of police arms and equipment in Direct Commercial Sales.

Table 5E. Direct Commercial Sales
1950-1982
(thousands $)

	FY 1950 FY 1980	FY 1981	FY 1982	FY 1950 FY 1982	Initially Proposed FY 1983
Belize	217	186	100	503	100
Costa Rica	1,170	57	150	1,377	150
El Salvador	2,220	17	300	2,537	200
Guatemala	5,091	7	750	5,848	100
Honduras	4,652	923	500	6,075	500
Nicaragua	4,243	-0-	-0-	4,243	-0-
Panama	38,625	752	1,000	40,377	2,050
Central America	*56,218*	*1,942*	*2,800*	*60,960*	*3,100*

Sources: Department of Defense, *Foreign Military Sales, Foreign Military Assistance Facts as of September 1981;* House of Representatives Hearings, *Foreign Assistance and Related Programs Appropriations for 1983, Part 6.*

Increased arms transfers to Central America through either FMS or Commercial Sales mean higher profits for U.S. arms manufacturers. The price tag on a single Huey helicopter ranges between $525,000 to $1.5 million. Bell Helicopters, the manufacturer of Huey helicopters, brings in 26% of the annual $3.3 billion sales of its parent company, Textron.[15] Bell has stepped up its emphasis on foreign military sales by giving international demonstrations of the uses of its military helicopters. A coalition of religious groups has formed to protest the company's profiteering with repressive regimes and has presented a shareholder's resolution that asks for "the establishment of social and ethical criteria to be used in the decision-making process for accepting foreign military sales/servicing contracts."[16] In addition to Textron's Bell Helicopters, the Institute for Policy Studies lists the following corporations as large contractors of military equipment to Central America:

Cessna Aircraft	Olin
Chamberlin Manufacturing	Polak, Winter and Company
Colt Industries	Remington Arms
FMC	Sentinel Electronics
Hercules	Smith & Wesson
ICI Americas	Sperry Flight Systems
Martin Marietta Aluminum Sales	

Commerce Department Sales

While Direct Commercial Sales refer to commercial sales of items included on the State Department's "U.S. Munitions List," Commerce Department Sales refer to items not on this official list of munitions but which can have a military use. Items exported this way include transport planes, and trainer aircraft, search radars, helicopter engines, computers, and "crime control and detection equipment." The last category comprises such items as "straightjackets, non-military gas masks, bullet-proof vests and shields," and "non-military protective vests, leg irons, shackles, handcuffs, thumbscrews, and other manufactures of metal."[17] It also encompasses such items as: "non-military arms such as shotguns, stun guns, dart guns, riot guns, and shock batons." Given the Reagan Administration's emphasis on greater exports and its tolerance of repressive governments, Commerce Department Sales are likely to steadily increase. Indicative of this trend was the $3.2 million sale of 50 military trucks and jeeps to Guatemala in June 1981 processed through the Commerce Department.

Economic Support Fund

The Economic Support Fund (ESF) was created by the Foreign Assistance

Act to provide aid under "special economic, political, or security conditions." The ESF comes under the security assistance budget, although the funds are administered by AID. In 1982, $260 million in ESF money was allocated for Central America. During a hearing on the proposed ESF appropriation for President Reagan's Caribbean Basin Initiative (CBI), Representative Clarence Long said the purpose of ESF grants is "largely military." In an exchange with the Assistant Secretary of Defense Francis West, Long said: "You know that economic supporting assistance is simply a device to say to a country, 'Look, take your money and buy weapons, and we will cover your exchange problems with it'."[18]

Lobbying for Security

Manufacturers of arms and defense-related items are the obvious beneficiaries of the FMS and Commercial Sales programs. Thirty-one defense manufacturers have formed a lobbying organization called the American League for Exports and Security Assistance (ALESA). Four unions are members of ALESA: Communications Workers of America, AFL-CIO; Teamsters Union; Marine Engineers Beneficial Association, AFL-CIO; United Brotherhood of Carpenters and Joiners, AFL-CIO. ALESA's principal goal is "to encourage the export of American goods and services in consonance with the security and economic goals of this nation."[19] In its support for increased levels of arms sales, ALESA noted that the U.S. human rights policy had been partially responsible for Nicaragua falling "into the hands of the Cuban-trained Sandinistas." Furthermore, ALESA noted that "in countries where we do have significant influence such as in South Korea, Saudi Arabia, or the Philippines, our human rights concerns often conflict with other perhaps more important considerations such as national security or economic necessity." ALESA has an accurate description of U.S. foreign policy: "Security assistance as well as economic assistance have been flexible implements in an integrated American foreign policy. These programs usually have been advantageous to the United States in that they have increased the prospects for regional stability in areas of the world important to the United States, thereby reducing the likelihood of direct U.S. military involvement."

MILITARY: COUNTDOWN BY COUNTRY

Belize

The United States is moving in as the British are moving out. Great Britain kept 1,600 soldiers in Belize after independence in 1981; but now that the United States has begun to train the 300-member Belize Defense Force (BDF), the British are beginning to leave. In 1982, 25 Belizean military students were scheduled for training in Panama and the United States. The Department of Defense is also sending U.S. advisors to Belize to train larger numbers of the country's military forces, and the United States is negotiating with Belize to construct a U.S. military base in the country.

Costa Rica

The Department of Defense says that 1983 "will be the first opportunity to make real progress in covering the training void created during the years 1967-1980 when no IMET [training funds] was provided to Costa Rica." In 1981, the U.S. military trained 37 Civil Guard members, in 1982, 56 members, and in 1983, the budget proposes training 103 members of the Civil Guard. Pressuring Costa Rica to step up its security programs, the United States has suggested that the country consolidate the various police and armed guards under one ministry. Although Costa Rica has no army, it has a 5,000-member Civil Guard and a 3,000-member Rural Guard. In addition, Costa Rica has a unit of 1,700 prison guards, and a 100-member intelligence service called the National Security Agency, and the 500-member Organization of Judicial Investigation (OIJ). OIJ is a well-trained and efficient repressive force, which has been trained by Chilean police. Many Costa Ricans object to the U.S.-sponsored military build-up because they feel that the security forces will provoke clashes with the Sandinista army. The U.S. Office of Defense Cooperation in San Jose administers the U.S. military activities in Costa Rica.[20]

El Salvador

The United States started pumping military aid to El Salvador shortly after the October 1979 coup that established the country's first civilian-military junta. Since then, military and economic aid to El Salvador has steadily increased beyond the original estimates of what was necessary to crush the guerilla resistance. In 1980, Congress budgeted no military assistance to El Salvador but by the end of the year it had authorized military aid totalling six million dollars. In 1981, five million dollars was originally authorized while $25 million was actually sent. And in 1982, the original figure was $26 million, but Reagan later decided that emergency aid was needed and brought the final amount of military aid to $81 million. The 1983 budget calls for $61.3 million in military aid to El Salvador.

El Salvador's combined armed forces number about 25,000,[21] including the army, navy, air force, national guard, national police, and treasury police. Forming part of El Salvador's offensive against the popular opposition are the paramilitary security forces which include ORDEN, the White Warriors Union, the Anti-Communist Armed Forces of Liberation (FALANGE), and the Organization for the Liberation from Communism (OLC). General Jose Alberto Medrano, a close ally of the United States, established ORDEN in 1968, "to make a barrier to the attempts of the communists to provoke subversion in the countryside." ORDEN is a paramilitary organization of 50,000 to 100,000, which enjoyed full government support until outlawed by the first civilian-military junta. It is now back, re-established as the National Democratic Front.[22] At least 56 U.S. military personnel, many of them members of the U.S. Special Forces, have been stationed in El Salvador where they have trained an elite Salvadoran strike force known as the Atlacatl Brigade. Salvadoran troops also receive training in the United States and Panama. In June 1982, Salvadoran pilots who finished their training in Panama flew back to El Salvador six Dragonfly counterinsurgency planes that commenced attacks against guerilla strongholds the very next day. The United States originally thought the guerillas could be defeated within a matter of months, but the guerillas continue to gain ground despite U.S. military aid. The State Department sees no light at the end of the tunnel and the Salvadoran government sees no limit to its need for U.S. assistance. "What we have received from the United States is not sufficient," said General Guillermo Garcia in 1982, who has asked that the United States send as many as 180 Huey helicopters.[23]

Guatemala

It's Saturday, a market day in a large mountain village in Guatemala, and the Indian farmers from the surrounding *aldeas* have come to sell their produce and socialize. Suddenly, an army truck pulls up. Several soldiers jump out and forcibly round up the teenage boys and young men. This system of conscription is common in Guatemala, which has the region's most well-equipped army. Most officers are *Ladinos* who come from middle-class backgrounds, while two-thirds of the troops are Indians. Cooperating with the 14,000-member army are 5,000 members of the National Police, 1,200 members of the Treasury Police, 450 members of the Judicial Police, and more than 1,000 members of the Mobile Military Police. Off-duty police and military compose the two most active right-wing terrorist units known as the Secret Anti-Communist Army and the Death Squad (*Esquadron de la Muerte*).

Since 1977, military aid to Guatemala has been obstructed by congressional human rights restrictions, but the Reagan Administration is determined to renew military aid to combat what the State Department calls "supported Marxist insurgency." For 1983, the United States has authorized $250,000 for the training of military students from Guatemala to "expose key officer personnel to U.S. military doctrine and practice." According to the Defense Department, "It is in the U.S. interest to maintain a relationship with the government of Guatemala which will enable us to increase the Guatemalan military's sensitivity to the control of abuses of the civilian population by the armed forces."

The first big step toward resuming military aid to Guatemala was the $3.2 million sale of trucks and jeeps, which, to avoid human rights regulations, were re-classified from military sales to sales for "regional stability." In April 1982, the United States announced plans to sell Guatemala four million dollars worth of helicopter parts and resumed training of the country's military. Most of the 450 members of the country's air force have been trained in the United States. Two allies of the United States, Argentina and Israel, have supplied arms and military training to Guatemala. The Reagan Administration has said that human rights violations do occur in Guatemala, but it has refused to admit that the government itself stands behind the repression and terrorist violence. Pleading ignorance, Assistant Secretary for Inter-American Affairs John Bushnell said, "There is very little public evidence as to who is responsible for any of the murders . . . . It is rather like El Salvador in the sense that a body turns up and you don't know what happened." Bushnell added that "given the extent of the insurgency and the strong Communist worldwide support for it, the administration would be very disposed to help Guatemala."

Lt. General Wallace Nutting told the *New York Times* in August 1982 that the United States should play "essentially the same role" in Guatemala as it is doing in El Salvador. He argued that the situation in Guatemala was potentially more serious than in El Salvador. "The population is larger, the economy is stronger, the geographical position is more critically located in a strategic sense," he said, adding that, "the implications of a Marxist takeover in Guatemala are a lot more serious than in El Salvador."[24]

Honduras

Honduras has become the staging ground for regional warfare. "The U.S. security assistance for Honduras," the Defense Department reports, "is designed to contribute directly to regional stability in Central America by enhancing Honduras' capacity to defend its sovereignty against increasing threats of subversion from guerilla terrorist groups." The most threatening development in 1982 was the decision by the United States to spend $21 million from the Air Force Military Construction Budget to improve three military air bases in eastern Honduras near Nicaragua.[25]

"The administration believes the improvement of these Honduran airfields," said a State Department spokesperson, "will enhance the long-term prospects for stability in Central America . . . . Improvement of these airfields so that U.S. aircraft could use them will . . . make it clear that we have the capability and the will to assist our friends if the need arises."[26]

The United States is increasing arms sales to Honduras. From 1950-1979, Honduras received an average of $333,000 per year in U.S. Foreign Military Sales (FMS). In 1980, FMS transfers jumped to five million dollars, and in 1981, to over eight million dollars for the year. The Defense Department says that Honduras is experiencing difficulty in purchasing "badly needed equipment" under FMS loan agreements so it has proposed that in 1983, arms go to Honduras on concessionary terms with a long grace period for repayment. The United States has provided Honduras with Huey helicopters and at least six A37B Dragonfly fighter-bombers, planes that were used for counterinsurgency in Vietnam.

The United States in 1982 had more military personnel in Honduras than in El Salvador. The Defense Department has reported that as many as 124 military personnel from Mobile Training Teams based in Panama are operating in Honduras, which in 1982 had the largest U.S. diplomatic mission of any U.S. embassy between Mexico and Brazil. Also reflecting the U.S. build-up in Honduras is the increased activity by AID's regional office for Central America and the American Institute for Free Labor Development, both of which have established offices in Tegucigalpa.

Honduras has combined armed forces numbering over 11,000.[27] Its special counterinsurgency unit, the Tesons, thought to number 700, has crossed into El Salvador on missions against the Salvadoran guerillas. In July 1982 the *New York Times* reported that a joint Honduran-Salvadoran operation against guerillas in El Salvador "has raised fears that the civil war may spread through the region."[28] In 1980, Honduras signed a peace treaty with El Salvador that committed Honduras to the task of policing the border area for political-security purposes and allowed the Salvadoran armed forces to enter Honduras on search and destroy missions.

The Honduran officers who began the reformist movement in 1972 have either been forced to resign or transferred out of the country, and the Honduran army is now controlled by its most reactionary and corrupt elements. In its attempt to use Honduras as a secure staging ground for counterinsurgency in Central America, the United States has promoted a plan for political reform and economic development accompanied by the expansion of the Honduran armed forces. As a Honduran officer said in a radio interview, "The U.S. will supply all the arms, equipment and body bags that we need, and all we have to do is supply the bodies."[29]

Nicaragua

"The revolution in Nicaragua has led the United States to crystalize its efforts to reassess and grapple with some decisions," said Lt. General Wallace Nutting. The apparent result of this reassessment has been a marked upswing in U.S. military assistance and counterinsurgency training in the region. Both open and covert assistance of counterrevolutionary forces is another part of the U.S. anti-Sandinista strategy. In 1981, President Reagan authorized $19 million in CIA funds to create a paramilitary force of up to 500 Latin Americans along the Nicaraguan/Honduran border. The *Washington Post* reported that, "The planned forces would attempt to destroy vital Nicaraguan targets, such as power plants and bridges, in an effort to divert attention and the resources of the government."[30] Figuring prominently in the U.S. plans for counterrevolution are the Miskito refugees from Nicaragua who are now living in Honduras. The two main counterrevolutionary groups are the Nicaraguan Armed Forces (FARN) and the Inter-American Defense Forces.

Unlike the other Central American armies, the Nicaraguan armed forces are more concerned about aggression from outside their borders than about internal insurgency. Regular troop strength numbers 22,000 soldiers who are backed up by 45,000 in volunteer militias. The Soviet Union and France have contributed arms, but Nicaragua's technological firepower is still unimpressive compared with that of its three northern neighbors.[31] The Sandinistas have charged that the U.S. support of counterrevolutionaries within Honduras is an attempt to provoke reaction from Nicaragua, thereby giving the United States an excuse to come to the rescue of its ally. Nicaragua's Minister of Defense, Humberto Ortega, says the country has built a defensive force, not an offensive one, and it will not be provoked by agitation along the Honduran border. "But," adds Ortega, "we have the right to defend our national sovereignty and the revolution."

Panama

The National Guard, which is the country's most powerful institution, has been largely equipped and trained by the United States. Under an agreement of the Panama Canal Treaty of 1977, the United States is providing Panama's National Guard with $50 million in Foreign Military Sales to upgrade its defensive capabilities. The treaty specifies that the National Guard coordinate the defense of the Canal. The Department of Defense says that this new security assistance arrangement "is a valuable foundation for close cooperation and coordination between Panamanian and U.S. forces." The National Guard with 6,500 soldiers works closely with the 4,500 members of the National Police. Reflecting on the increased role of the armed forces in Panama, the National Police Training School in Panama now schools its students in political methods and philosophy. The National Guard, dropping its previous nationalistic rhetoric, has taken a pronounced turn to the right, and its leadership has announced support for U.S. foreign policy in Central America. The conservative leader of the National Guard, General Ruben Dario Paredes, has announced candidacy for president of Panama in 1984.

REFERENCE NOTES

1. Hearings before the Foreign Affairs Committee, House of Representatives, *The Foreign Assistance Act of 1962*, pp. 267, 268.
2. Department of Defense, Security Assistance Program, Fiscal Year 1981, p. 16, cited by Michael T. Klare and Cynthia Arnson, *Supplying Repression: U.S. Support for Authoritarian Regimes Abroad* (Washington: Institute for Policy Studies, 1981).
3. "Bridge of the Americas," *Army Digest*, September 1968, pp. 12-14, cited by Michael T. Klare in *War Without End* (New York: Alfred A. Knopf, 1972).
4. Steve Weissman, *The Trojan Horse* (San Francisco: Ramparts Press, 1974), p. 78.
5. *Ibid.*
6. *Ibid.*, p. 77.
7. Jenny Pearce, *Under the Eagle: U.S. Intervention in Central America and the Caribbean* (London: Latin American Bureau, 1981), p. 250.
8. "Integrating the Big Guns," *NACLA Report on the Americas*, May-June 1973, (New York: the North American Congress on Latin America), referred to as *NACLA* in all reference notes that follow.
9. *Central America Report*, June 16, 1982, p. 210.
10. *Latin America Weekly Report*, January 20, 1982.
11. *Central America Report*, July 16, 1982, p. 211.
12. Klare and Arnson, p. 51.
13. Hearings before the Subcommittee on Foreign Operations Appropriations of the Committee on Appropriations, House of Representatives, *Foreign Operations Appropriations for 1963, Part 1* (Washington: Government Printing Office, 1962), p. 359.
14. Klare and Arnson, p. 56.
15. *Annual Report 1981*, Textron, p. 46.
16. Vincent Brevetti and Fay Hansen, "U.S. Profits from El Salvador Arms Sales," *Guardian*, June 9, 1982, p. 10.
17. Klare and Arnson, pp. 78-83.
18. Hearings before the Subcommittee on Foreign Operations and Related Agencies of the Committee on Appropriations, House of Representatives, *Supplemental Appropriations for 1982, Part 2* (Washington: Government Printing Office, 1982), p. 43.
19. Hearings before the Committee on Foreign Relations, Senate, *Foreign Assistance Authorization for Fiscal Year 1982* (Washington: Government Printing Office, 1982), pp. 299-303.
20. "Moves to Strengthen Police," *LARR*, September 9, 1981.
21. *Washington Report*, Council on Hemispheric Affairs, July 13, 1982.
22. *Resource*, Institute for Policy Studies, March 1980.
23. "Arming El Salvador," International Policy Report, Center for International Policy, August 1982.
24. Alan Riding, "U.S. General Calls Guatemala Aid 'Imperative'," *New York Times*, August 22, 1982.
25. Department of Defense, International Assistance Office, Interview with Lt. Colonel Ralph Novac, September 1982.
26. Hearings before the subcommittee of the Committee on Appropriations, House of Representatives, *Military Construction Appropriations for 1983* (Washington: Government Printing Office, 1982), p. 337.
27. *Washington Report*, July 13, 1982.
28. *New York Times*, July 7, 1982.
29. *Boston Globe*, August 12, 1982.
30. *Washington Post*, March 10, 1982.
31. *Washington Report*, July 13, 1982.

Chapter Six

Foreign Aid: Rewards of Giving

The first priority is a regional effort to revitalize the private sector and to reduce the acute shortage of foreign exchange and working capital impeding the private sector's recovery.

— Regional Office for Central
America and Panama (ROCAP),
Agency for International
Development, 1982

Foreign aid just doesn't make sense to most people in the United States. What's the logic to spending billions of dollars overseas when we have such serious economic problems of our own? And what's the sense in having a professed fiscal conservative as president who keeps increasing foreign aid?

The first hard truth of foreign aid is that its main purpose has never been to help the world's starving masses or to develop the underdeveloped world. The nation's first food aid law didn't include even a hint of humanitarian concern. It's not difficult to figure out the real reasons for foreign aid. In fact, they are set forth by U.S. presidents when they talk to the elite world of corporate executives and policy-makers about international development. From John F. Kennedy's Alliance for Progress to Reagan's Caribbean Basin Initiative (CBI), the U.S. government has always protected the interests of the private sector. In 1962, Kennedy said the primary goal of the Alliance for Progress "relates to our increased efforts to encourage the investment of private capital in the underdeveloped countries."[1] While past foreign aid programs have all emphasized the participation of private capital, the Reagan Administration has made the benefit to private investment the acid test of all foreign aid programs. In a national policy statement delivered in Philadelphia in October 1981, President Reagan outlined the main objectives of U.S. international aid and development programs. These objectives include: 1) the stimulation of "international trade by opening up markets," 2) the improvement of the "climate for private investment," and 3) the creation of a "political atmosphere in which practical solutions can be applied."[2]

Reagan's approach to international development and foreign aid corresponds with the dictates of the Foreign Assistance Act of the United States. The first administrative provision of the act, entitled "Encouragement of free enterprise and private participation" states:

> "It is declared to be the policy of the United States to encourage the efforts of other countries to increase the flow of international trade, to foster private initiative and competition . . . and to encourage the contribution of United States enterprise toward the economic strength of less developed friendly countries through private trade and investment abroad [and] private participation in programs carried out under this Act . . . ."

The Foreign Assistance Act regulates foreign aid programs and obligates the recipient government to promote U.S. business in the following ways:

> - make arrangements to find opportunities for investment for private enterprise,
>
> - discourage nationalization of private investment and other actions that divert essential resources and impair the climate for new private investment,
>
> - utilize wherever practical the services of U.S. private enterprise including the services of consultants,
>
> - accelerate a program of negotiating treaties for commerce and trade that facilitate the flow of private investment,
>
> - utilize the services of private enterprise to manage programs of foreign assistance, and
>
> - procure commodities within the United States unless the President authorizes foreign purchases.

The benefits of U.S. foreign aid to U.S. business fall into three categories: 1) promotion of U.S. foreign investment, 2) expansion of a market for U.S. exports, and 3) facilitation of the import of food and natural resources. Most U.S. aid to Central America is geared to help U.S. business, but another factor explains the recent increases in economic aid to the "friendly countries" of the region. Economic aid accomplishes things that guns and bombs can't do. Foreign aid to Central America, for example, funds road construction projects in El Salvador and Honduras that give the military better access to critical border areas. U.S. aid also props up governments that would otherwise fall due to economic problems and domestic insurgency. The more a government receives in foreign economic aid, the more of its own budget is available for the purchase of guns and bombs. As the director of the Agency for International Development (AID), Peter McPherson, said, "There's a real interchangeability here between economic assistance and internal security."[3]

AID, a division of the State Department, is the lead agency for U.S. foreign assistance. Other government institutions involved in foreign aid programs and international development are as follows: Overseas Private Investment Corporation (OPIC); Export-Import Bank (Eximbank); and the United States Department of Agriculture (USDA) through the PL 480 program and the Commodity Credit Corporation (CCC).

AID:
DEVELOPMENT FOR WHOM?

AID administers four kinds of assistance: 1) Development Assistance Grants, 2) Development Assistance Loans, 3) Technical Assistance, and 4) Economic Support Fund (ESF) assistance. AID programs are planned unilaterally, without the input of the recipient country. The countries can, of course, decline AID assistance, but that would signal a complete break with the U.S. financial and trade network — something underdeveloped countries are hesitant to do. Development grants, development loans, and technical assistance from the United States are the regular forms of assistance offered by AID. Economic Support Fund aid is available when the State Department determines that deteriorating economic and political conditions within a country threaten the "internal security" of the United States. All AID-administered funds are tied to policies that promote the expansion of U.S. investment and the increase of U.S. exports. The recipient country must sign a letter of agreement that describes the manner in which the funds will be spent and the conditions required by AID. These agreements encourage "sound recipient economic policies and the creation of an environment which is hospitable to both local and foreign private initiative and investment."[4]

Most foreign aid money never leaves the United States. As Dean Hinderliter, AID regional inspector general for Latin America, explained: "A lot of money would never go to a developing country as dollars. It would go in goods and services. In most cases, the aid money is deposited into a U.S. bank directly by AID, which opens an account for the recipient country. Those funds are then used to buy the goods and services."[5] In the last several years, about 96% of commodities financed by AID grants were U.S.-made.[6] Most AID loans are also tied to the purchase of U.S. goods and services. Commodities purchased through AID grants generally must be shipped on U.S. flag vessels, while goods purchased through loans must be shipped on either vessels of the United States or other friendly nations.[7]

Most AID funds go to the poorer nations of the world not through grants but through loans. And the ratio of loans to grants has shown a steady increase for Central America. From 1946-80, 68% of the funds for Central America from AID and predecessor agencies were loans. By 1981, loans accounted for 74% of the AID program, and 76% in 1982. With loans come debts. The Central American nations (excluding Belize) owed AID over $726 million at the beginning of 1982, as shown in Table 6A. Under this debt-for-development system, Panama and Costa Rica in 1980 had debt payments to AID that were higher than what they received from AID in direct grants. AID charges an interest rate of only three to four percent. This low interest attracts the financially strapped nations, but causes further indebtedness and deepens their unequal debtor/creditor relationship with the United States.

Table 6A. Cumulative Debts to AID by Country as of 1/31/82
(millions $)

Costa Rica	$ 73
El Salvador	118
Guatemala	80
Honduras	111
Nicaragua	204
Panama	140
TOTAL	**$726**

Source: Senate Hearings before the Committee of Appropriations for Assistance and Related Programs Appropriations Fiscal Year 1983, p. 69.

Bureau of Private Enterprise

President Reagan is trying to let loose the "magic of the marketplace" in the underdeveloped world through his new Bureau of Private Enterprise within AID. Chief magician is Elise Du Pont, wife of Delaware's governor, who was hired for the famous magic touch of her corporate family. Du Pont said that the Bureau's programs differ from past AID practices in that the Bureau focuses more on direct arrangements with the private business sector rather than basing aid on government-to-government relationships. "Our new emphasis," explained AID Director Peter McPherson, "seeks a partnership of government and the private sector in the total development — not just involvement at the implementation stage."[8] In 1981, the Bureau of Private Enterprise began to investigate possible investment opportunities in each Central American country. Once the Bureau staff finds a Central American business with profit potential, they then try to hook the business up with interested private investors from the United States. The Bureau has concentrated on building U.S. investment in non-traditional exports and agro-industrial ventures such as a processing plant for vegetables. The local partners of such a project are farmers who contract with a U.S. company to sell their produce to the company's processing plant. The Bureau either directly finances the project or provides indirect financing through an intermediary like a credit union.

"We envision some projects, when fully developed, being primarily managed by the private investors, but with AID oversight," Du Pont explained. She believes "that there are many cases in the developing world where the U.S. investor would be more comfortable in assessing risks and making an investment decision if the U.S. government had an investment in the project in some way."[9]

The Bureau is looking to sink as much as $2.5 million in projects in Central America, but "prefers that most of its financial participation be in the $250,000 to one million dollar range." President Nixon once said, "To guide this capital to higher-risk areas, the federal government offers a system of insurance and guarantees."[10] Not only does the federal government offer insurance and guarantees to U.S. investors in foreign countries, but now it finances U.S. foreign investment. Four types of financing are in the works: 1) direct loans to existing indigenous enterprises, 2) loan participation with U.S. lending institutions, 3) capitalization of private financial intermediaries, and 4) credit and seed capital to venture-capital firms. The Reagan Administration's new financing schemes for U.S. foreign investment are steps ahead of the practices of past administrations. The range of the Bureau's work covers planning the project, doing feasibility studies, providing infrastructure, providing credit, financing demonstration projects, and even taking a financial position in a project to get it started.

Another focus of the Bureau is to improve "the indigenous climate and infrastructure for private enterprise." Du Pont said these efforts will create "strong, sophisticated markets for U.S. products and services, providing hospitable locations for investments and joint ventures by U.S. companies seeking stable risk-taking environments."

The Bureau also oversees the Housing Guaranty Program which insures loans from the U.S. private sector for housing projects in underdeveloped nations. Since its formation in the early 1960s, the Housing Guaranty Program has backed more than $1.5 billion in U.S. financing. The program's regional offices for Central America are in Tegucigalpa and Panama City. The amounts of authorization for 1982 and 1983 for Central American projects are as follows: Belize, $9 million; Costa Rica, $20 million; El Salvador, $15 million; Guatemala, $20 million; Honduras, $25 million; and Panama, $23 million.[11]

AID in Central America

Congress responded to the crisis in Central America with a dramatic increase in AID funds and programs. For example, AID and ESF funds for El Salvador from 1980-82 amounted to $335.3 million, which represents a threefold increase over the previous 33 years. In 1981, Central America received 54% of all the funds for Latin America and the Caribbean. Explaining the 1983 AID budget for the region, AID Director McPherson said, "I think that I can say without fear of contradiction that our program embodies all of President Reagan's principles."[12] The following are brief descriptions of AID's regional and country programs for Central America.*

Regional Programs

"U.S. objectives can be met only if the region is peaceful and politically stable," says AID's Regional Office for Central America and Panama (ROCAP). ROCAP, which has its office in Guatemala City, funds regional rather than country-specific programs. The region is important, says ROCAP, because of the high levels of U.S. investment in Central America and because it is the fourth largest U.S. trading partner in Latin America. "The private sector's ability to maintain production, employment, and the flow of trade" has been identified as the key solution to the economic crisis in Central America. ROCAP's budget jumped from four million dollars in 1980 to eighteen million dollars in 1982. ROCAP is sponsoring a six million dollar Private Sector Export Promotion project to increase non-traditional exports from the region. Recently ROCAP issued a five-year, $42 million loan to the Central American Bank for Economic Integration for a Private Sector Promotion Fund to "help finance the requirements for essential imports, working capital, and investment opportunities."[13]

Belize

Before independence Belize was the beneficiary of AID assistance indirectly through the U.S. controlled Caribbean Development Bank (CDB). One of the AID-financed projects through the Caribbean Development Bank was the construction of a factory in Belize City for assembly industries. Belize started receiving direct AID funding in 1981. One of the first AID projects was a study by Coopers & Lybrand to identify possibilities for U.S. investment in Belize. A sign of the incorporation of Belize into the U.S. sphere of economic and political influence was Prime Minister George Price's eagerness to receive ten million dollars in ESF money in 1982 to develop U.S. investment and trade in that country. As U.S. aid to Belize increases, it is likely that Belize will become another U.S. client state in Central America.

*Information from AID's Congressional Presentations Annex III, Fiscal Year 1982 and 1983.

Costa Rica

In 1981, AID slowed down its development assistance to Costa Rica because the country had failed both to meet its international debt payments and to maintain an economic austerity agreement with the International Monetary Fund (IMF). Costa Rica has promised the IMF and other international creditors that it will impose harsh economic measures and cut back its social services programs, so in 1982 AID resumed and increased its funding to Costa Rica. The United States is providing emergency aid through the Economic Support Fund and PL 480, the food aid program. In 1981, AID made a $10 million loan to Costa Rica's only private bank, Agro-Industrial and Export Bank of Costa Rica (BANEX), to promote non-traditional exports to the United States. AID's Cooperative Development and Marketing Program also promotes the export economy by funding the National Institute for Cooperative Development which provides credit for processing plants that will help produce food for export.

El Salvador

The AID program in El Salvador supports the private sector through the Industrial Recovery Program and the Private Sector Support Project. In 1982, AID provided an emergency $10 million Public Services Restoration loan "to restore vital public services that have been damaged or destroyed by terrorist activities." AID's development strategy for 1983 includes programs to 1) arrest the sharp economic decline and begin the process of economic recovery, 2) prevent collapse of the private sector and restore its productive capacity, 3) increase government employment, and 4) consolidate and strengthen the agrarian reform program. AID's Agrarian Reform Project in El Salvador provides credit and supplies to small farmers in the hope that a conservative class of small farmers will develop.

Guatemala

Guatemala is receiving funding for a Small Farmer Diversification Project that "will develop and disseminate diversified crop technologies and imports required by small farmers to switch production from basic grains to higher-value fruits and vegetables." This and other agricultural development projects in Guatemala reflect the AID campaign to encourage the production of non-traditional crops for export. Grants to the government will fund the construction of infrastructure projects in the Altiplano region of Guatemala to facilitate export production. The Private Sector Development Initiatives project started in 1982 by AID "will attempt to bring the private sector more fully into the socio-economic development process" by channeling "the dynamism of the private sector" into creating employment, increasing productivity, and stimulating community development. The Foreign Assistance Act (Section 116) prohibits aid to any government that engages in a consistent pattern of gross negligence of human rights. However, a big loophole in the human rights provision permits assistance if it meets basic human needs. Both AID and the Guatemalan government say their programs are "helping needy people." In August 1982, Congress allocated ten million dollars of Economic Support Funds to Guatemala.[14]

Honduras

A focal point of AID activities in Honduras is the Honduran Development Foundation (FUNDAGRO), an AID creation designed to pool private capital in rural Honduras. FUNDAGRO is one of a growing number of credit organizations sponsored by AID in Latin America. Through foundations like FUNDAGRO, AID encourages export production and inputs of U.S. farm technology. AID says that "Honduras is eager for private foreign investment," and that the country needs U.S. funds to increase credit and construct infrastructure projects. AID channels emergency Economic Support Fund money through the private banking system to "revitalize the economy." AID has a Forestry Development Project of $20 million that is providing technical assistance and planning to the Honduran Forest Development Corporation.

Nicaragua

In April 1981 the Reagan Administration announced that the United States was cutting off aid to Nicaragua, charging that the country was a conduit for Cuban arms to the Salvadoran insurgents. Reagan halted AID development assistance funds and $9.6 million in wheat shipments under the PL 480 program. Financial support for private sector and private voluntary organizations, however, was not terminated. "The principal U.S. interest in Nicaragua," said AID in 1981, "is the evolution of a pluralistic society with a mixed economy, not hostile to the United States." The AID budget presentation outlined the U.S. foreign aid strategy for Nicaragua:

> A pluralistic Nicaragua governed by a moderate government provides the best hope for sustained economic, political, and social progress of its citizens and for the long-term stability of the country. A stable Nicaragua will also contribute to peace, stability, and moderation in other areas of the politically volatile Central American region.

> The AID program strategy is to assist in establishing the economic framework within which Nicaragua's forces of moderation can operate and prosper . . . . The program also supports the private sector, which is the strongest force of democratic pluralism in Nicaragua, activities of other private and voluntary organizations, and people-to-people projects.

The initial postwar recovery grant to Nicaragua went to a "leading private sector organization, FUNDE, for expansion of its program in cooperative development." FUNDE or the Nicaraguan Development Foundation is the counterpart of the Honduran Development Foundation established by AID. FUNDE is an associate organization of the High Council of Private Enterprises (COSEP). FUNDE has worked at cross-purposes with the Sandinista government by sponsoring small agricultural cooperatives. Besides providing agricultural credit, FUNDE had an educational component that subsidized both short-term and long-term schooling.

Congress authorized funds for Nicaragua in 1982 but held most funds in abeyance. "We are seeking these funds to keep our options open in Nicaragua and to be prepared to deal with future developments there," reported AID in a congressional hearing, "Nicaragua's private sector and other moderates who can influence Nicaragua's path toward pluralism continue to need our help."[15]

The Sandinista Government prohibited COSEP from receiving a $5.1 million grant authorized by Congress in March 1982. Members of COSEP are the Nicaraguan Development Foundation, the Nicaraguan Chamber of Commerce, the Chamber of Nicaraguan Industries, the Chamber of Nicaraguan Builders, the Confederation of Nicaraguan Professionals, and the Union of Nicaraguan Agricultural Producers and Cattle Ranchers. The Sandinista Workers Union (CST) charged that the objective of the AID grant was "to finance movements that try to destabilize the Nicaraguan process." Nicaragua pointed to a statement made by a U.S. State Department official that U.S. "aid is a symbol of political and moral support for Nicaraguans discontented with the Sandinista regime."[16]

Panama

"The primary interest of the United States in Panama," reports AID, "is to foster a democratic political system and an economic and social environment conducive to the successful operation of the Canal." In agriculture, AID aims to "strengthen the private sector . . . by building private sector organizations and by providing public infrastructure and services needed by independent and private organizations to operate effectively." Beneficiaries of AID's private sector aid are business organizations like the Panamanian Chamber of Commerce, the National Council of Private Enterprise, and the Panamanian Association of Business Executives. Funding is planned for the Pan-American Development Foundation for its activities in assisting *mini-empresas* (small businesses). AID is also considering the allotment of funds to Technoserve, a U.S. voluntary organization, to organize and assist small business in Panama.

Farming But No Food

About 50% of the AID budget goes for agriculture, rural development, and nutrition, but that doesn't mean much has been done to alleviate hunger and malnutrition in the underdeveloped world. The focus of AID programs is to increase agricultural production and to increase the input of U.S. technology and farm products like fertilizer and pesticides. AID programs encourage small farmers to move away from low-priced basic agricultural commodities like corn and beans into production of the more lucrative export crops. An AID deputy said that AID programs allow small farmers "to grow, process, and package fresh vegetables for export to a more affluent country that can afford them."[17] The rationale behind this emphasis on export crops is that it improves the income of the small farmers and increases the underdeveloped country's trade balance.

"We will discourage policies which reduce incentives for rural producers, such as food price policies which favor the consumer and over-valued exchange rates which discourage exports," said AID Director McPherson.[18] Many AID programs include agreements with the recipient nations that change their internal economic policies and facilitate the import of U.S. farm inputs. While increased agricultural production for export is the thrust of the AID program, there has been some criticism of this orientation within the agency. "We have thus far not utilized the concept of hunger alleviation as a basic organizing principle of our activities," stated an AID memo. "Instead we have fallen back on more manageable sub-objectives, particularly that of increasing agricultural productivity, an area where the U.S. has considerable expertise . . . ."[19] The author of the memo noted that of the $175 million appropriated to the AID's food and nutrition account in 1980, less than five percent was specifically related to nutrition activities.

An executive of a U.S. fertilizer firm presented another side of the issue. He said, "I must emphasize that there would be scarcely any investment if it were not for the infrastructure, the education, the training, and the support provided by our aid program."[20] In 1982, AID reported that one of its largest programs was a $17 million project for agrarian reform in El Salvador that provides credit for fertilizers and other inputs.[21]

Funding for Loyalty

Private Voluntary Organizations (PVOs) receive about 14% of the annual AID budget for their work in underdeveloped countries. Their roles range from strictly humanitarian and relief efforts to business consulting and planning. Some PVOs, like Church World Service and Catholic Relief Services, have little to do with the political purposes of the foreign aid program, whereas others like the American Institute for Free Labor Development (AIFLD) are closely tied to AID's foreign policy strategy. Others play into that strategy through their own practices and principles. World Vision, a fundamentalist, anti-communist Christian relief organization, has met with frequent criticism dating back to the Vietnam War that it allows the CIA and the Defense Department to use its organizations for their own political purposes. In Honduras, Father Fausto Mills, a priest working with refugees, reported that World Vision members "landed helicopters in places where there were large concentrations of refugees, and told them 'communism is your enemy and it has ruined Honduras'."[22] In one way or another, the PVOs that receive funding from AID fit into the overall objectives of the United States in the region.

AID also funds population control organizations and in the last two years has been decreasing assistance to public and government agencies concerned with population planning in favor of increased funding to private organizations. The U.S. government provides 94% of the budget of the Association for Voluntary Sterilization and 88% of the Pathfinder Fund's budget. Pathfinder "assists innovative pioneering programs which will lead to lower rates of population growth." Retired General William C. Westmoreland submitted a statement to the U.S. Senate Committee on Foreign Relations that favored increased funds to population control programs.[23] Westmoreland said:

> "It seems to me that there has been a missing element in strategic planning in the national interest of our country. The long-range security interests of America involve sources of raw materials, routes of sea and air transportation, possibly base areas in an emergency, and a military posture designed to deter the persistent adventurism of the Soviet Union. A missing element is inadequate attention, in a strategic context, to uncontrolled population growth in those selected countries. We have observed that population explosion in underdeveloped countries can result in political unrest, temptations to cross international boundaries, and the creation of a breeding ground for terrorist organizations. Control of population growth can foster viable economies and simplify the problems of government.

Such arguments have also been used for the control of minority populations in the United States. Population control organizations give little attention to the roots of underdevelopment and poverty that make it difficult for many Third World families to support themselves.

AID has also been committing more of its money to non-profit consulting companies that manage AID organizing projects and programs in Central America. Three such organizations are the New Transcentury Foundation

(100% government-funded), Technoserve Inc. (50%), and the International Executive Service Corps (28%). The executive corps works with the private sector in Central America to increase its organizational abilities. Founded in 1964 by David Rockefeller and other national business leaders, the executive corps had gained the sponsorship of over 175 multinational corporations by 1969. It is consultant to U.S. foreign investors in Guatemala, Honduras, El Salvador, Panama, and Costa Rica.

AID also funds Private Agencies Collaborating Together (PACT), which is an alliance of private organizations coordinating development activities in underdeveloped countries. AID provides 100% of the funding of this private group and partially funds 155 other PVOs, some of which are listed in Table 6B.

Table 6B. Some Private Voluntary Organizations With Operations in Central America and Receiving Funds from AID in 1980

Business

Credit Union National Association — credit unions

International Executive Service Corps — consulting

National Association of the Partners of the Alliance — business exchanges

New Transcentury Foundation — consulting

Pan American Development Foundation — business development

Technoserve — agricultural processing development

Winrock International Livestock Research and Training Center — animal agricultural training

Wisconsin-Nicaragua Partners — business development

Development

CARE — community development

Hermandad — community development

Inter-American Development Institute — credit unions

Save the Children Federation — community development

Volunteers in Technical Assistance — community and business development

Religious

Catholic Relief Services — relief and community development

Church World Service — relief and community development

Seventh-Day Adventist World Service — community development

World Vision Relief Organization — community development and refugees

World Relief Corporation — refugees

Services

Agua del Pueblo — health programs

American Institute for Free Labor Development — labor organizing

Amigos de las Americas — health programs

Direct Relief Foundation — medical aid

La Leche League International — breastfeeding encouragement

People-to-People Health Foundation — health education

Project Concern International — health programs

Boy Scouts — youth programs

Population

Pathfinder Fund — family planning

Planned Parenthood Federation of America — family planning

Source: Bureau of Food for Peace and Voluntary Cooperation, *Voluntary Foreign Aid Programs, 1980.*

Each year, the PVOs come to Congress to ask for increased appropriations from the AID budget. In 1982, Douglas Hellinger of the Development Group for Alternative Policies in testimony before the House Committee on Foreign Operations criticized the close relationship that many PVOs maintain with AID. Hellinger said: "Private and voluntary organizations are . . . private entities free to work with and assist the world's poor in a spirit of volunteerism and collaboration. There are signs, however, that many PVOs are increasingly willing to compromise their independence for additional funding. It is clear that AID is intent to utilize PVOs to its own advantage." Hellinger said that AID and its director Peter McPherson consider partnership in this case to mean "funding for loyalty." "This loyalty," explained Hellinger, "has two components: the willingness to carry out AID-defined projects on AID's terms, rather than AID building on the independent grassroots work of PVOs; and the support of not simply the PVO line item in the AID bill in Congress, but rather the entire bill, no matter its composition."[24]

AID increased assistance to the private sector and PVOs in Nicaragua after the Sandinistas took power in 1979. Most aid went to what AID calls "indigenous PVOs." Nicaragua received more aid through PVOs in 1980 than any other nation in Latin America. Listed in Table 6C is the AID assistance to PVOs in Central America for 1980.

Table 6C. AID Assistance to U.S. and Indigenous PVOs for Fiscal Year 1980
(thousands $)

	U.S. PVOs	Indigenous PVOs
Costa Rica	$ 366	$ 265
El Salvador	758	49
Guatemala	287	-0-
Honduras	92	480
Nicaragua	800	1,423
Panama	86	125
TOTAL	$2,389	$2,342

Source: Hearings before a Subcommittee of the Committee on Appropriations, House of Representatives, *Foreign Assistance and Related Programs Appropriations for 1982,* Part 5, p. 83.

AID funded a number of U.S. Private Voluntary Organizations for projects in Nicaragua, including:

- Wisconsin Partners of Americas, for services to Miskito Indians

- The New Transcentury Foundation, for community rehabilitation

- Partners of the Americas, for a regional educational radio program

- The American Institute for Free Labor Development (AIFLD) for AFL-CIO associated labor union organizing

- COSEP, for organizing small farmers and ranchers

- Red Cross

- Technoserve, for technical and managerial advice to small business

- CARE, for *campesino* training and food programs

In addition to the other PVOs, the government has one of its own. The Inter-American Foundation (IAF) was founded in 1969 as a semi-autonomous organization to "strengthen the bonds of friendship between Latin America and the United States." AID and the Inter-American Development Bank (IDB) provide the funding to IAF, which aims to "support self-help efforts and encourage the growth of democratic institutions." Decisions are made by a board of directors appointed by the president of the United States, and a majority of the board must come from the private sector. Current board members of IAF include Peter McPherson, administrator of AID; Thomas O. Enders, Assistant Secretary for Inter-American Affairs; and Viron P. Vaky, Associate Dean at Georgetown University's School of Foreign Service and former assistant secretary of state under Carter. Other board members hail from Levi Strauss, Hartford National Bank, Amex Systems, Quaker Oats, and Sears Roebuck and Company. In the last ten years, IAF has funded over 900 projects, with Chile being the leading recipient of its funds. In Central America, the Inter-American Foundation has funded the following number of projects between 1971 and 1981: Guatemala, 41; Panama, 41; Nicaragua, 32; Honduras, 25; Costa Rica, 24; Belize, 19; and El Salvador, 15. Pre-revolutionary Nicaragua led in terms of the amount of funding, which amounted to $5 million during the last decade.[25] Current funding in Nicaragua is channeled through the Nicaragua Development Foundation, a private sector outreach and promotion organization under the High Council on Private Enterprises (COSEP). COSEP has placed itself squarely in opposition to Nicaragua's Sandinista government.

ECONOMIC SUPPORT FUND

Foreign aid from the Economic Support Fund (ESF) falls somewhere between economic development aid and military aid. The State Department says ESF "is used to promote economic or political stability in regions where the United States has special security interests, and promote peaceful solutions to international problems which affect U.S. interest, national security, and achievement of foreign policy objectives." The tremendous increases in aid to Central American countries in 1982 came from ESF authorizations.

The State Department says that social upheaval and economic disarray in Central America threaten the vital interests of the United States, and it has asked Congress for substantial increases in ESF money for the region. Most ESF loans and grants in Central America are designed to encourage private enterprise. The recipient country signs an agreement with AID that describes the way the funds will be used. AID program managers, economists, and development specialists work with the country on the actual implementation of the ESF loan or grant program. This often puts AID in a position to make crucial decisions about the country's economy and to directly promote U.S. business interests. In March 1982, President Reagan announced his Caribbean Basin Initiative (CBI) to provide emergency assistance to selected countries in the region.

Congress altered the president's original request and allocated $200 million in ESF appropriations for Central America. In addition, $25 million in ESF funds will be available for future allocation, $2 million was allocated for the Inter-American Development Foundation, and $2 million to the American Institute for Free Labor Development. Table 6D shows the distribution of ESF funding from 1981-1983. The proposed 1983 budget includes another $190 million for Central America, with $50 million allocated to "permit quick U.S. response to unforeseen needs in the Caribbean Basin."[26] ESF assistance is earmarked for the following purposes.[27]

Belize: To provide private sector credit for both foreign exchange and local currency costs and to stimulate private sector expansion.

Honduras: To assist the private sector by financing the creation and expansion of industries.

El Salvador: To aid the private sector by funding the importation of raw materials and intermediate goods, to help reopen and rehabilitate a selected number of industries, and to repair infrastructure damaged by war.

Costa Rica: To finance necessary imports and technical assistance required to spur production, employment, and exports.

Table 6D. ESF FUNDING
(millions $)

	1981	*1982*	*CBI*	*1983 Proposed*
Belize	-0-	-0-	10	-0-
Costa Rica	-0-	20	70	60
El Salvador	44.9	40	75*	105
Guatemala	-0-	-0-	10*	-0-
Honduras	-0-	-0-	35	25
Nicaragua	56.6	-0-	-0-	-0-
Panama	-0-	-0-	-0-	-0-
ROCAP	0.9	-0-	-0-	-0-

*not more than

Sources: Congressional Presentation for Fiscal Year 1983; Congressional Quarterly Weekly Report, August 21, 1982, pp. 2104-2105.

FOOD FOR PEACE

"Food is a weapon," said Secretary of Agriculture John R. Block, "but the way we use that weapon is to tie countries to us. That way they'll be reluctant to upset us."[28] Block was referring to the PL 480 food aid program that sells and distributes U.S. agricultural products overseas. The budget of the PL 480 program for Central America in 1982 was $65.7 million — about 15% of total U.S. agricultural exports to the region. In the post-World War Two era, the United States used surplus agricultural commodities as "defense support." This program of food aid was expanded by Public Law 480 (PL 480) in 1954, which was designed "to increase consumption of U.S. agricultural commodities, to improve the foreign relations of the United States, and for other purposes." PL 480 comprises two main types of food aid.[29] Title I sells food to friendly governments on concessionary terms with 20 to 40-year credit agreements. This part of PL 480 allows the recipient government to sell the food to its own citizens and then to use the profit from the sales to finance its public expenditures. Title II refers to the more commonly known type of food aid whereby a Private Voluntary Organization (PVO) like CARE distributes free food. A recent provision of the Title II program allows a government to receive and sell food as in Title I, but it requires the sales income to be used to develop agricultural programs to expand food production.

The State Department often utilizes the PL 480 program for political purposes. The United States cut off $9.6 million in wheat shipments to Nicaragua in 1981 as part of the U.S. government's program of destabilization of the Sandinista government. In contrast, the amount of PL 480 'food credits scheduled for El Salvador from 1981-83 is nearly three times the amount of food aid given to that country during the first 26 years of the program. Over 74% of this food aid comes under Title I,[30] thereby giving the government great flexibility in the use of the food and sales income. Food aid as a way to provide military aid has been a common practice of the PL 480 program. During the Vietnam War, one half of the total PL 480 credits went to South Vietnam and Cambodia. The South Vietnamese army sold the food and used the income to pay its soldiers. From 1966-71, over $690 million of PL 480 went to generate funds for military equipment purchases.[31] In 1982, El Salvador received 43% of the total PL 480 food credits for Central America.

A 1982 report by the United States Department of Agriculture (USDA) said that, "PL 480 is one of the United States' most successful market development tools."[32] The USDA reported seven of the top ten nations which purchased U.S. farm products were formerly recipients of U.S. food aid. A prime beneficiary of the food aid program has been the U.S. grain corporations. Since the program's birth 28 years ago, over $32 billion of U.S. agricultural products have been shipped out of the country under the PL 480 program. The amount of food distributed and sold by the United States each year depends on the agricultural market in the United States and the exigencies of foreign policy. The U.S. president can increase or decrease PL 480 shipments to a country without congressional approval.

PL 480 has been especially valuable in opening up markets for U.S. grain producers, who exported more than $20 billion worth of grain under the program since its inception in 1954. Wheat and wheat products have accounted for over 70% of the program's tonnage and roughly half of its value. "The PL 480 program has given a big impetus to U.S. flour exports," said the USDA, "Nearly two-fifths of the U.S. flour exports in 1980 were under PL 480."[33] The Food for Peace program currently accounts for three to four percent of the total U.S. agricultural exports. During years of wheat surpluses, however, this percentage increased to 33% of total farm exports in 1958 and 29% in 1963.

Occasionally the food aid given through Title II actually hinders local economic development. Such was the case with the emergency food aid given to Guatemala after the 1976 earthquake that had left thousands homeless. Two voluntary organizations, CARE and Catholic Relief Services, distributed 27,000 tons of grain to rural victims of the quake, though it hadn't ruined their grain reserves. The effect of the donated grain was to knock the bottom out of the local grain market since the influx of the free food caused the prices to drop below the costs of production. "The people of the highlands grow their corn, and if they have some left over from their needs, they sell it," explained an Indian leader from Chimaltenango, "When all that food came in, there was no longer a market for corn, and the farmers lost out."

One relief worker from the United States said that "even outside disaster situations, food handouts weaken minimum social structures and they discourage farmers from growing their own food." He added, "If a voluntary agency wants food to support a specific program it can buy it locally and help national farmers rather than import it from the United States." PL 480 frequently contributes to the breakdown of community social structures by giving power to people associated with the U.S. programs. Roland Bunch, a volunteer worker in Guatemala, said that "largely because of the give-aways the villages started to turn more to leaders who could produce free things . . . whether they were honest or dishonest, rather than to the leaders they'd been putting their trust in for years."[34] A study by the Presbyterian Church criticized the PL 480 program. While the food aid has done some good, the study reported, "It has also helped unpopular governments remain in power . . . discouraged local food production, and increased the dependence of some developing nations on imported foodstuffs." The study advocated that all foreign assistance go to meet basic human needs, not to achieve short-term foreign policy goals, to promote U.S. market development, or to dispose of surplus U.S. products.[35]

EXIMBANK: SUBSIDIZING EXPORTS

The Export-Import Bank of the United States (Eximbank) is a leading proponent of U.S. corporate control of international markets. Eximbank provides government credit for financing, insurance, and bank guarantees for U.S. exports in order to give U.S. corporations a competitive edge in international trade. In 1981, Eximbank had a total financing authorization of $452 million.[36] The Eximbank lends to U.S. corporations, foreign businesses, and foreign governments that purchase U.S. products. Under the insurance program, a corporation like Deere and Company could receive reimbursement from Eximbank if an agricultural cooperative in Guatemala failed to meet its payment schedule for farm machinery bought from the company. Closely related to Eximbank is the private Foreign Credit Insurance Association (FCIA), an association of over 50 major insurance companies that work directly with Eximbank and U.S. exporters to insure repayment for their financing to foreign buyers. In 1981, the association paid $19.7 million to cover losses. An article in the Department of Commerce magazine *Business America* reported that "over the past two years especially, a combination of economic and political factors worldwide has made the extension of export credit increasingly risky."[37]

The bank's direct credit program finances large mining and infrastructure projects with long-term repayment periods. It also offers bank guarantees and export credit insurance for less expensive operations. Eximbank maintains relations with a network of over 300 U.S. commercial banks through its bank guarantee program, which insures their loan payments against the possible failure of a foreign purchaser to pay for the products. Eximbank's financial picture is not looking good. In 1980, one of the few times since its inception, the bank did not pay the Treasury a dividend on the government's equity in the bank. It had a net income of $30 million in 1981 down from $110 million in 1980. In 1982, an $18 million deficit is projected.[38]

Eximbank has a history of using its financial resources with political motives. In Chile, the Eximbank cut off all loan guarantees to the Allende government, making it extremely difficult for Chilean businesses to obtain products such as machinery and spare parts from the United States. Such policies also have the indirect effect of making it difficult for the country to obtain other external financing. Eximbank President Henry Kearns said that if a borrower "is in trouble with us, there's literally no private institution in the U.S. that will lend to him."[39] Nicaragua has been the latest victim of such discriminatory practices. After the Sandinistas took power in 1979, Eximbank's program of loans, grants, and insurance dropped off drastically. Total Eximbank loans to Nicaragua amounted to $38.3 million from 1962-1978, but since 1979 there have been no new loans to Nicaragua. In 1981, all Eximbank guarantees and insurance in Nicaragua amounted to only $11,514 — a sharp decline from $8.9 million in 1979.

Commodity Credit Corporation

The Commodity Credit Corporation (CCC) offers another kind of credit and financing for U.S. exports. Administered by the U.S. Department of Agriculture (USDA), the CCC promotes export of U.S. agricultural products to selected foreign countries. GSM-102, a CCC program, encourages U.S. banks to provide credit for agricultural export sales. Under this program, the U.S. exporter receives immediate payment from a U.S. bank for its export sales. The U.S. bank then gets its money back plus interest from the foreign purchaser of U.S. agricultural commodities. If the purchaser fails to pay, the CCC reimburses the bank. In this way, the U.S. exporter receives immediate payment for foreign sales, and the U.S. bank receives additional foreign loan business that is guaranteed by the U.S. government. In 1981, the export guarantee program meant over $1.8 billion in credit business for U.S. banks.[40] One advantage of this program for the United States is that all the financial transactions of export sales stay within the country. Over $42 million in agricultural exports to Central America were covered by the CCC guarantee program in 1981.[41]

OPIC: INSURANCE FOR THE TRANSNATIONALS

The Overseas Private Investment Corporation (OPIC) is the government insurance company for the transnationals. Congress created OPIC in 1969 to foster the "participation of U.S. private capital and skills in the economic and social progress of developing countries through programs of political risk insurance."[42] The U.S. Treasury backs up the insurance policies issued by OPIC. Since 1971, OPIC has been insuring and guaranteeing U.S. investors against potential risks of loss from their overseas investments due to expropriation, inconvertibility of currency, and wars, revolution, or insurrection. In 1981, Congress approved new legislation that expanded the definition of "political risk" to include "civil strife," which covers more limited forms of violence against U.S. business property. This increased coverage "is expected to involve lower-value claims, windows broken rather than whole factories blown up."[43]

"OPIC is unquestionably a valuable development and export promotion tool," said Henry Geylin, the president of the Council of the Americas, "but not to be overlooked is its important value as a tangible and flexible instrument of foreign policy." OPIC is one of the many instruments of foreign policy that Reagan has used to fashion his Caribbean Basin program. OPIC President Craig A. Nalen said, "The administration has placed a high priority on strengthening U.S. ties with this area whose economic and political development objectives are so closely allied with our own."[44]

Active insurance contracts in the Caribbean/Central American region amounted to $2.4 billion by the end of 1981. OPIC's largest insured project in Central America in recent years has been the oil pipeline in Panama; Northville Terminal Corporation and Chicago Bridge and Iron Company received a total of $33 million in OPIC coverage in 1981 for the project. In Honduras, Rosario Resources, owned by Amax, announced a $16 million expansion of their silver and zinc mine which will be insured by OPIC. Table 6E lists OPIC's insured investors in Central America during 1979, 1980, and 1981.

Table 6E. OPIC Insured Investors
1979, 1980, 1981
(thousands $)

Year	Company	Location	Project	Maximum single coverage
79	American Standard International	Costa Rica	Plastic faucets & sanitary wares manufacturing (expansion)	496
79	Bankers Trust	Panama	Oil storage & transshipment facility (expansion)	2,500
79	Beckman Instruments	El Salvador	Electronic components assembly	3,330
79	Chase Manhattan	Panama	Oil storage & transshipment facility (expansion)	7,500
79	Chemical Bank	Panama	Oil storage & transshipment facility (expansion)	2,000
79	Chemtex Fibers	Costa Rica	Polyester filament manufacturing (expansion)	1,350
79	Delmed	El Salvador	Medical products manufacturing (expansion)	1,993
79	First National Bank of Boston	Panama	Oil storage & transshipment facility (expansion)	1,000

Year	Company	Location	Project	Maximum Single Coverage
79	International Proteins	El Salvador	Seafood catching & processing	450
79	Kimberly-Clark	El Salvador	Paper products manufacturing (expansion)	8,100
79	Manufacturers Hanover Trust	Panama	Oil storage & transshipment facility (expansion)	2,500
79	Shrimp Culture	Honduras	Shrimp farming (expansion)	1,729
80	Joseph Master, et al	Costa Rica	Ornamental plants farm	648
80	Rosario Resources	Honduras	Silver, lead, & zinc mining (expansion)	16,000
80	Wallis & Company	Honduras	Silver & gold mining	1,186
80	Harold W. Whitney	Belize	General farming	1,620
81	ABA Industries	Costa Rica	Metal machine parts manufacturing	63
81	BankAmerica International	Honduras	Electric wire & cable manufacturing	3,000
81	James L. Boudet, et al	Costa Rica	Lime & orange groves	840
81	William C. Brothers	Belize	Cedar shingle mill (expansion)	290
81	Chicago Bridge and Iron	Panama	Petroleum pipeline construction	11,966
81	Crescent Corset	Honduras	Pre-cut textiles processing	635
81	Northville Terminal	Panama	Petroleum pipeline construction	20,820
81	Tri-State Culvert	Guatemala	Metal culvert pipe, flood protectors, & grain silos manufacturing	810

Source: OPIC Annual Reports 1979, 1980, 1981.

Kimberly-Clark made the news when it dropped sponsorship of the *Lou Grant* television series in reaction to actor Ed Asner's public opposition to U.S. policy in El Salvador. In 1979, the company received four million dollars in OPIC insurance for a new factory in San Salvador. Justifying its involvement in the project, OPIC said, "The project will increase the amount of hygienic paper products available to local distributors. Professional and technical training will be provided by the project which will employ 304 workers."[45]

Several electronics assembly companies doing business in San Salvador's Free-Trade Zone have received OPIC insurance. AVX Ceramics has a plant insured for $3.8 million that employs Salvadorans to assemble ceramic capacitors, which are shipped back to the company's headquarters in South Carolina for testing and packaging. Former OPIC President Bruce Llewellyn told a congressional hearing that the AVX assembly plant in El Salvador allows the company to compete better against Japanese manufacturers. Llewellyn said, "In this case, it is not a runaway shop; it is simply the ability to get half a loaf, if you will, a very important half a loaf, rather than giving up the entire chip manufacturing operation to the foreigners."[46]

Not only does OPIC insure the overseas investment of U.S. firms, but it also has a fund to finance foreign business operations and has recently begun to promote distributorships and leasing programs that assist U.S. companies. OPIC has provided $1.4 million for a Mack Truck dealership in Honduras and a Caterpillar machinery distributorship in Belize. OPIC's main priority is the promotion of U.S. exports. Bruce Llewellyn said, "About 100 of the largest companies in the U.S. account for half of U.S. exports, and a total of 250 for about 75%. About 33% of all U.S. exports go overseas to affiliates or subsidiaries of domestic companies, which points up . . . the fact that exports and investments go hand in hand."[47]

In 1981, Congress extended the life of OPIC for another four years, and President Reagan directed OPIC to place increased emphasis on Central America. OPIC insurance increases the U.S. government's vested interest in upholding "friendly" Central American governments, no matter how repressive they may be. Conversely the United States has a stake in toppling governments that threaten U.S. interests. The claims on OPIC by companies nationalized by the Allende government in Chile almost drained OPIC reserves before a U.S.-backed coup ousted the progressive Chilean government. In Nicaragua, U.S. investors have claimed losses due to the revolution. Corporations that have made claims against OPIC for losses in Nicaragua include American Standard, General Mills, Citizens Standard Life Insurance, Sears Roebuck and Company, and Ralston Purina. In 1980 and 1981, several companies in El Salvador presented their cases to OPIC for insurance settlements.

AIFLD

Since 1950 the U.S. Department of Defense has trained over 22,000 Central American soldiers. But even more enthusiastic about training Central Americans is a non-profit organization funded by AID called the American Institute for Free Labor Development (AIFLD). Since 1962, AIFLD has trained over 90,000 Central American workers in labor organizing and political theory.[48] U.S. corporate and labor leaders came together in 1962 to establish AIFLD. The purpose of the new organization was to train Latin American union leaders and to encourage the formation of trade unions that would combat communist influence.

U.S. concern for Latin American organizing existed before the development of AIFLD. In 1918, the American Federation of Labor (AFL), under the leadership of Samuel Gompers, took the first step to form a hemispheric labor federation. Gompers brought together the AFL and Mexican labor to establish the Pan-American Federation of Labor (PAFL). President Wilson, who saw PAFL as a potential vehicle for U.S. foreign policy in Latin America, offered covert financial assistance to PAFL. At the PAFL founding convention in

Laredo, Texas, the AFL representative Santiago Iglesias described the new federation as the instrument "through which constructive trade unionism can gain ascendency in Latin America."[49] Delegates from El Salvador, Honduras, and Nicaragua attended the second convention in 1919, and the organization grew slowly over the next ten years. PAFL, however, didn't survive the tough years of the Depression, and an equivalent organization didn't appear until some 20 years later.

During the 1930s and 1940s, the AFL and the Congress of Industrial Organizations (CIO) developed an analysis of foreign affairs strikingly similar to the official foreign policy of the United States. A case in point is a speech given in 1939 by John L. Lewis. In the name of the CIO, Lewis said that "Central and South America are capable of absorbing all of our excess and surplus commodities . . . . Obviously, increased trade volume with the Latin American countries would result in improved political and cultural relationships and make for increased security for the United States when the day comes that some imperialistic foreign power challenges the Monroe Doctrine."[50] Both the AFL and the CIO cooperated with the Office of Inter-American Affairs (OIAA) in the early 1940s when the OIAA organized State Department tours to the United States for Latin American union leaders. OIAA Director Nelson Rockefeller later commented on his association with labor during those years. He said, "George Meany's cooperation, as well as that of [other labor leaders], was tremendously helpful to setting up many of the Latin American programs . . . . We saw eye to eye on these matters."[51]

Labor leader Serafino Romualdi, who worked for the OIAA under Nelson Rockefeller, spearheaded the U.S. government's attack on progressive unionism in Latin America in the 1940s. Romualdi called for the creation of an AFL-affiliated labor federation in Latin America that would promote anti-communist unions. In 1951, Romualdi was instrumental in setting up the Inter-American Regional Organization of Workers (ORIT), which became a branch of the anti-communist International Federation of Free Trade Unions. Romualdi, the first director of ORIT, later wrote a book about his labor union work in Latin America. He said: "Had not organized labor and peasants of Latin America actually opposed the subversive programs of the communists, the political map of our hemisphere today would be quite different. Venezuela, Colombia, Guatemala, Peru, and above all Brazil also would probably be another communist nation."[52] According to Romualdi, ORIT was not based "on the concept of class struggle, but aimed at rapprochement with free enterprise – as a partner."[53]

In the United States, federations of unions in the same industry called International Trade Secretariats worked through ORIT to gain a hold on Latin American unions. One such international secretariat called the Post, Telegraph and Telephone Workers International (PTTI) had the Communications Workers of America (CWA) as its largest affiliate. Former CWA president, Joseph A. Beirne, played a key role in the formation of AIFLD. Beirne said in an interview with Readers Digest that the idea for labor training for Latin

Americans came to him when looking out a plane window while flying over the Andes. While reflecting on the misery of the people, he "suddenly realized that this would never be cleared up unless it could be put in the minds of these people to change their outlook, their view of the world."[54] Following the suggestions of Beirne, the CWA sponsored a three-month training school for PTTI-affiliated unions throughout Latin America. When the union members returned home, they received a nine-month stipend to promote anti-communism and free trade unionism in their own countries. The success of these early CWA labor courses sparked the formation of AIFLD in 1962. U.S. business and labor leaders decided that an expanded training program would be a perfect companion to ORIT. The founders of AIFLD saw it as an organization that would respond to the "threat of Castroite infiltration and eventual control of major labor movements within Latin America."[55]

The AFL-CIO's George Meany served as the first president of AIFLD, while J. Peter Grace of the W.R. Grace Company was the organization's first chairperson. Grace was a good friend of President Kennedy, who appointed Grace to head the influential Department of Commerce Committee on the Alliance for Progress. The committee's task was to evaluate the Alliance for Progress and to recommend ways the Alliance could further the interests of private enterprise in Latin America. At the same time, through his involvement in AIFLD, Grace had a part in directing the course of labor organizing in the hemisphere. "We must bear in mind," said Grace, "that we cannot allow communist propaganda to divide us between liberals and conservatives, or between business and labor, or between the American people and their government."[56] The Grace Foundation of the W.R. Grace Company was a financial contributor to AIFLD. The foundation also gave to groups such as the American Council for the International Promotion of Democracy Under God and an organization called Citizens for a Free Cuba.[57] Other corporations that offered financial support to AIFLD were United Fruit, Anaconda, Merck and Company, and Pan American World Airways. Nelson Rockefeller, the acknowledged spokesperson for corporate capitalism's march into Latin America, was an early member of AIFLD's board of trustees. With the structure and personnel ready, AIFLD was set to make its mark in Latin America.

AIFLD in the Eighties

The AIFLD sponsored sixteen courses in 1981 on "Political Theories in Central and South America" that offered "intensive and comprehensive training for trade union leaders in the complex field of ideologies as they affect trade union development."[58] Four courses took place in Honduras where AFL-CIO and AIFLD staff trained trade union leaders from Honduras, El Salvador, and Guatemala. One special two-week seminar in Honduras in 1981 taught Salvadoran *campesino* leaders "political philosophy."

The AIFLD Education Department in 1981 provided specialized training at

AIFLD AND THE CIA

AIFLD has frequently been accused of having close connections with the CIA. On one occasion, *Business Week* called the international apparatus of the AFL-CIO, "labor's own version of the CIA." In 1968, the *Washington Post* mentioned that William C. Doherty Jr., the executive director of AIFLD, was involved in CIA operations. But it was Philip Agee, former CIA operative and author of *Inside the Company: CIA Diary*, who detailed the alliance of the CIA and AIFLD in Latin America. Agee described AIFLD as a "CIA-controlled labor center financed through AID [with] programs in adult education and social projects used as a front for covering trade-union organizing activity." Agee also made the following observations about organizations and labor leaders associated with AIFLD.

International Confederation of Free Trade Unions (ICFTU): Labor center established and controlled by the CIA to oppose the progressive World Federation of Trade Unions.

Inter-American Regional Labor Organization (ORIT): Organization under the ICFTU for the Western Hemisphere, headquartered in Mexico City and a principal mechanism for CIA labor operations in Latin America.

Inter-American Labor College: Training school of ORIT in Cuernavaca, Mexico, financed and controlled by the CIA.

Communications Workers of America (CWA): U.S. trade union utilized by the CIA for operations through the Post, Telegraph, and Telephone Workers International.

Joseph Beirne: President of the CWA and founder of AIFLD, Beirne was an important collaborator in CIA labor operations.

William Doherty: Inter-american representative of the Post, Telegraph, and Telephone Workers International, and CIA agent in labor operations as Executive Director of AIFLD, Doherty was considered to be one of the CIA's most effective agents.

Jose Figueres: Costa Rica's president three times and leader of the anti-communist "revolution" in that country in 1948, Figueres was front man for CIA operations such as AIFLD and the Institute for Political Education and in general a longtime CIA collaborator.

Serafino Romualdi: Representative of the American Federation of Labor (AFL) and later director of AIFLD, Romualdi was a longtime principal CIA agent for labor operations in Latin America.

Source: Philip Agee, *Inside the Company: CIA Diary* (New York: Stonehill, 1975).

the George Meany Center in Maryland to 234 Latin American trade unionists. Six programs lasting seven weeks contained four areas of instruction: political aspects of development, economics, trade unions and productivity, and democracy and development. At the conclusion of their studies in the United States, the trade unionists began a nine-month "salaried internship program" financed by AIFLD.[59] Graduates of the course returned home to organize free trade unions and to spread their newly acquired political knowledge. Through the international secretariats, AIFLD has operated a program that since 1976 has brought about the enlistment of "128,000 new union members and the formation or re-establishment of more than 1,000 unions in Latin America and the Caribbean."[60]

The Agrarian Union Development Department (AUDD) is a branch of AIFLD that "seeks to bring to bear the inherent philosophy – the mystique – of the U.S. trade union movement's tradition of social struggle into play on behalf of rural workers."[61] AUDD focuses more on organizing small farmers rather than landless farmworkers who compose the vast majority of rural workers. Rather than organizing *campesinos* into unions, AUDD establishes associations to improve the farmers' situation through credit and community services, with the goal to develop a small farmers class with capitalistic tendencies. The most active AUDD program is in El Salvador, with other rural organizing projects in Honduras and Costa Rica.

Extolling the virtues of the American Institute for Free Labor Development to his corporate colleagues, J. Peter Grace said, "Through the AIFLD, business, labor, and government have come together to work toward a common goal in Latin America, namely supporting the democratic form of government, the capitalistic system and general well-being of the individual. It is an outstanding example of a national consensus . . . . "[62] This unity among labor, business, and government is now less official since J. Peter Grace stepped down from his position with AIFLD, and all board members are now representatives from labor. Grace assured the board, however, that he and other corporate leaders would maintain "close and friendly" ties with AIFLD and its membership.

Although corporations with Latin American investments have good reason to back AIFLD, private business has not paid AIFLD's way. Rather it has been the government that has kept AIFLD alive. The institute's information specialist Jack Heberly said that of the 1981 $7.7 million AIFLD budget only 5% was contributed by the AFL-CIO and 95% by the Agency for International Development. AID Director McPherson told a 1981 congressional hearing: "As you probably know, the AFL-CIO has a fairly substantial contract with AID in Latin America. My recollection is that, for fiscal year 1981, it amounted to something like eight million dollars . . . . We need to have a free labor movement in these countries and there needs to be some recognition of the role they can play in a private enterprise environment."[63] The Reagan Administration, recognizing this role, asked that two million dollars of his Caribbean Basin Initiative (CBI) go to AIFLD activities in Central America and the Caribbean alone. Table 6F lists Fiscal Year 1980 AID contracts to ORIT and AIFLD. AID contracts AIFLD to perform services of mutual interest to the government and the AFL-CIO.

Table 6F. AID Contracts to AIFLD and ORIT in Latin America
Active* October 1, 1979 - September 30, 1980

Amount	Contract description
$ 625,000	revolving loan fund
682,120	support for non-communist labor program in Uruguay
231,000	support for Inter-American Regional Workers Organization (ORIT) to strengthen free trade union institution in Latin America
1,406,000	contract to coordinate and administer a program of technical assistance to the free trade unions throughout Latin America
12,826,880	cooperative agreement to support the development of democratic trade unions in Latin America
500,000	strengthening of free labor, democratic labor, and related organizations in Nicaragua and Caribbean area
2,600,000	a special three-month program to support land reform in El Salvador
100,000	provide support for a program of union-to-community food distribution centers in urban El Salvador

*Contracts often span over more than one year's time.
Source: Agency for International Development, Department of State, Current Technical Service Contracts and Grants Active During the Period October 1, 1979 through September 30, 1980.

AIFLD's current operations in each of the seven Central American countries are outlined below.

El Salvador: AIFLD's largest program is in El Salvador, where the institute has focused on the agrarian reform as a way of organizing *campesinos*. Current AIFLD Executive Director William Doherty has been active in El Salvador since 1966, when he helped form the Salvadoran Communal Union (UCS)[64] as a conservative alternative to progressive rural unions. The AIFLD's agrarian reform program was an attempt to undercut the power of the oligarchy and to build an anti-communist base in Salvadoran politics. The Land to the Tiller agrarian reform program was designed by Roy Prosterman, who had created a land reform program with the same name in South Vietnam. AIFLD reported that through the agrarian reform program, UCS identified 67,000 potential voters and offered them free transportation to the election centers in March 1982. The AIFLD and AID covered the costs of an extensive UCS campaign to publicize the agrarian reform program. The campaign included radio and television advertising and the work of 400 organizers to promote and explain the agrarian reform to *campesinos*. John McAward of the Unitarian Universalist Service Committee, which has sponsored several congressional study missions to El Salvador, said that AIFLD has been discredited in many Salvadoran circles due to the allegations that the institute is connected with the CIA and the fact that it is funded by the U.S. government. McAward added that AIFLD has "a lot of clout in Congress."[65]

Guatemala: Shortly after the CIA-engineered coup in 1954, head of state Colonel Castillo Armas invited representatives of the AFL-CIO and the Cuban Federation of Labor (under the Batista dictatorship) to "reorganize" the country's trade union movement. In 1955, the Trade Union Council of Guatemala formed as an affiliate of ORIT. AIFLD is currently working with the Independent Campesino Union and continues to train other union leaders in government-associated unions like SITTIGUA, the trade union of Guatemalan telephone workers.

Honduras: ORIT gained control of the banana workers union after a major strike in 1954. At that time the ORIT advisor was Andrew McClellan, who later became the AFL-CIO's Inter-American Representative. Attempts by progressive workers to regain control of the unions of Standard Fruit and United Fruit have been repeatedly destroyed by repressive government action removing union leadership and opening up the union for ORIT operations. AIFLD has ties with the Honduran Workers Federation, the Federation of Unions of National Workers of Honduras, and the National Association of Campesinos.

Nicaragua: The Confederation for Trade Union Unity (CUS) is an ORIT affiliate which receives AIFLD training. During the reign of dictator Anastasio Somoza, CUS opposed Somoza less actively than any other union and consequently enjoys little support in post-Somoza Nicaragua. AID's annual contract with AIFLD for CUS averaged $100,000 to $150,000 before the 1979 triumph by the Sandinistas. The first year after the triumph, AID authorized an expenditure of $500,000 primarily for AIFLD-supported projects in Nicaragua. CUS Assistant Secretary General Frank Jimenez, now living in the United States, pledged the loyalty of CUS to the overtly counterrevolutionary group, Nicaragua Democratic Union and its military wing, the Nicaragua Revolutionary Armed Forces (FARN).[66]

Other Central American countries: In Panama, the Secretary of the Confederation of Panamanian Workers sits on AIFLD's board of trustees. AIFLD regularly conducts seminars in Panama and maintains connections with the cargo, transport, and oil pipeline transshipment workers. In Costa Rica, AIFLD has an AID grant to assist the Campesino Union Strengthening and Credit Program, and it has a $500,000 project with the Federation of Democratic Workers (CCTD) to organize agricultural workers. Former president of Costa Rica, Jose Figueres, is a longtime supporter of AIFLD in Central America. San Jose, Costa Rica is the home of AIFLD's main research center. In Belize, AIFLD sponsors seminars in political theory and trade union rights in an effort to build a U.S.-affiliated union movement in that newly independent nation.

A transnational union would be an ideal way to present a united front against the exploitative and runaway practices of the transnational corporations. But AIFLD has been more interested in uniting workers with U.S. owners than in uniting workers themselves. Addressing the graduation class of AIFLD in January 1982, AFL-CIO President Lane Kirkland said that the problem with Latin America today is that extremists "seek to debase trade unionism by linking it to the question of who owns the means of production." Kirkland called such concerns "esoteric theories about social organization."[67]

TWO DECADES OF DEVELOPMENT

By the late 1950s business and political leaders in the United States came to recognize that Latin America would soon explode in violent revolution if something wasn't done to improve the living conditions of the vast majority of Latin Americans. In 1956, Nelson Rockefeller hosted the "Panels of Prospects for Latin America," which brought together the nation's top scholars and financial leaders to discuss the future of Latin America.[68] A participant in these seminars was the junior senator from Massachusetts John F. Kennedy, who later formulated the Alliance for Progress. The Alliance and related U.S. programs ushered in an era of U.S.-sponsored development for the region.

President Kennedy promised to "complete the revolution of the Americas," but the legacy of the Alliance hasn't been as grand as the rhetoric that accompanied the early Latin American aid programs. The best (or the worst) that U.S. foreign aid has accomplished has been to delay the inevitable development of popular revolutions. It was fashionable in the 1960s to say that poverty — not communist-inspired insurgency — was responsible for the social unrest of the southern part of the hemisphere. If the Alliance could only soften the harsher effects of unequal land and income distribution, then there would be no need for radical changes. But this liberalism didn't set well with the members of the oligarchy who weren't about to budge from their position of power and privilege. Lofty phrases about developing Latin America temporarily improved the image of the United States, but the actual results of U.S. aid programs were marginal. The reformist aspects of U.S. foreign policy continue to appear in current development assistance programs, but the designers of these programs are careful not to challenge the country's base of real political and economic power. The United States isn't about to encourage the workers and *campesinos* to wage their own struggle for long overdue reforms. When it comes down to it, the United States has regularly sided with the elite of Latin America, not the masses. The word "revolution" had a positive connotation in presidential speeches, but it had an entirely different meaning when it came from the people of Latin America. As a result, the United States found itself embracing the military leadership as the only sector that could guarantee the security of Latin America for U.S. political and economic interests.

Congressional Representative Clarence Long, expressing a commonly-held cynical view of U.S. foreign assistance, said, "Foreign aid takes money from poor people in rich countries and gives it to rich people in poor countries."[69] Corruption certainly has been part of the foreign aid story in Central America. Funds that were allocated for a country's poor often ended up in the nation's central bank or in the pockets of the military dictators of the region. The aid seldom reached the poor but it did serve to reinforce governments favored by the United States. Repression wasn't the preferred alternative, but it suited the United States better than revolution. The Alliance for Progress became the Alliance for Stability.

There's no denying that the $2.8 billion in economic aid that has gone to Central America from 1962-82 has produced some identifiable results. AID points to a long list of projects as visible proof of its contribution to development and progress in Central America — roads, communications systems, credit programs, and irrigation systems. But this infrastructure development is much like the government trying to improve the conditions of Navajo Indians by building a road to facilitate the coal stripmining of the reservation. AID's development assistance programs for the private sector in Central America are as ineffective as domestic programs that aim to solve the problems of the ghettos and barrios by creating a sub-class of Chicano and Black entrepreneurs. The aid simply does not "trickle down" like all the development economists say it will. The U.S. government's program to "develop" Central America has operated within impossibly narrow definitions of reform and development. In review, some of the ways that U.S. dollars have contributed to the underdevelopment of Central America are the following:

- the assumption that infrastructure development is synonomous with social development,

- the emphasis on small farmers while ignoring the problems of the majority of the landless poor,

- the support of the expansion of U.S. investment which has the predictable result of pushing local capitalists out of business,

- the promotion of export production to the detriment of production for local food needs,

- the uncontrolled transfer of U.S. technology that has contributed to the region's indebtedness and increased unemployment,

- the reinforcement of patterns of power that prevent wider social development.

Dramatic changes have occurred in Central America in the last twenty years. The industrial sector has grown tremendously, and a new agricultural sector of non-traditional export crops has boomed. U.S. investment has increased 500% in the last two decades for the seven nations of Central America, and a new middle class has sprung up. Accompanying these signs of development have been worsening trade deficits and external indebtedness. The poor haven't seen the promised development. Infant mortality rates have increased in El Salvador, Honduras, Panama, and Nicaragua. Per capita food production has declined in Central America. The bottom 20% of the population still gets only 3-4% of the income, and the oligarchy still owns most of the land. An all too visible development of the last two decades has been the rise of terror and repression in Central America. The Nicaraguan people triumphed over the Somoza dictatorship, but U.S. foreign aid continues to bolster the military regimes in Honduras, Guatemala, and El Salvador.

In the 1980s, the pretension of reformism and social justice that characterized early foreign assistance and development programs has fallen away to reveal the true purpose and intent of foreign aid. AID means aid for private enterprise; international development means expansion of U.S. trade and investment; support for democracy means support for anti-communism; and peace means stability and the maintenance of the status quo. President Reagan has stepped up economic aid to Central America not to develop the region but as a last ditch attempt to prevent the spread of the real "revolution of the Americas."

REFERENCE NOTES

1. Steve Weissman, *The Trojan Horse*, (San Francisco: Ramparts Press, 1974), p. 83.
2. *Congressional Presentation: Agency for International Development Fiscal Year 1983*, (Washington: AID, 1982), p. 2.
3. *Ibid.*
4. *Ibid.*, p. 321.
5. *Miami Herald*, March 12, 1982.
6. Interview by Tom Barry, September 9, 1982.
7. *Ibid.*
8. *Business America*, November 30, 1982, p. 2.
9. *Ibid.*, p. 3.
10. *NACLA*, April 1970, p.9.
11. AID Fiscal Year 1983, p. 141.
12. *Ibid.*, p. 3.
13. *Congressional Presentation: Agency for International Development Fiscal Year 1983*. Annex III Latin America and the Caribbean, (Washington: AID, 1982), p. 40.
14. Congressional Quarterly *Weekly Report*, August 21, 1982, p. 2104.
15. Hearing before the Subcommittee on Foreign Operations and Related Agencies of the Committee on Appropriations, House of Representatives, *Foreign Assistance and Related Programs Appropriations for 1982, Part 5*, (Washington: Government Printing Office, 1981), p. 104.
16. *Central America Report*, July 16, 1982, p. 213.
17. *Food Monitor*, January-February 1982, p. 5.
18. Hearing before the Subcommittee on Inter-American Affairs of the Committee on Foreign Affairs, House of Representatives, *Review of Revised Fiscal Year 1982 Economic Assistance Proposals for Latin America and the Caribbean*, December 15, 1981, (Washington: Government Printing Office, 1982), p. 7.

19. *Food Monitor*, January-February 1982, p. 8.
20. Susan George, *How the Other Half Dies*, (New Jersey: Allanheld, Osmun, 1977), p. 132.
21. *Review of Revised Fiscal Year 1982*, December 15, 1981, p. 8.
22. Frank Viviano, "CIA Church Group in Honduras," *Guardian*, August 26, 1981, p. 13.
23. Hearing before the Subcommittee on Foreign Operations and Related Agencies of the Committee on Appropriations, House of Representatives, *Foreign Assistance and Related Programs Appropriations for 1982, Part 3*, (Washington: Government Printing Office, 1981), p. 403.
24. *Ibid.*, p. 240.
25. "Voluntary Foreign Aid Programs," U.S. International Cooperation, (Washington: AID, 1982); *Foreign Assistance and Related Programs Appropriations for 1982, Part 3*, pp. 233-316.
26. Hearings before the Subcommittee on Foreign Operations and Related Agencies of the Committee on Appropriations, House of Representatives, *Foreign Assistance and Related Programs Appropriations for 1983, Part 6,* (Washington: Government Printing Office, 1982), p. 995.
27. *Ibid.*, p. 300.
28. *Multinational Monitor*, January 1981, p. 8.
29. *Annual Report 1979*, Food for Peace, p. 29.
30. *Foreign Assistance and Related Programs Appropriations for 1983, Part 6*.
31. Weissman, p. 157.
32. *Foreign Agriculture*, July 1982, p. 6.
33. *Ibid.*, pp. 8, 9.
34. Alan Riding, "U.S. Food Aid Seen Hurting Guatemala," *New York Times*, November 6, 1977.
35. *Multinational Monitor*, January 1981.
36. *Annual Report Fiscal Year 1981*, Eximbank.
37. *Business America*, August 23, 1982, p. 6.
38. *The Banker*, June 1981, p. 61.
39. "Helping U.S. Business Sell More Abroad," *U.S. News and World Report*, July 19, 1971, cited in *NACLA*, August 1974.
40. *Foreign Agriculture*, p. 10.
41. "CCC Guarantee Program Fiscal Year 1981," U.S. Dept. of Agriculture.
42. "Description of U.S. Aid Programs," U.S. Dept. of Commerce, December 1980.
43. Hearings before the Subcommittee on International Economic Policy and Trade of the Committee on Foreign Affairs, House of Representatives, *Review of Activities of the Overseas Private Investment Corporation*, (Washington: Government Printing Office, 1980), July 17, 1979 and February 7, 1980.
44. "Nalen Sworn in as OPIC President; Caribbean Push Begins," *Topics*, (Washington: OPIC, 1981), June-July 1981, p. 1.
45. *Review of Activities of the Overseas Private Investment Corporation*.
46. *Ibid.*, p. 108.
47. *Ibid.*, p. 106.
48. *Annual Progress Report 1962-1982*, AIFLD.
49. *American Federationist*, October 1925, cited in Jack Scott, *Yankee Unions, Go Home*, (Vancouver: New Star Books, 1978), p. 174.
50. *United Mine Workers Journal*, September 15, 1939, cited in Scott, p. 201.
51. AFL Convention Proceedings 1954, cited in Scott, p. 204.
52. Serafino Romualdi, *Presidents and Peons: Recollections of a Labor Ambassador in Latin America*, (New York: 1967).
53. Weissman, p. 88.
54. "AIFLD: A Union to Union Program for the Americas," AIFLD, p. 9.
55. Scott, p. 218.
56. "AIFLD: A Union to Union Program," p. 7.
57. "Amazing Grace," *NACLA*, March 1976, p. 13.
58. *Annual Progress Report 1962-1982*.
59. Scott, p. 228.
60. *Annual Progress Report 1962-1982*.
61. "AIFLD's Agrarian Union Development Department," AIFLD.
62. J. Peter Grace, "Labor Boosts Living Standards," *Journal of Commerce*, April 14, 1966.

63. Hearings before the Subcommittee on International Economic Policy and Trade of the Committee on Foreign Affairs, House of Representatives, *Is Partnership Possible?*, (Washington: Government Printing Office, 1981), p. 37.
64. *Fortune*, May 4, 1981, p. 226.
65. Congressional Quarterly *Weekly Report*, April 24, 1982, p. 897.
66. "Target Nicaragua," *NACLA*, January-February 1982, p. 21.
67. *Guardian*, March 24, 1982, p. 2.
68. Weissman, p. 75.
69. Hearing before the Subcommittee on Foreign Operations and Related Agencies of the Committee on Appropriations, House of Representatives, *Foreign Assistance and Related Programs Appropriations for 1982, Part 4*, (Washington: Government Printing Office, 1981), p. 179.

PART TWO

GUATEMALA

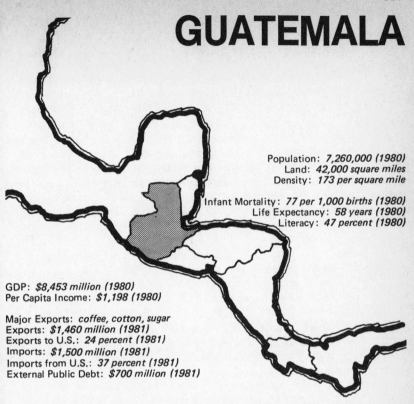

Population: *7,260,000 (1980)*
Land: *42,000 square miles*
Density: *173 per square mile*

Infant Mortality: *77 per 1,000 births (1980)*
Life Expectancy: *58 years (1980)*
Literacy: *47 percent (1980)*

GDP: *$8,453 million (1980)*
Per Capita Income: *$1,198 (1980)*

Major Exports: *coffee, cotton, sugar*
Exports: *$1,460 million (1981)*
Exports to U.S.: *24 percent (1981)*
Imports: *$1,500 million (1981)*
Imports from U.S.: *37 percent (1981)*
External Public Debt: *$700 million (1981)*

Guatemala "has come out of the darkness and into the light," said U.S. Ambassador Frederic C. Chapin, after a 1982 coup toppled one military government only to replace it with another.[1] Having been shunned for several years because of its blatant human rights violations, Guatemala is back in the good graces of the United States. To keep the country in the U.S. orbit, the United States has given moral and military support to the government's long-running counterinsurgency campaign, an effort that has lately focused on eliminating Indian participation in the popular revolutionary movement.

The Spanish Crown in the 1500s regarded Guatemala as its most important colonial outpost in Central America. For the Spaniards, Guatemala was not a country to be developed but simply a source of wealth for the royal coffers. Finding no gold, the Spanish colonizers turned to the land to make their fortunes. Expansive haciendas removed Indians from their land and used Indian slave labor to grow cocoa, indigo, and cochineal dye for export. Then, as now, the ruling classes and army in Guatemala didn't value Indian life; between 1519 and 1610, two-thirds of the Indian people in Guatemala were killed.[2]

The Spanish Crown prohibited Guatemala from manufacturing products that would compete with its own trade to the Latin American colonies. Frustrated by this colonial control, the *criollos* (native-born Spanish) declared their independence from Spain in 1821. This new political independence neither ended the region's economic dependence on the European market nor improved the dire lot of the Indian population.

The beginning of cultivation and export of the coffee bean in the mid-1800s created an oligarchy of wealthy families, some of whom have passed on their riches and power to the present generation. From the outset, however, the financing, processing, and marketing of Guatemalan coffee were in the hands of outside interests, particularly Germans. During World War Two the United States confiscated German coffee interests and forced German citizens into confinement, allowing U.S. interests to gain hold of the coffee market.

U.S. investors first came to Guatemala, however, not for coffee but for bananas. In 1904, dictator Manuel Estrada Cabrera granted United Fruit's affiliate, International Railways of Central America (IRCA), a ninety-nine year concession to finish the construction of Guatemala's principal railroad which ran from the capital to the Atlantic harbor of Puerto Barrios. In return for completing the railroad, United Fruit received a contract in 1906 for 170,000 acres of some of the country's best land for banana production on the Atlantic coast. By the 1930s, the United Fruit Company had become the largest landowner, employer, and exporter in Guatemala. In 1936, the company signed another ninety-nine year lease with General Jorge Ubico, then dictator of Guatemala, to operate another banana plantation on the Pacific coast.[3] "Ubico granted the company the kind of concessions to which it had become accustomed: total exemption from internal taxation, duty-free importation of all necessary goods, and a guarantee of low wages."[4]

Reflecting on the company's history and its significance in Guatemala, Thomas McCann, a former official of United Fruit, wrote the following: "Guatemala was chosen as the site for the company's earliest development activities at the turn of the century because a good portion of the country contained prime banana land and because at the time we entered Central America, Guatemala's government was the region's weakest, most corrupt, and most pliable. In short, the country offered an 'ideal investment climate,' and United Fruit's profits there flourished for fifty years."[5]

In 1944, a popular coalition formed to break the power of the oligarchy and to modernize the country by instituting reforms.[6] The coalition, supported by 85% of the (literate male) vote, elected intellectual Juan Jose Arevalo as president, bringing more than one hundred years of dictatorship to an end. Arevalo initiated labor rights legislation, overturned the unfair vagrancy laws, and created a state bank to help small landowners. In 1951, Jacobo Arbenz succeeded Arevalo as president, promising to carry out a complete land reform to redistribute the country's idle land. Arbenz said: "First [we have] to convert our country from a dependent nation with a semi-colonial economy into an economically independent country; second, to transform our nation from a backward past with a predominantly feudal economy into a modern capitalist country; and third, to see that this transformation is carried out in such a way that it brings with it the highest possible elevation of the standard of living of the great masses of people."[7]

Chief target of the Agrarian Reform Law of 1952 was the United Fruit Company, which kept 85% of its 500,000 acres of land idle. Expropriating 387,000 idle acres, the government offered to compensate the company $1,185,115 based on the company's own tax declaration.[8]   The Agrarian Reform Law exempted all cultivated land no matter the size of the plantation. It established agrarian committees to administer the law which allowed *campesinos* 42.5 acres "in ownership or in use for life." By 1954, 100,000 families had received land, credit, and technical aid.

Reactions to the Guatemalan reforms were immediate. Nicaragua's dictator Anastasio Somoza and an attorney for United Fruit together attempted to pressure President Harry Truman for approval of "Operation Fortune." Without President Truman's okay, this early plan to overthrow Arbenz floundered. United Fruit then mounted an extensive press campaign to discredit Arbenz, with claims that "an iron curtain is falling over Guatemala."

U.S. Ambassador to Guatemala John Peurifoy said: "The candle is burning slowly and surely, and it is only a matter of time before the large American interests will be forced out completely." A.A. Berle of the State Department declared that Guatemala was "in the grip of a Russian-controlled dictatorship."[9]   Arbenz was hardly the communist leader that United Fruit and the State Department claimed him to be. Though he did recognize the Communist Party of Guatemala, he himself rejected a class analysis in favor of a reformist ideology. But his liberal reforms and insistence on independent economic development were enough to threaten the United States.

The Eisenhower Administration approved a plan called Operation Success, which was organized, inspired, and financed by the CIA. In 1954, Colonel Castillo Armas overthrew Arbenz. Thomas McCann of United Fruit wrote that "United Fruit was involved at every level" in the CIA's successful Guatemalan coup.[10]

United Fruit had connections in the Eisenhower Administration that led to the coup. Secretary of State John Dulles had been a senior partner of Sullivan and Cromwell, United Fruit's New York law firm and its principal advisor on foreign operations; CIA Director Allen Dulles was also a former member of the law firm. John Moors Cabot, the Assistant Secretary of State on Inter-American Affairs, was the brother of Thomas Dudley Cabot, former president of United Fruit. Eisenhower's personal secretary, Ann Whitman, was married to Ed Whitman, director of United Fruit's public relations department. General Walter Bedell Smith, a trusted advisor of Eisenhower and former CIA director, oversaw the destabilization of the Arbenz Administration and then later joined the board of United Fruit.[11]

In her book, *The Declassified Eisenhower*, Blanche Cook wrote that, "Guatemala represented a new level of political warfare, including a fully orchestrated cover-up and significant aerial bombing."[12]   The cover-up hid the fact that

Castillo Armas' army had trained on a United Fruit plantation in Honduras with arms flown in from a clandestine Miami airport. On the day of the coup, Castillo Armas flew into Guatemala City in a U.S. embassy plane.

During and after the 1954 coup, over 9,000 people were arrested and many tortured. Over 1.5 million acres were returned to the large landowners including United Fruit, and the Armas government abolished 533 unions.[13] The ten-year Guatemalan experiment with political freedom and bourgeois democracy ended only to begin a series of military dictatorships, each more repressive and blood-thirsty than the one before it. The 1954 coup dashed any hope that future governments could address the vital issues of Guatemala, namely: inequitable land distribution, transnational control of the economy, reliance on export crops, and military rule.

Trained at the U.S. Command and General Staff School in Fort Leavenworth, Castillo Armas received the immediate backing of the United States, which rushed money and advisors to the new regime. The U.S. government increased by sevenfold its personnel in its Guatemala aid mission after the coup.[14] U.S. salvage operations for the first few years after the coup, excluding military aid, cost $80 to $90 million,[15] while the entire U.S. economic aid program for Latin America each year was about $60 million.[16] This assistance, in addition to funds from multilateral agencies, particularly the World Bank, financed massive infrastructure projects such as roads and electrical networks. A condition attached to these funds was that the road building contracts be given to private construction firms which were primarily U.S. companies.[17]

After a trip to Guatemala to give the unpopular government a boost, Vice-President Nixon said: ". . . President Castillo Armas' objective to do more for the people in two years than the Communists were able to do in ten years is important. This is the first instance in history when a Communist government has been replaced by a free one. The whole world is watching to see which does the better job."[18]

POLITICS

A change of pace in Guatemala's history of military dictatorships occurred in June 1982 when General Efrain Rios Montt, upon declaring himself President of Guatemala, said: "Thank you God, for you have put me here." Rios Montt is a preacher for the Church of the Complete Word, a branch of a California evangelical organization called Gospel Outreach. Jim Durkin, founder and presiding elder of Gospel Outreach, said, "God has raised up a leader of this nation." He called Rios Montt "a man of destiny, a man of God."[19]

The religious dictator had come close to becoming Guatemala's president in 1974; but, after agreeing not to contest a fraudulent vote count, Rios Montt left for Madrid as the country's military attache with a sizeable deposit for his

Swiss bank account. He also served at one time as Guatemala's military attache in Washington and as a director of the Inter-American School in Panama.

The Rios Montt coup gave the United States the opening it needed to resume economic and military aid to the repressive Guatemalan government. In recognizing it, the U.S. government said it was looking forward to having a "friendly and fruitful" relationship with Guatemala. Although repression slowed down in the cities, the military escalated its search-and-destroy missions in the countryside especially against the Indian communities which it suspected of supporting the guerillas.

Military governments and fraudulent elections have been a way of life in Guatemala since the 1954 coup. Liberal candidates have been gunned down, and leftist groups have been prohibited from participating in elections. Many Guatemalans believe that the political/military organizations which have coalesced to form the Guatemalan National Revolutionary Unity (URNG) are the only remaining hope for necessary social, political, and economic changes in Guatemala. The four political/military organizations that compose the URNG are the following: Guatemalan Workers Party (PGT), Rebel Armed Forces (FAR), Guerilla Army of the Poor (EGP), and the Revolutionary Organization of People in Arms (ORPA).

The five main points of the URNG coalition, which have been endorsed by all the major mass organizations in Guatemala, are the following:

1. The Revolution will eliminate repression and guarantee life and peace;
2. Distribution of the properties of the very rich, agrarian reform, price control, and the allowance of reasonable profits;
3. Guarantee of equality between Indians and *Ladinos*;
4. All patriotic, popular, and democratic sectors will be represented in the new government, equal rights for women, protection for children, and a guarantee of freedom of expression and religion;
5. Based on the principle of self-determination, the Revolution will guarantee a policy for non-alignment and international cooperation which poor countries need.

In the last two years, the Indian population has begun to integrate itself into the armed struggle. "The traditionally passive peasantry's new found resistance to stand up for itself in the face of officially-sponsored violence has been the key to the recent successes of EGP," stated the *Latin America Regional Report*.[20] The EGP, which more than any other group has Indians in their forces and leadership, cited the "awakening of the broad Indian masses" as the most hopeful sign in their revolutionary movement. Indeed, the Indians have become the heart of Guatemala's revolution.

U.S. Military Involvement

Guatemala's armed forces are the largest and most highly trained and equipped in all of Central America. The army consists of 14,000 men divided into infantry, artillery, and parachute battalions.[21] Most of the pilots in the 450-member air force have been trained in the United States.

In 1957, the U.S. Office of Public Safety (OPS) provided training for 404 Guatemalan police at the International Police Academy in Washington and another 31 at the Inter-American Police Academy in Panama. In the 1960s and early 1970s, OPS paid for pistols, revolvers, carbines, shotguns, ammunition, vehicles, tear gas grenades, gas masks, radios, helmets, and safety shields with the explanation that this aid "provided essential riot control equipment as an interim measure to establish the predicate for more humane treatment of persons involved in civil disturbances."[22]

The United States became further enmeshed in the Guatemalan military in the late 1960s when the U.S. military mission tapped Colonel Carlos Arana to direct the counterinsurgency program. Arana coordinated the slaughter of 8,000 Guatemalans between 1966 and 1968 in an attempt to wipe out a small group of guerillas. On hand to help were 1,000 Green Berets accompanying Guatemalan patrols on counterinsurgency raids. Official denials not withstanding, U.S. pilots flew U.S. planes that dropped napalm on the peasants. Under the leadership of the U.S. military attache, Colonel John Webber, paramilitary groups associated with large landowners were encouraged to collaborate with the army in hunting down "subversive" peasants.[23] These groups were forerunners of the White Hand, a right-wing vigilante organization responsible for the deaths of thousands.

At least partial responsibility for the existence of the death squads lies with the United States. Colonel Webber said in 1968: "That's the way the country is. The communists are using everything they have, including terror. And it must be met." Webber admitted in an interview with *Time* magazine that it was at his instigation that "the technique of counter-terror had been implemented by the Guatemalan army in the Zacapa and Isabel areas."[24]

When Colonel Arana became president in 1970, a second reign of terror was unleashed, this time with the assistance of 32,000 Guatemalan police trained through the OPS program. Arana stated: "If it is necessary to turn the country into a cemetery in order to pacify it, I will not hesitate to do so."[25] Over 15,000 Guatemalans died from political violence during his first three years in office. General Rios Montt served under Arana as Chief of General Staff and was personally responsible for several massacres of Indian villages. Amnesty International reported that after the guerillas were suppressed the right-wing para-military death squads "continued to operate, abducting and assassinating opposition leaders and their sympathizers and sometimes killing at random for the purpose of general intimidation. . . . Between 1966 and 1976, some 20,000 people had died at the hands of these para-military squads."[26]

Amnesty International reported that the para-military organizations are connected with the Guatemalan government: "The selection of targets for detention and murder, and the deployment of official forces for extra-legal operations, can be pinpointed to secret offices in an annex of Guatemala's National Palace, under the direct control of the president of the republic."[27]

U.S. business leaders in Guatemala have supported the military. Fred Sherwood, former president of the American Chamber of Commerce in Guatemala, said in 1980: "Why should we be worried about the death squads? They're bumping off the commies, our enemies. I'd give them more power. Hell, I'd get some cartridges if I could. . . . Why should we criticize them? The death squads — I'm for it. . . . We all feel that he [Reagan] is our savior."[28]

President Jimmy Carter's human rights policy ostensibly stopped military aid to Guatemala, but deliveries of military aid from previous arrangements continued throughout his term. And before he left office, Carter began to advocate the reinstatement of military aid and sales to Guatemala.[29]

Explaining that it would like "to establish a more constructive relationship with the Guatemalan government," the Reagan Administration has by-passed human rights legislation on military and economic aid to Guatemala. In June 1981, the administration approved a $3.2 million cash sale of military vehicles by the Commerce Department under the category of "regional stability equipment," and it supported a proposed grant of $4 million for spare parts for Huey helicopter gunships.

Since the 1954 coup, $66 million in U.S. military aid has been sent to the military governments.[30] Elias Barahona, EGP member who infiltrated the Ministry of Interior under President Lucas Garcia, revealed that the pacification plan initiated in 1982 which utilizes para-military forces rather than the army in attacks on peasant villages, was produced in the mid-1970s in conjunction with U.S. advisors.[31]

ECONOMY

The economy grew at the rate of five to six percent during the 1970s, but it lost speed in 1980 and is now slowing to a standstill.

During the 1960s and 1970s, the Guatemalan economy seemed immune to the country's endemic political violence, but the increasing repression and the expanding guerilla war combined with regional instability has caught up with the nation's economy. Land owners have left the country rather than risk guerilla attacks, while those who have stayed complain of inadequate protection by the government's security forces. Guerilla groups, realizing the important role of export crops in upholding the country's financial stability, have targeted cotton, sugar, and coffee harvests. As the repression and violence worsen, business and land owners have been transferring their capital to foreign countries. Other reasons for the stagnating economy include a declining balance of trade and consequent drop in international reserves, undependable and low commodity prices, inflationary pressures, regional market instability, and the decline of the tourist trade.

The import bill, largely from oil, machinery, and food products, has increased at an alarming rate, giving Guatemala a negative balance of trade despite its large export market. Foreign exchange reserves are also dropping rapidly, threatening the country's ability to pay the large import bill. Net international reserves dropped from $445 million at the end of 1980 to $150 million at the end of 1981, meaning that at the start of 1982 Guatemala had only enough reserves to cover a little more than a month of imports.[32] Since 1925, the Guatemalan *quetzal* has had a one-to-one parity with the U.S. dollar, but the demand for dollars in 1982 has for the first time created a black market at 12-18% over the official rate.

Social and economic differences are more striking in Guatemala than in other Central American countries. Guatemala City, with its skyscrapers and modern pavilions, is the Central American mecca for capitalists, while the squatter settlements that line the city's ravines belie the first impression of Guatemala as a developed economy. Outside the city, a shocking poverty pervades rural Guatemala.

According to the World Bank, over half of the country's population lacks the financial resources to purchase adequate food, housing, and other basic necessities. Malnutrition ranks as one of the three principal causes of hospitalization and unemployment is estimated at 31% of the economically active population.[33] One-half of the maternal deaths are due to septic abortions. Seventy-five percent of rural Guatemalans are malnourished; 50% die before age five.[34]

Public Finance

Public works is about the only forward moving sector of the Guatemalan economy. After the 1976 earthquake, public spending jumped drastically, not to meet the basic needs of the poor, but rather to finance large infrastructure projects. Three major ventures are in progress: a $170 million deep-water port on the Pacific, a $1.4 billion ring road linking major national highways, and a huge hydro-electric plant in Quiche, to which the Inter-American Development Bank (IDB) has committed a $70 million loan. A province with a largely Indian population, Quiche has been under military siege since 1975. The United States, obliged to oppose loans to countries with human rights violations, abstained during the vote for the Quiche plant loan, but privately lobbied in favor of the loan. The International Monetary Fund (IMF) has approved a generous loan package for Guatemala of $110 million to compensate for declining profits from coffee and cotton exports and tourist income in 1981. The IMF noted in its announcement that the precarious state of the economy is in large part due to the outflows of private capital. Critics of this loan point out that Somoza and the desperate government of El Salvador received similar aid from the IMF to hold up their unstable regimes.[35]

A major weakness in the Guatemalan budget is its lack of a strong tax base from income and property. In 1980, taxes amounted to just 8.7% of the GDP. Three-fourths of all central government funding comes from indirect taxes that originate primarily from consumers. Direct taxes, mostly on income, have fluctuated between 15 and 20% of revenues over the past decade, while taxes on property and inheritance are negligible. The lack of property taxes and the nominal income taxes make Guatemala attractive to foreign corporations.[36]

U.S. Interests

Over 300 firms with U.S. interest are doing business in Guatemala. Bank of America and Del Monte (owned by R.J. Reynolds) are the largest U.S. interests in Guatemala. Bank of America is the largest financier of agricultural projects in the country and Del Monte is the largest U.S. landholder and agricultural producer. Also prominent in Guatemala is the Latin American Agribusiness Development Corporation (LAAD) which finances non-traditional agricultural exports such as flowers, cattle, and vegetables. Among the largest industrial investors in Guatemala are Goodyear, Coca-Cola, Colgate Palmolive, Philip Morris, Warner Lambert, American Standard, United Brands, U.S. Steel, and Weyerhaeuser. In 1980, U.S. imports increased 13.5% to $544 million. Exports to the U.S. also rose sharply, totalling $412 million in 1980, an increase of 26.3% over 1979.[37]

Concerning the country's investment climate, the U.S. Embassy stated: "With only a few exceptions, the industrial, commercial, and agricultural sectors are open to foreign investors on a 100% equity basis. The new exchange controls permit full repatriation of earnings and payment for all imports without exception."[38]

Apologists for U.S. foreign investment in Guatemala point to the country's relatively large GDP and increasing rate of growth for the past 20 years as evidence of a healthy, developing economy. Economic development in Guatemala, however, has only been a boom for a minority of producers and exporters, with the financial situation of the vast majority of the population worsening.

Agriculture

Agriculture accounts for more than one-fourth of the country's GDP, three-fifths of the total employment, and two-thirds of its exports. The main agricultural exports are coffee, cotton, and sugar. Other agricultural exports include meat, bananas, vegetable oils, and spices. The oligarchy of Guatemala has its roots in the rich coffee *latifundia* in the rolling slopes of the Pacific coastal region. Between 1930 and 1934, Central America sold 20% of its total coffee harvest to the United States and 75% to Europe; between 1940 and 1944, the United States share increased to 87% of the market.

The first transnational corporation to come to Guatemala was United Fruit. In 1972, United Fruit sold its banana operation in Guatemala to Del Monte for

$20.5 million and its International Railways of Central America to the government. The company, however, maintained three subsidiaries: Numar (oil and margarine), Polymer (plastic products), and Unimar (marketing).

A *latifundia/minifundia* (large farm/small farm) system of livelihood and production dominates rural Guatemala. Every year, over 500,000 Indians descend from their small mountain plots to the Pacific coastal plain to pick cotton, cut cane, and harvest the coffee from the plantations of the landed oligarchy. In Guatemala, 80% of the land is held by two percent of the farm families, and 83% of the farm population lives on tracts too small to maintain a family.[39] Unable to grow enough food on their tiny plots, the Indians sell their labor for a couple of dollars a day. A study by the International Labor Organization found that working conditions on the *latifundia* were "totally unacceptable with regard to hygiene, health and education."

Dr. Lou Falcon, an entomologist who has worked in Guatemala, said, "The people who work in the fields are treated like half-human slaves. When an airplane flies over to spray, they can leave if they want to. But they won't be paid. They often live in huts in the middle of the field, so their homes, their children, and their food all get contaminated."[40]

Although they constitute a majority in Guatemala, Indians are a super-exploited sub-class that work in the society's lowest-paying jobs as domestic servants, farmworkers, and vendors. The three major ethnic groups and 22 sub-groupings of Indians live mostly in the central and western highlands when not working on the *latifundia*. It wasn't until the Arevalo-Arbenz era that the Indian population obtained full legal rights as citizens, but the *Ladinos* (Mestizos) still treat the Indians with disdain. Life expectancy for *Ladinos* is 60 years, while Indians average a 50 year life span.[41]

Rampant malnutrition and disease are among the products of the skewed land distribution and export-oriented economy in Guatemala. The fertile and well-drained soil of the coastal lands could be a breadbasket for the country instead of a series of plantations for export production. In the last thirty years, attracted by U.S. prices, growers have turned their land over to the export market. The post-World War Two market in the United States encouraged Guatemalan growers to expand their plantations, thereby narrowing the land available for the *Ladino* and Indian *campesinos*. In the 1950s, cotton production boomed, and then the U.S. embargo on Cuban sugar opened a new market for cane production in Guatemala.

In 1980, the value of Guatemala's food imports from the United States increased 52% over 1979, while the value of exports to the United States decreased one percent. Wheat and wheat flour from the United States, worth nearly $22 million, led the imports, followed by corn, rice, beans, soybean cake, and grease.[42]

Bank of America, known as the agricultural bank in Guatemala because of its emphasis on agricultural loans, is the only U.S. bank with full service facilities in Guatemala. Local banks are prohibited from loans of more than $5 million, guaranteeing Bank of America an important role in the economy.

Bank of America is a founder of the Latin American Agribusiness Development Corporation (LAAD). Second only to the Guatemalan government itself as a source of capital for the export sector, Bank of America has invested heavily in beef, sesame, cardomom, quinine, and rubber — industries which keep the economy afloat. U.S. church and solidarity groups have protested Bank of America's involvement in Guatemala. The Guatemalan News and Information Bureau is conducting a campaign against the Bank of America's "patronage of the Guatemalan regime's campaign of military terror." Bank of America has a history of financing private land deals for the military and for government officials. Shareholders registering complaints against Bank of America include the United Church Board for World Ministries, California State Teachers Retirement System, and the state's Public Employee Retirement System. Allan Nairn reported in the *Multinational Monitor* that the bank is the only foreign firm known to have representation in *Amigos del Pais*, an exclusive Guatemalan business and professional club that has conducted an expensive program of lobbying and public relations in the U.S. to help gain support for the military regime. "Some *Amigos* members," wrote Nairn, "have been directly linked to the financing of death squads responsible for the murders of thousands of Guatemalans."[43]

Robert Morris of the Interfaith Center on Corporate Responsibility said, "The Bank of America corporate secretary even tried to intimidate one of the religious investors by asking that they seriously consider what would happen to their representatives in Guatemala should the stockholder action be made public."[44]

In a 1980 interview, Keith Parker of the Bank of America said: "When you've got a situation like you have here, you need the strongest government you can get. If you use human rights in a country with guerillas, you're not going to get anywhere."[45]

Industry

Guatemala is the most industrialized Central American nation. Industrial activity, which accounts for 16% of the GDP and about 20% of the labor force, comprises the following industries: food processing, textiles, construction materials, tires, and pharmaceuticals. The oil industry is also becoming a major source of foreign exchange.

More than any other Central American country, Guatemala benefits from the Central American Common Market (CACM), the main source of its income after the U.S. market. In 1980, the CACM received 29% of Guatemalan exports.[46] Since 1964, because of the country's large quantity of exports, Guatemala has enjoyed a trade surplus with other CACM members and in 1980, it was the only CACM nation with a positive balance.

The industrial sector, based in Guatemala City, hasn't been able to absorb the labor surplus created by the expansion of export agriculture and its increased mechanization. The government has offered additional incentives to investors who locate outside Guatemala City, but has had little success. As part of a drive to decentralize industry from the heart of Guatemala City, the government is sponsoring a 70-acre industrial park called the Atlantic Coast Trade Center to be built by Brown and Root Overseas with financing from U.S. Eximbank. Also in government plans is the increased promotion of the labor-intensive finishing industries called *maquiladoras*.

In its report on Guatemala, the American Chamber of Commerce in Guatemala said that none of the U.S. businesses it contacted "are experiencing or expecting to experience any unmanageable labor problem." According to the Chamber, "The general feeling is that political agitation is imported rather than internal. . . ."[47]

A prime example of transnational investors collaborating with repressive military dictatorships is Coca-Cola's relationship with the Guatemalan government. One U.S. investor in Guatemala commented in an interview with *Newsweek*: "Coca-Cola is becoming a leading brand name of oppression here, and believe me, they've got heavy competition." In the mid-70s, workers began to organize at the Coca-Cola bottling company called Embotelladora Guatemala. Four years of assassinations, military raids, and mass firings followed. Franchise owner John Trotter was a leading member of the Freedom Foundation, a right-wing group in Guatemala which had connections with the military and right-wing death squads.

Coca-Cola, which has 800 franchises in 135 countries, backed down in 1980 under international labor and church pressure and agreed to the removal of the military from the plant, union recognition, and a negotiated collective wage and work agreement. The agreement also required Coca-Cola to terminate Trotter's franchise and to establish a relief fund for the families of assassinated organizers.[48]

Government and business regard oil as the last chance for the Guatemalan economy; the U.S. State Department calls Guatemala "the plum of Central America" because of its tremendous oil reserves.[49]

Basic Resources, a Luxembourg-based firm and Guatemala's largest oil well driller, teamed up with U.S. firms after the 1954 coup to redesign the country's natural resources. General Vernon Walters, one of the architects of Reagan's Central America policies, worked for the company until early 1981 using his influence with the Guatemalan military to permit increased oil production. The two oil refineries in the country are owned by Texaco at Escuintla and Standard Oil of California (Chevron) at Puerto Barrios.[50]

The Eximbal nickel mine near Lake Isabel was operating with generous, tax-exempt concessions until it stopped production in 1980. Owned jointly by International Nickel Corporation and Hanna Mining, Eximbal had given the Guatemalan government hope that the mining and smelting operation would soon be a leading producer of foreign exchange. The joint venture decided to mothball the project citing high energy costs, faltering prices, and world-wide recession. International Nickel, a Canadian based but U.S. controlled corporation, received financial help from the World Bank, U.S. Eximbank, and the Canadian Export Development Corporation to finance the Eximbal project.

Two prominent members of a Guatemalan inquiry commission investigating the Eximbal contract were killed after they criticized the give-away terms of the lease.

Tourism has traditionally provided Guatemala with its third largest source of income, but in the year 1980, tourism dropped $30 million – a full 50% from the year before.[51] Guerilla and opposition groups consider tourism to have perpetuated the outside control of Guatemala's economy and politics. In October 1981, the Guerilla Army of the Poor (EGP) bombed Eastern Airlines and the American Chamber of Commerce in Guatemala City. Their reason for the attack on Eastern was that the airline was "actively participating in a campaign to promote U.S. tourism to our country at a time when hundreds of Guatemalans are being assassinated by the repressive forces armed by the U.S. government. . . . The Guerilla Army of the Poor wishes to emphasize that its revolutionary actions are not directed against North American firms or citizens just because of their nationality. Rather they are designed to hit those firms or individuals which are actively collaborating with the barbaric regime which is oppressing our people." In December 1981, Eastern Airlines decided to pull out of Guatemala because of the falling tourist trade.

Guatemalan and U.S. business owners eagerly awaited the 1980 U.S. presidential election results. Candidate Ronald Reagan had assured the business community in Guatemala that it could count on him to hold the line against the country's growing opposition movement. After meeting with Reagan during the campaign, Roberto Alejos Arzu, who had made his plantation available as a training site for the CIA's Bay of Pigs invasion in 1961, said: "Reagan is one of the few people in the high political sphere who understands what's going on down here."[52]

As subsequent events have proved, the business owners and foreign investors in Guatemala had good reason to celebrate the Reagan victory. The U.S. government has stepped up its economic and military assistance to the Guatemalan government. The resource wealth of Guatemala, its concentration of U.S. investment, and its strategic position next to Mexico are reasons that the United States will not let Guatemala slip from its imperial grip without a long, fierce struggle. But the country's unified opposition is equally determined to create a popular government in what is often considered the keystone nation in Central America.

References for Introductory Statistics

Business America, March 8, 1982; *Business Latin America*, July 7, 1982; Inter-American Development Bank, *Economic and Social Progress in Latin America 1980-81; Latin America Regional Report*; United Nations, *Monthly Bulletin of Statistics*, April 1982; U.S. Department of State, *Background Notes – Guatemala*, July 1981.

REFERENCE NOTES

1. Juan Vasquez, "Guatemala Now Deserves Aid," *Miami Herald*, April 17, 1982.
2. Eric Wolf, *Sons of the Shaking Earth*, (Chicago: University of Chicago Press, 1959), pp. 31, 195.
3. Stephen Schlessinger and Stephen Kinzer, *Bitter Fruit: The Untold Story of the American Coup in Guatemala*, (Garden City, N.Y.: Doubleday, 1982), p. 70.
4. *Ibid.*
5. Thomas McCann, *An American Company: The Tragedy of United Fruit*, (New York: Crown, 1976), p. 45.
6. Susanne Jonas and David Tobis, Editors, *Guatemala*, (Berkeley and New York: NACLA, 1974), p. 49.
7. Blanche Cook, *The Declassified Eisenhower: A Divided Legacy of Peace and Political Warfare*, (Garden City, N.Y.: Doubleday, 1981), p. 224.
8. Jonas and Tobis, p. 49.
9. Cook, *Declassified Eisenhower*.
10. McCann, *An American Company*.
11. Jonas and Tobis; Cook; Schlessinger and Kinzer; Lars Schoultz, "U.S. Policy toward Guatemala," (unpublished University of North Carolina paper, 1981).
12. Cook, p. 278.
13. Jonas and Tobis, p. 75.
14. *Ibid.*, p. 81.
15. U.S. General Accounting Office, Comptroller General, *Report: Examination of Economic and Technical Assistance Program for Guatemala*, International Cooperation Administration, Dept. of State, 1955-60, Washington DC, GPO 1960, p. 19.
16. Jonas and Tobis, p. 81.
17. *Ibid.*, p. 79.
18. Richard Nixon, "What I Learned in Latin America," *This Week*, August 7, 1955.
19. Loren Jenkins, "Leader's Faith Puzzling," *Washington Post*, April 6, 1982.
20. "Swimming Against the Tide," *LARR*, April 2, 1982, p. 10.
21. "Guatemala, a Country at War," National Network in Solidarity with the People of Guatemala (NISGUA), June 1982, p. 4.
22. U.S. Office of Public Safety, *Termination Phase-out Study of the Public Safety Project: Guatemala*, Washington DC, U.S. AID, July 1974, as cited in "Background Information on Guatemala," Institute for Policy Studies, June 1981.
23. Penny Lernoux, *The Cry of the People*, (Garden City, N.Y.: Doubleday, 1980), p. 186.
24. Jenny Pearce, *Under the Eagle*, (London: Latin American Bureau, 1981), p. 68.
25. James Y. Bradford, "Guatemala: A People Besieged," American Friends Service Committee, January 1978.
26. Amnesty International, "Memorandum Presented to the Government of the Republic of Guatemala Following a Mission to the Country from 10 to 15 August 1979," (London: 1979).
27. Amnesty International, Guatemala: A Government Program of Political Murder, (London: 1981), p. 3., as cited in Institute for Policy Studies' Background Notes.
28. Pearce, p. 176.
29. Shoultz, pp. 7, 8.
30. Cynthia Arnson, "Background Information on Guatemala, the Armed Forces and U.S. Military Assistance, (Washington DC: Institute for Policy Studies, June 1981).
31. *LARR*, June 4, 1982.
32. "Basic Economic Troubles Belie Recovery," *Business Latin America*, May 2, 1982, p. 12.
33. World Bank, *Guatemala: Economic and Social Position and Prospects*, (Washington DC: World Bank, 1978), pp. 12, 19.
34. *New York Times*, July 20, 1982.
35. *Update on Guatemala*, November 30, 1981.
36. "Guatemala," *Foreign Economic Trends*, August 1981, p. 9.
37. *Ibid.*, p. 13.
38. *Ibid.*, p. 4.
39. World Bank, pp. 12, 19.
40. David Weir and Mark Schapiro, *Circle of Poison: Pesticides and People in a Hungry World*, (San Francisco: Institute for Food and Development Policy, 1981), p. 7.

41. *Economic and Social Progress in Latin America*, (Washington DC: Inter-American Development Bank, 1981), p. 254.

42. "U.S. Farm Export Gain in Central America," *Foreign Agriculture*, October 1981, USDA, p. 21.

43. Allan Nairn, "Bank of America Asked to Explain its Support for the Guatemalan Death Squads," Multinational Monitor, March 1982, p. 14.

44. *Ibid.*

45. *Ibid.*

46. "Background Notes: Guatemala," U.S. Dept. of State, (Washington DC: Superintendent of Documents, July 1981), p. 1.

47. Association of American Chambers of Commerce, Fourth Quarter, 1980.

48. "Coca-Cola Backs Down," *Multinational Monitor*, July 1980.

49. *Wall Street Journal*, May 28, 1981.

50. *Market Strategy for the Eighties*, Metra Consulting, (London: 1980).

51. *Central America Report*, April 28, 1982, p. 116.

52. "The Reagan Connections: The Military, the Ultra-Right, and Big Money Keeping the Plantation Pacified," *Green Revolution*, Winter 1981, p. 50.

UNITED STATES BUSINESS IN GUATEMALA*

Abbott Laboratories
 Abbott Laboratorios; *pharmaceutical manufacturing*

ACLI International
 Internacional de Comercio; *commodities brokerage; LAAD equity*

Action Enterprises
 Covington Aircraft International; *used aircraft sales*

ADELA Investment Company
 ADELA de Centroamérica; *investing*

Agencias Angel; *car importing and distribution*

Agro-Inversiones; *ornamental plant production*

Alberto Culver; *cosmetic manufacturing and distribution*

Alexander & Alexander
 Alexander de Centroamérica; *insurance brokerage*

Alexander & Baldwin Agribusiness
 Alexander y Baldwin Agro-Industrial; *agricultural and industrial consultants*

American Cyanamid
 Cyanamid Interamerican; *cosmetic and pharmaceutical distribution*
 Shulton; *cosmetic manufacturing and distribution*

American Enterprises
 Danny's Pancakes; *restaurant*

American Express; *credit card service*

American Home Products
 Productos del Hogar; *pharmaceuticals*

American International Group
 American International Underwriters; *insurance*
 La Seguridad de Centroamérica, Compañía de Seguros; *insurance*
 La Seguridad de Centroamérica, Compañía de Fianzas; *bonds*

American Motors
 Agencias Nicol; *auto importing and retailing*

American Standard
 Standard Industria Centroamericana de Sanitarios (INCESA); *bathroom fixture manufacturing*

*An indented item is a subsidiary, affiliate, or branch of the corporation immediately above it.

Americana Hotels
  Hotel El Dorado Americana

Arthur Andersen & Company
  Arevala, Perez y Asociados; *public accountants*

Atico Financial Corporation
  Comercial Aseguradora Suizo-Americana (CASA); *insurance*

Avon Products
  Productos Avon de Guatemala; *perfume and cosmetic manufacturing and distribution*

BankAmerica
  Bank of America; *banking; three branches*
  Credomatic de Guatemala; *Master Charge credit card services*

Bank of California
  Banco de Comercio e Industria; *banking*

Baroid; *chemical product distribution*

Bawden Drilling; *oil drilling*

Beatrice Foods
  Asunta; *cookie manufacturing*
  Asunta Carimba; *textile manufacturing*
  Fábrica de Productos Alimenticios Peter Pan; *food processing*
  Fábrica de Productos Alimenticios RENE; *food processing*

Bemis
  Bemis Internacional; *packing plastics manufacturing*

Bendix
  Industria Filtros FRAM de Centroamérica; *oil filter manufacturing*

Blue Bird Body
  Blue Bird Centroamericana; *bus body manufacturing*

Boise Cascade
  Bolsas de Papel; *lumbering, paper manufacturing*
  Industria Papelera Centroamericana; *paper manufacturing*
  Litografía de Guatemala; *printing supplies*
  Empresa Comercial y Industrial Hispaña

Borden
  Compañía Internacional de Ventas Centroamérica; *food and cement distribution*

Boyle Midway International
  Productos del Hogar; *cleaning products manufacturing and distribution*

C. Brewer & Company
  Agronómicas de Guatemala; *agricultural business*

Bristol-Myers
  Bristol-Myers de Centroamérica; *pharmaceutical and cosmetic manufacturing*
  Unitek de Centroamérica; *dental supplies*

Caballero International
  Kima y Asociados; *tire, industrial lubricant, steel and machinery importing and distribution*

Cargill
  Cargill Americas; *fats and animal feed commodity trading*

CBS
  Distribuidora Guatemalteca de Discos; *record distribution*
  Industria de Discos Centroamericanos

Celanese
  Celanese de Guatemala; *chemical and plastic manufacturing*
  Cementos Novela
  Compañía Comercial e Industrial Celanese Guatemala; *synthetic fiber and plastic manufacturing*

Central Soya
  Alimentos Mariscal; *feed mill*
  Central Soya de Guatemala; *animal feed production*
  Industria Nacional de Concentrados Integrales Centroamericanos; *poultry*

Chesebrough Ponds
  Chesebrough Ponds International; *cosmetic manufacturing*

Citicorp
  Citibank; *banking*

Clark Equipment
  Atlas Eléctrica; *refrigeration equipment and supplies*

Cluett, Peabody & Company
  Arrow de Centroamérica; *shirt manufacturing*

Coca-Cola
  Embotelladora Guatemalteca; *soft drink manufacturing*
  Industria de Café; *instant coffee manufacturing*
  Industrias del Pacífico; *soft drink manufacturing*
  Productos Alimentos Sharp; *canned food processing*
  Tenco

Codell Construction; *construction*

Colgate Palmolive
  Agencia Maritima; *marine cargo handling*
  Alimentos Kern de Guatemala; *canned goods manufacturing*
  Colgate Palmolive; *toiletries manufacturing*
  Empresa Agro-Mercantil y de Servicio
  Helena Rubenstein de Centroamérica; *cosmetic manufacturing*
  Industria Química; *bath products, toothpaste manufacturing*
  Riviana Foods; *food processing*
  TEMCO; *toothpaste tube production*

Colt Industries Group
  Fairbanks Morse de Centroamérica; *electrical machine manufacturing*

Compañía Comercial e Industrial de Supertiendas; *supermarket; LAAD equity*

Compañía de Distribución Centroamericana; *food distribution; LAAD equity*

Condominio El Golf; *condominium project; ADELA equity*

Continental Grain
  Compañía Continental Centroamericana; *grain brokers*

CPC International
  Productos de Maíz y Alimentos; *food production*

Dart & Kraft
  Plásticos Centroamericanos Tupperware; *plastic manufacturing*
  Alimentos Kraft; *food production*
  Electrodos de Centroamérica
  Hobart Ayau y Compañía; *electrical equipment manufacturing*

Dataram
  Dataram Guatemala; *electronics manufacturing*

Davy
  Arthur G. McKee & Company; *contracting and engineering*

Diners Club
  Diners Club de Guatemala; *credit card*

Diversey Chemicals
  Diversey Química; *cleaning agent manufacturing and distribution*

Dometic
  Industria Metalúrgica Centroamericana; *household appliance and machine manufacturing*

Dow Chemical
  Dow Química de Centroamérica; *chemical product manufacturing*

E.I. Du Pont de Nemours & Company
  Química Du Pont de Centroamérica; *pesticide distribution*

Eaton
  Cutler-Hammer; *electrical control panel and box manufacturing*

Economy Forms; *steel forms manufacturing for concrete construction*

K.R. Edwards Leaf Tobacco
  Casa Export; *tobacco exporting*

Eli Lilly & Company
  Eli Lilly de Centroamérica; *pharmaceutical manufacturing and agricultural and industrial product distribution*

ESB
  Distribuidora MA Nicol y Compañía
  Duralux; *battery and accumulator manufacturing*

Exxon
  Esso Centroamérica; *petroleum product distribution*
  Essochem de Centroamérica; *chemical product marketing*
  Esso Standard Guatemala; *exploration*

Fact O Bake; *automobile paint and body shop*

Financiera Industrial y Agropecuaria; *private development; ADELA equity*

Finca Oro Blanco; *cotton production*

Firestone Tire & Rubber
  Firestone de Guatemala; *rubber tires*
  Plantaciones de Hule Firestone; *rubber production*

FMC
  FMC Guatemala

Foremost-McKesson
  Foremost Dairies de Guatemala; *dairy product manufacturing and distribution*
  Cocinas Foremost

H.B. Fuller
  Kativo de Guatemala; *paint manufacturing and distribution*
  Fuller y Compañía de Centroamérica; *Fuller products*
  Kioskos de Pinturas; *paints*
  Punto de Viniles; *vinyls*
  Adhesivos Industriales de Guatemala; *adhesives*

General Mills
  Industria de Maíz; *corn flour production*
  Industrias Gem-Ina
  Industria Harinera Guatemalteca;
    wheat flour production
  General Mills de Guatemala

General Telephone & Electronics (GTE)
  GTE Sylvania; *electric housewares and*
    lighting manufacturing

GENESCO
  Formfit de Guatemala y Compañía;
    clothes manufacturing

Geosource Exploration Company; *oil*

Getty Oil

Gibbs & Hill
  Compañía Minera de la Sierra;
    consulting engineers

The Gillette Company
  Gillette de Centroamérica; *razor*
    blade and cosmetic manufacturing
    and distribution

Goldsmith Seeds
  Jardines Mil Flores; *seed production*

Goodyear Tire & Rubber
  Gran Industria de Neumáticos
    Centroamericana (GINSA); *rubber*
    tire manufacturing and distribution
  Plantaciones de Hule Goodyear; *rubber*
    production
  Goodyear International; *rubber tire*
    manufacturing and distribution

W.R. Grace & Company
  Productos Darex; *food processing*
    equipment manufacturing
  Ducal; *food processing*

Green Thumb
  Plantadores Ornamentales Unidos;
    ornamental plants

Greyhound
  Armour-Dial International; *detergent*
    manufacturing

Griffith Laboratories
  Laboratorios Griffith de Centroamérica;
    raw materials and additives for the
    food industry

Grolier
  Grolier International; *reference book*
    publishing

Gulf Oil
  Petroleos Gulf de Guatemala

Gulf + Western Industries
  Cinema International; *motion picture*
    distribution

Halliburton
  Brown & Root Overseas Corporation;
    contractors

Hanna Mining Company
  Exploraciones y Explotaciones Mineras
    Izabal; *mining*

Hanover Brands
  Alimentos Congelador Montebello
    (ALCOSA); *frozen vegetable*
    processing

Harza Engineering; *consulting engineers*

Helmerich & Payne
  Helmerich & Payne Guatemala; *oil and*
    gas drilling

Hemco; *agricultural consulting*

Hercules
  Hercules de Centroamérica; *agricultural*
    chemical manufacturing

Hertz
  Rentautos; *auto renting*

Hinkle Contracting
  Construciones Hinkle de Guatemala;
    asphalt and paving contracting

Hockman Lewis
  Equigas de Guatemala; *gasoline service*
    station and industrial equipment
    distribution

IBM World Trade Corporation
  IBM de Guatemala; *office equipment*
    sales, renting, and servicing

IC Industries (Pet)
  Compañía América de Refrigeración;
    commercial refrigeration
    manufacturing
  Hussman Refrigeration; *commercial*
    refrigeration manufacturing

IMCO Services; *oil drilling*

INA
  Contabilidad Mecanizada
  Compañía de Seguros Cruz Azul;
    insurance

Industria Superior; *pickup shell*
  manufacturing

Industrias Sésamo; *grain production;*
  LAAD equity

International Dairy Queen
  Dairy Queen; *fast food*

International Executive Service
  Cuerpo Internacional de Servicios
    Ejecutivos; *business consulting*

Internorth; *natural gas and liquid fuel*
  distribution

The Interpublic Group of Companies
McCann-Erickson Centroamérica;
advertising

Inversora Pinares; *low cost housing project;*
ADELA equity

ITT
Conquistador Sheraton Hotel
ITT de Guatemala; *communications*
equipment distribution and repair

IU International
Agronomics de Guatemala
Empresa Agricol el Pacayal
Empresa Agropecuaria Patzulin
Industria Guatemalteca de Macadamia
Monte de Oro

Johnson & Higgins
Consultores de Seguros; *insurance*

Johnson & Johnson
Johnson & Johnson de Centroamérica;
cosmetic and toiletry manufacturing
Compañía de Productos para la Salud,
Johnson & Johnson

JWT Group
APCU-Thompson Asociados;
communications company

Kellogg
Kellogg de Centroamérica; *cereal*
processing and distribution

Kem Manufacturing
Kem Centroamericana;*chemical cleaner*
manufacturing and distribution

Kimberly-Clark
Kimberly Clark de Centroamérica;
paper products distribution

Koppers
Impregnadora de Madera de Guatemala;
wood treating
Maderas del Norte; *wood treating*

Latin American Agribusiness Development
(LAAD); *agribusiness financing;*
ADELA equity

Lemarco International
Lemarco de Guatemala; *fertilizer*
formulation, importing and exporting

Litton Industries
Royal MacBee de Guatemala;
accounting
Western Geophysical; *geophysical*
seismic exploration

Materiales de Construcción; *concrete*
block manufacturing; ADELA equity

McCormick & Company
McCormick de Centroamérica; *spice*
and seasoning distribution

McDonald's
Servirápido de Guatemala; *fast food*

McKessen Laboratories
Laboratories McKessen de Guatemala;
pharmaceutical manufacturing

Merck & Company
Merck, Sharp, & Dohme;
pharmaceutical distribution

Meridian Engineering; *construction*

Miles Laboratories
Laboratorios Miles de Centroamérica;
pharmaceutical manufacturing
Miles Overseas; *pharmaceutical*
manufacturing

Minnesota Mining & Manufacturing
Minnesota 3M Interamericana
Minas de Oriente
3M Centroamericana

Mister Donut of America
Don Doña; *doughnut shop*

Mobil
Mobil Oil

Monsanto
Monsanto Centroamericano de
Guatemala; *agricultural product*
distribution
Monsanto Indem
Monoil Guatemala

Moran Enterprises
Autoquímicas de Centroamérica;
auto chemicals

Morris Silver & Associates; *consulting*

Morrison-Knudsen; *contractors and*
engineers

Nabisco Brands
Dely; *food processing and distribution*
Pan American Standard Brands; *fruit*
and vegetable production and
distribution
Salvavidas; *candy manufacturing and*
distribution
J.B. Williams y Compañía; *toiletry*
manufacturing

National Car Rental Systems

National Cash Register (NCR)
Cajas Registradoras Nacional Azmitia
y Compañía; *office equipment*
distribution

Nello L. Teer; *general contracting*

NFC Industries
NFC de Centroamérica; *food processing*
equipment distribution

R.J. Noble
Arena y Grava; *aggregate production*

North American Culvert
Drenajes y Tubería Corrugada
(DRETUCO); *corrugated metal pipe
manufacturing and distribution*

Northwest Industries
Velsicol de Centroamérica; *agricultural
chemical distributor*

Norton Simon
Avis Rent-A-Car
Max Factor de Centroamérica; *toiletries*
Norton Simon; *paint*

Owens-Illinois
Maderas el Alto; *sawmill*
Premadas

PADEC; *food processing plant engineering
and design*

Pan American Life Insurance
Compañía de Seguros Panamericana;
insurance

Pan American Mail Lines
Flomerca Trailer Service; *shipping*

Pan American Paint Manufacturing
PanTex Pinturas Nacionales; *paint
manufacturing*

Pan American World Airways; *air
transportation*

Parker Drilling; *oil drilling*

Peat, Marwick, Mitchell & Company;
accounting and auditing

PepsiCo
Comidas; *Pizza Hut restaurant*
Comigua; *Pizza Hut restaurant*
Pepsi Cola Interamericana; *soft drink
bottling*

Pfizer; *pharmaceutical, chemical, and
veterinary product manufacturing
and distribution*

Phelps Dodge
Facelec; *electrical conductor
manufacturing*

Philbro
Engelhard Minerals; *chemical and
industrial distribution*

Philip Morris
Tabacalera Centroamericana (TACASA);
*cigarette manufacturing and
distribution*

Picker; *x-ray equipment distribution*

Pillsbury
Fábrica Kugarts, Matheu, Garin y
Compañía; *food production*
Molinas Modernos; *flour mill*

Pillsbury Holdings Canada; *food
production*
Productos Alimenticios Imperial;
food production

Los Pinos; *mushroom production; LAAD
equity*

Pittsburgh-Des Moines
Cilindros de Centroamérica (CILCASA);
propane cylinder manufacturing
Transformadora Industrial Pittsburgh-
Des Moines (TIPIC); *metal structure
manufacturing*

Prefabricados de Madera Simco; *wood
product manufacturing; ADELA
equity*

Price Waterhouse & Company; *accountants
and auditors*

Productos Alimenticios Grandel y Alpina;
meat processing; LAAD equity

Productos el Delfin; *fish importing and
exporting*

Promotora Mercantil; *financial services;
ADELA equity*

Propane
Distribuidora Centroamericana de Gas
(DIGAS); *propane gas distribution*

Quaker Oats
Quaker de Guatemala

Ralston Purina
Auto Cafés Purina; *animal feed
processing*
Incubadoras Centroamericanas;
chicken production
Purina de Guatemala; *feed mill*

Ramset Fastening Systems
Ramset de Guatemala; *construction
materials and equipment*

Reforestadora Industrial; *reforestation;
ADELA equity*

Retzloff Chemical
Agro-Químicas de Guatemala;
*pesticide manufacturing and
distribution*

Revlon
Armour de Centroamérica;
pharmaceuticals
Revlon Guatemala; *cosmetics*

Rey Café; *coffee production*

R.J. Reynolds (Del Monte)
Compañía de Desarrollo Bananero de
Guatemala (BANDEGUA); *banana
production*
Sealand Service; *international maritime
transportation*

Richardson-Vicks
  Richardson-Merrell Interaméricas;
    *pharmaceutical manufacturing and
    distribution*
  Vick Chemical; *pharmaceutical
    manufacturing*

Rio Colorado Drilling
  Beta Drilling Guatemala; *oil drilling*

Robert Consolidated Industries
  Quindeca; *adhesives, waterproof
    products and finishes manufacturing
    and distribution*

Rohm & Haas
  Rohm & Haas Centroamérica; *chemical
    manufacturing*

Rolling
  Orkin International; *exterminator*
  Compañía Exterminadora Orkin de
    Guatemala

Roy Jorgenson Associates; *technical
    assistance for road construction*

Santa Lucrecia; *cattle production; LAAD
    equity*

Schering-Plough
  Plough Export; *drugs, toiletries, and
    cosmetics manufacturing and
    distribution*

SCM
  Empresa Nacional de Plásticos
    (ENAPLA); *resins manufacturing*
  Galvanizadora Centroamérica
    (GALCASA); *galvanized sheeting
    manufacturing and distribution, and
    resins and adhesives manufacturing*
  Industria Química Guatemalteca de
    Adhesivos y Derivados (INDUCOL)
  Pinturas Centroamericanas (PINCASA);
    paint manufacturing and distribution
  Servicios Minimax; *trucking*

G.D. Searle
  G.D. Searle International;
    pharmaceuticals

Sears Roebuck & Company; *department
    store*

Servicios; *commercial activities; ADELA
    equity*

Servicios Educacionales y de Desarrollo de
    Centroamérica (SEDECA);
    development of educational programs

Sherwin-Williams
  Sherwin-Williams Centroamericana,
    Guatemala; *paint distribution*

Singer Manufacturing Company of New
    Jersey
  Dinah; *sewing machine distribution*

Squibb
  Laboratorio Farmacéutico Squibb;
    pharmaceutical manufacturing
  Salvidas de Guatemala; *pharmaceuticals*
  Squibb Mathieson International

Standard Oil of California
  Compañía Petrolera Chevron;
    petroleum product distribution
  Refinería de Asfaltos Chevron
  Refinería Petrolera de Guatemala
    Centroamérica

Standard Oil of Indiana
  Amoco Guatemala Petroleum; *oil
    exploration and production*

The Stanley Works
  Herramientas Collins; *machete
    manufacturing*

Sterling Drug
  Sterling Products International;
    *cosmetic and pharmaceutical
    manufacturing and distribution*

Sunnyside Nurseries
  Industria Floradol; *ornamental plant
    production*

Superior Oil

C. Tennant & Sons
  Industria Timba; *steel cylinder
    manufacturing*

Tenneco
  Tenneco Far East Exploration &
    Development; *oil exploration*
  Tenneco Guatemala; *petroleum*

Texaco
  Texaco Caribbean; *petroleum*
  Texaco Exploration Guatemala;
    oil exploration
  Texaco Guatemala; *petroleum
    production*
  Texas Petroleum; *oil refining*

Transamerica
  Autorentas; *car rental*

Transway International
  Coordinated Caribbean Transport
    (CCT); *shipping line*
  Terminales de Gas
  Tropical Gas de Guatemala (Tropigas);
    gas distribution

Trans World
  Plas-Tikal; *export management*

Travelodge International
  Hotel Guatemala Fiesta

Union Carbide
  UNICAR; *agricultural product
    manufacturing*

United Air Lines (UAL)
  Hoteles Biltmore de Guatemala
  Hoteles Camino Real

United Brands
  Compañía Agrícola de Guatemala;
    bananas
  Numar; *vegetable oil processing*
  Polymer; *plastics*
  Unimar; *marketing*
  United Fruit; *banana production*

U.S. Geosource Exploration; *oil exploration
  and exploitation*

U.S. Steel
  Industria de Tubos y Perfiles
    (INTUPERSA); *steel products
    manufacturing*

United Technologies
  Otis Elevator; *elevator sales*

Universal Flavors; *food and flavor
  manufacturing and distribution*

Universal Food Products
  Lavaduras Universal; *yeast
    manufacturing and distribution*
  Central Productos Universal

Upjohn
  Compañía Farmacéutica Upjohn;
    *pharmaceutical manufacturing and
    distribution*
  Upjohn; *pharmaceutical manufacturing
    and distribution*

Universal Leaf Tobacco; *tobacco
  production and cigarette
  manufacturing*

Varisur
  Compañía Minera del Caribe; *mineral
    exploration*

The Wackenhut Corporation
  Wackenhut de Guatemala; *security*

Warner Lambert
  Laboratorios de Productos
    Farmacéuticos (LAPROFA);
    pharmaceutical manufacturing
  Productos Adams; *candy and gum
    manufacturing*
  Compañía Farmacéutica Parke Davis;
    *pharmaceutical manufacturing and
    distribution*

Weyerhaeuser
  Cajas y Empaques de Guatemala;
    cardboard box manufacturing

Wilbur Smith and Associates;
  transportation and financial studies

The Wilkinson Company
  Industrias Wilkinson de Guatemala;
    precious metal sales

Xerox
  Xerox de Guatemala; *copier marketing
    and servicing*

REFERENCES

Directory of American Firms Operating in Foreign Countries, 1979; *Directory of Corporate Affiliations*, 1982; Dun & Bradstreet, "Principal International Businesses," 1982; *Export/Import Markets*, 1982; *Foreign Index to the Directory of Corporate Affiliations*, 1981; *Million Dollar Directory*, 1982; *Moody's*, 1981; *Rand McNally International Bankers Directory*, 1982; 10-K Reports, 1981; *World Directory of Multinational Enterprises*, 1980.

ADELA, Annual Report, 1981; *Agribusiness in the Americas*, 1980; BankAmerica, "Bank of America Worldwide Facilities," May 1981; Donald Castillo Rivas, *Acumulacion de Capital y Empresas Transnacionales en Centroamerica*, 1980; Latin American Agribusiness Development Corporation (LAAD), Annual Reports, 1976-1981; *Mergers & Acquisitions*, Spring 1982; Overseas Private Investment Corporation (OPIC), Annual Reports, 1978-1981; United States Embassy in Guatemala, "Subsidiaries and Affiliates of American Firms," 1981.

BELIZE

Population: *160,000 (1980)*
Land: *8,866 square miles*
Density: *18 per square mile*

Infant Mortality: *40 per 1,000 births (1980)*
Life Expectancy: *60 years (1980)*
Literacy: *80+ percent (1980)*

Gross Domestic Product (GDP): *$135 million (1981)*
Per Capita Income: *$755 (1980)*

Major Exports: *sugar, citrus, bananas*
Exports: *$103 million (1981)*
Exports to U.S.: *50 percent (1980)*
Imports: *$141 million (1981)*
Imports from U.S.: *46 percent (1980)*

Categorizing Belize is difficult. Some say it's a Caribbean country; others say Belize is Central American. Great Britain has for many years claimed Belize as its territory, while Guatemala still considers Belize as its own.

At least part of this identity crisis was resolved on September 21, 1981, when Belize, formerly British Honduras, gained its independence from Great Britain. Dancing and celebration marked this long-awaited event in Belize City, but this small, sparsely-settled nation faces an uncertain future. The British influence and the majority Black population have oriented Belize more to the Caribbean economic community, but the escalating crisis in Central America is reminding Belize that it can't escape its geographic circumstances. Salvadoran and Guatemalan refugees now pour over its border; heavily-armed Guatemala is ready at any time to pounce on its tiny neighbor. Prime Minister George Price asked that 1,600 British troops remain to protect Belize. Meanwhile, the U.S. is prevailing upon the new fledged country to snuggle up under the wing of the U.S. economic and political domain.

The U.S. moved in quickly to replace the British influence in Belize through military aid, economic aid, and aid for private investment. It began negotiations with Belize in 1981 to establish an airfield and military base. Immediately after Belizean independence, the United States announced that it would send military advisors to train the 200-person Belizean army, and members of the defense force are to receive training at U.S. facilities in Panama. The U.S. government is also providing Belize with $1 million in sophisticated electronic equipment with potential military use. The opposition weekly, *The Beacon*, reported that U.S. soldiers will soon be going to Belize for jungle training.

Most multilateral aid to Belize has been provided by the United Nations and the Caribbean Development Bank, which has financed the expansion of a deep-water port near Belize City, a citrus project, and electrification projects. U.S. firms are in an excellent position to receive contracts for agriculture and infrastructure projects since the United States funds the Caribbean Development Bank through the Agency for International Development (AID) and through multilateral bank loans from the World Bank. Now that Belize is independent, it's eligible for concessionary loans from the Inter-American Development Bank which will further U.S. presence in Belize.

Belize was incorporated into the USAID program through an assistance project that contracted the U.S. consulting firm Coopers & Lybrand to identify possibilities in Belize for U.S. investment, especially the potential for joint ventures with local firms. The project will also seek out sources of investment finance for new U.S. private investment in Belize. The focus of the AID project is in keeping with the principles of President Reagan's policy to increase investment opportunities for U.S. corporations and to tie the region economically to the United States. The U.S. has recently offered Belize economic and technical assistance in exchange for establishing an open door policy for Haitian refugees, many of whom have been living in the United States. The Belizean government has started to settle 2,500 Haitians in the southern part of the country.[1]

Although U.S. influence is spreading rapidly, Belize has failed to fall completely in step with U.S. policy for the Caribbean and Central America. Belize maintains friendly ties with Cuba and the revolutionary government of Grenada, and Prime Minister Price declined the U.S. invitation to join the Central American Democratic Community (CDC) with Guatemala, El Salvador, Honduras, and Costa Rica.

ECONOMY

Belize's colonial heritage with the British Commonwealth has hindered the development of a national bourgeoisie, forcing the country to rely on foreign manufacture for even the most basic items. Replacing Britain as chief supplier of imported goods to Belize, the U.S. was the source of 46% of Belize's imports in 1980, up 36% from 1978. Principal U.S. exports to Belize include processed food items, manufactured goods, and machinery and transportation equipment.[2] The country's small, undeveloped manufacturing base and its narrow range of agricultural products for domestic consumption make it import-dependent and vulnerable to international levels of inflation.

In 1980, Belize received $25 million or 15% of its Gross Domestic Product (GDP) in external financing from the European Development Fund, the Caribbean Development Bank, and the United Kingdom. With independence Belize is losing much of this funding and it will lose an additional $10 million when the British military force withdraws.[3]

The People's United Party (PUP), with George Price at the helm, has maintained control of the government since 1964 when British Honduras was granted full internal self-government under a ministerial system. PUP's economic program for 1980-83 calls for the continued development of the agricultural base of the economy and the growing role of the public sector, calling for $180 million in public sector investment through 1985.

Agriculture

Agriculture plays the leading role in the Belizean economy, accounting for 32% of the GDP, 85% of the exports, and 40% of the employment.[4] Large plantations produce sugar, citrus crops, bananas, and cocoa for export, while the output of small-scale farms goes to domestic markets. Assad Shoman, a government minister, confirmed that in Belize 80% of the land is in the control of foreigners, many of them absentee owners. Most of the land is unfarmed. Of a total of 5.7 million acres, 2.2 million are considered suitable for agriculture and half for grazing. Only 15% of land suitable for agriculture is being used.[5] Food constitutes 25% of Belize's total imports. One of the stated aims of PUP's economic development plan is self-sufficiency in food through comprehensive land reform, agricultural education and training, increased funding for crop development, and improved distribution and marketing facilities.

The British sugar giant Tate & Lyle operates Belize Sugar Industries which exports most of its sugar and molasses to the United States. U.S. interests are giving a great deal of consideration to cattle raising projects that would use land resources for pasture development and feed grain production. According to the U.S. Department of Commerce, a good beef market in the Caribbean and a USDA approved slaughterhouse already located in Belize makes the country a profitable place for investment in cattle.

Local demand for wood necessitates the importation of timber, but a United Nations study estimated that about 49 million cubic feet of tropical hardwood could be cut on a sustained yield basis. Currently only two million are cut. Only one small kiln exists in Belize, used for experimental purposes by the government, but a U.S. investor is setting up a large kiln for a furniture-making business. Other new U.S. ventures in Belize include two companies which process and distribute shrimp and lobster caught off Belize's Caribbean coast.

Industry

The manufacturing sector in Belize is small. Local products include beer, cigarettes, batteries, flour, fertilizer, nails, and roofing. Most other products are imported. Import-substitution industries in Belize don't contribute to the economy substantially because most of them are the so-called "wrap and pack" or "screwdriver" industries that use Belize at the final stage of a long production line. Toilet paper manufacturing in Belize, for example, involves little more than cutting huge rolls made in the U.S. into small rolls.

Belize's foreign investment law allows exemption from income taxes and import duties for as long as 15 years. The country is trying to attract more offshore industries which do both the buying of materials and the selling of their products entirely outside the country. The Williamson Corporation, for example, employs about 500 women workers to assemble Dixie Jeans for sale in the U.S.

The mounting pressure from the United States for Belize to accept its money, investment, and foreign policy is manifested in the heated left-right political polarization within Belize. An anti-communist society has formed, and a faction of the business community has red-baited several government officials. The people of Belize will have to decide whether their new nation can maintain an independent political stance or whether it will be pulled into the military and economic orbit of the U.S. like so many other Latin American and Caribbean nations.

References for Introductory Statistics

Inter-American Development Bank, *Economic and Social Progress in Latin America 1980-81*; U.S. Department of Commerce, *Foreign Economic Trends - Belize*, October 1981; U.S. Department of State, *Background Notes - Belize*, May 1982.

REFERENCE NOTES

1. "Guatemalans Protest Haitian Resettlement," *Central America Report*, July 1982, p. 219.
2. "Belize," *Business America*, September 21, 1981, p. 24.
3. *Belize*, Foreign Economic Trends, October 1981.
4. Ibid.
5. Ibid.

UNITED STATES BUSINESS IN BELIZE*

Air Florida; *air transportation*

Aqua Lodge

Barrier Reef; *hotel*

Barrow Logging; *logging and sawmill*

Belize Beef; *cattle*

Belize Cemcol; *Caterpillar tractor*

*An indented item is a subsidiary, affiliate, or branch of the corporation immediately above it.

Belize Estate & Produce

Belize International; *rock quarry*

Belize Pharmaceutical

Big Falls Ranch; *rice production and processing; ADELA equity*

Brothers, Wm. C.; *sawmill*

Carr, John; *cattle production*

Carver Tropical Ranch; *cattle production*

Castle & Cooke
Belize Brewing; *beverage bottling*

Caterpillar Americas; *Caterpillar tractor distribution*

Caye Chapel; *hotel and resort*

Chase Manhattan
Atlantic Bank; *banking*

Collier, John; *cattle production*

Collins Foods
Kentucky Fried Chicken; *restaurant*

El Pescador; *hotel*

Hershey
Hummingbird Hershey; *cocoa production*

Hide-A-Way Lodge

Hurley, Robert; *cattle production*

IM Brokers of Florida; *lobster and fish processing*

Keller Caribbean Sports; *fishing lodge*

Kellogg
Belize Citrus; *fruit production*
Belize Feed; *feed processing*
Belize Food; *food processing*
Caribbean Foods; *food processing*
Salada Foods; *food processing*

Manatee Lodge

Mariah Reef Resort

Minter Naval Stores; *pine resin extraction and sawmill*

Misener Marine Construction; *port construction*

Paradise House; *hotel*

Placencia Cove; *hotel*

Prosser Fertilizer and Agrotec; *fertilizer mixing*

Pyramid Island; *hotel*

Rebco; *diesel engine sales*

Renco Battery Factory; *manufacturing*

Robinson Lumber

Seminole Steel Erectors; *cattle production*

Shore Lobster; *shrimp and lobster distribution*

Snell Environmental Group; *shrimp production*

Stone, Cecil Albert; *ranch*

St. George's Lodge

Swingle, Dean; *ranch*

Texaco
Texaco Belize

Tropical Produce; *mango production*

Turneffe Island Lodge

Victoria House; *hotel*

Westmoreland, William; *farming*

Whitney, Harold; *farming*

Williamson Industries; *garment manufacturing*

Wyatt, John; *farming*

REFERENCES

Directory of American Firms Operating in Foreign Countries, 1979; *Directory of Corporate Affiliations*, 1982; Dun & Bradstreet, "Principal International Businesses," 1982; *Export/Import Markets*, 1982; *Foreign Index to the Directory of Corporate Affiliations*, 1981; *Million Dollar Directory*, 1982; *Moody's*, 1981; *Rand McNally International Bankers Directory*, 1982; 10-K Reports, 1981; *World Directory of Multinational Enterprises*, 1980.

ADELA, Annual Reports, 1981; *Agribusiness in the Americas*, 1980; Latin American Agribusiness Development Corporation (LAAD), Annual Reports, 1976-1981; Overseas Private Investment Corporation (OPIC), Annual Reports, 1978-1981; United States Department of State, List of U.S. Investors in Belize, July 1982; Interview with Belizean Embassy staff.

PANAMA

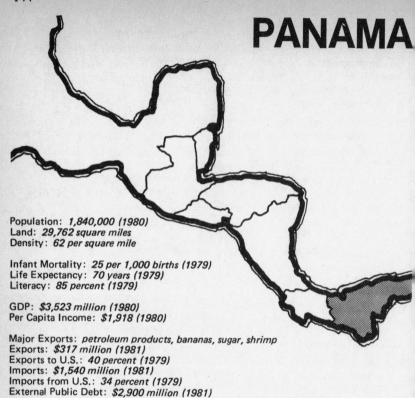

Population: *1,840,000 (1980)*
Land: *29,762 square miles*
Density: *62 per square mile*

Infant Mortality: *25 per 1,000 births (1979)*
Life Expectancy: *70 years (1979)*
Literacy: *85 percent (1979)*

GDP: *$3,523 million (1980)*
Per Capita Income: *$1,918 (1980)*

Major Exports: *petroleum products, bananas, sugar, shrimp*
Exports: *$317 million (1981)*
Exports to U.S.: *40 percent (1979)*
Imports: *$1,540 million (1981)*
Imports from U.S.: *34 percent (1979)*
External Public Debt: *$2,900 million (1981)*

Explaining the early history of the Panama Canal, President Theodore Roosevelt said, "I took the Canal, and let the Congress debate."[1] Like gunboat diplomacy and Big Stick policies in Latin America, official arrogance toward Panama has also continued into modern times. Presidential candidate Ronald Reagan, echoing a common U.S. conservative slogan, said: "We bought it, we paid for it, we built it, and we intend to keep it."[2]

It was the California Gold Rush of 1848 that first brought Panama into the widening sphere of U.S. economic and military control. Tens of thousands of adventurers from the East Coast rushed through Panama on their way to the riches of California rather than risk the arduous, often dangerous trans-continental trip across the United States. Recognizing the importance of the isthmus, New York financiers secured an exclusive concession from Colombia to construct a railroad across its territory of Panama.[3] The railroad, completed in 1855, substantially reduced the cost of transporting goods, raw materials, and passengers from one ocean to the other. The U.S. Army intervened five times between 1856 and 1865 to guarantee the investment of the Panama Railroad Company and to suppress protests for Panamanian independence from

Colombia.[4]

The Spanish-American War of 1898 marked the birth of the United States as an imperial power. U.S. military leaders, concerned that their gunboats had to travel the long route around Cape Horn, started lobbying for the construction of a trans-isthmian canal across Panama. Though the Senate of Colombia rejected a U.S. petition in 1903 to build a canal through Panama, it didn't stop the United States or President Roosevelt. The *U.S.S. Dixie* and the *U.S.S. Nashville* sailed to Panama to prevent Colombia from squashing a U.S.-instigated revolt. A major figure in these machinations was William Nelson Cromwell, founder of the prestigious New York law firm, Sullivan & Cromwell; Cromwell represented and owned stock in the French Canal Company and also directed the Panama Railroad. The first canal treaty was signed with the U.S. only five days after securing Panama's independence from Colombia. Signing the treaty for Panama was Frenchman Philippe Bunau-Varilla, who, like Cromwell, was interested in selling the remaining assets of the French company that had earlier tried to build a canal. No Panamanian signed the Panama Canal Treaty of 1903.

The treaty gave the U.S. the right to intervene in the internal affairs of the new country, which essentially became a protectorate of the United States. U.S. government officials and the U.S. military supervised the national elections in Panama in 1908, 1912, and 1918. Unlike other sectors of the population, the Panamanian oligarchy supported the U.S. presence in Panama and often requested the intervention of U.S. forces to control popular protests and uprisings. In 1918, a detachment of Marines remained in the Chiriqui province for two years to maintain public order; and in 1925, 600 U.S. Army troops carrying rifles with fixed bayonets entered Panama City to break a rent strike. For twelve days, American troops patrolled the streets to keep order and guard U.S. property.[5]

Popular opposition forced the Panamanian government to reject a largely concessionary treaty with the U.S. in 1926, and it wasn't until the General Treaty of Friendship and Cooperation of 1936 that the United States relinquished the right to unilateral intervention in Panama's political affairs. In that treaty, the U.S. obtained the right of further access to additional lands and waters for the defense and modernization of the Canal. In 1942, the U.S.-Panama Base Convention allowed the United States over 100 new military and telecommunications facilities in Panama, marking the beginning of the extensive and permanent U.S. military presence in the Canal Zone. In 1947, popular protests prevented the authorization of increased U.S. military presence, but the Treaty of Mutual Understanding and Cooperation of 1955 permitted the United States to locate another large military base in Panama in exchange for increased access to the Canal Zone by local business people.[6]

Pent-up resentment against the United States surfaced in the Flag Riots of 1964 when U.S. authorities prevented Panamanian students from raising their national flag alongside the U.S. flag at a high school in the Canal Zone. "Within hours, 30,000 Panamanians were in the streets of Panama City, confronting

U.S. troops who had orders to fire warning shots before shooting to kill. The riot soon spread to Colon, on the Atlantic side of the Zone, then deep into the interior. . . . By the time this explosion of anti-Yankee fury was contained, over $2 million in property had been burned or otherwise destroyed — almost all of it American. Twenty-eight people had been killed, 300 wounded, and 500 arrested, almost all of them Panamanian."[7] When the government of Panama reacted by breaking relations with the United States, the U.S. conceded to raise the Panamanian flag at the high school in the Canal Zone and also agreed to negotiate a new canal treaty. After three years of negotiations, the U.S. proposed a treaty that was roundly rejected by the Panamanian masses. Finally in 1977, under the leadership of Brigadier General Omar Torrijos Herrera, Panama and the United States reached an agreement over the ownership and operation of the Panama Canal. Actually there were two new treaties: The "Panama Canal Treaty" and the "Treaty on the Permanent Neutrality and Operation of the Panama Canal."

Torrijos, reluctantly signing the agreement, said: "Mr. President [Carter], . . .I want you to know that this treaty, which I shall sign and which repeals a treaty not signed by any Panamanian, does not enjoy the approval of all our people, because the twenty-three years agreed upon as a transition period are 8,395 days, because during this time there will still be military bases which may make our country a strategic reprisal target, and because we are agreeing to a treaty of neutrality which places us under the protective umbrella of the Pentagon. This pact could, if it is not administered judiciously by future generations, become an instrument of permanent intervention."[8]

Since the first treaty in 1903, the United States has resisted attempts by Panamanians to gain more control over the Canal and the Canal Zone. In the 1960s, however, U.S. military analysts reported that the Canal was no longer of strategic military importance since 24 of the largest U.S. aircraft carriers could no longer fit through the Canal.[9] Military experts have also noted that the most likely threat to the operation of the Canal would come from within Panama by insurgents frustrated by continued U.S. domination of the Canal and the Canal Zone. The military generally agreed that the best defense of the Canal would be a cooperative, protective contract involving Panama's National Guard.

After some initial hesitation, the U.S. corporations backed the canal treaties which they felt would reduce anti-imperialist sentiment in Panana, thereby improving the prospects for investment. An array of U.S. business organizations including the Council of the Americas and the National Association of Manufacturers lobbied for the ratification of the treaties, but in Panama the people were less than enthusiastic. Many Panamanians regarded the treaties as the best compromise agreement possible, given the unequal power relationship between the two nations. In support of the treaties, the Committee for the Ratification of the Panama Canal Treaties in New York noted that the rent received by the Empire State Building in 1970 exceeded $13 million while Panama was receiving only $2.3 million for the lease of 553 square miles occupied by the Canal and 14 U.S. military bases. Organizing to oppose the treaties, the Conservative Caucus, and the American Security Council formed the Emergency Coalition to Save the Panama Canal, but the overwhelming corporate support for the treaties insured ratification.[10]

Provisions of the 1977 treaties include:

> The right of the U.S. to manage and operate the canal until the year 2000.
>
> The perpetual right of the U.S. to protect and defend the Canal.
>
> All key bases and training areas operated by the U.S. will remain under U.S. control until 2000.
>
> Panama will assume territorial jurisdiction in 1982 over the Canal Zone (five mile area on either side of the Canal).
>
> The perpetual right of the U.S. to build a new sea-level canal ten miles to the west.
>
> An increase of toll fees received by Panama from $2.3 million to approximately $70 million annually.
>
> The establishment of a nine-member Canal Commission, composed of five U.S. members and four Panamanian members to manage the Canal (in 1989, to change to four U.S. and five Panamanian members).

In 1981, Ambler H. Moss Jr., the U.S. Ambassador to Panama, summarizing the U.S. position in regard to the canal treaties, said: "Panama, which could well have been another source of agitation and disturbance in the area, is now one of the bright spots in an otherwise confused and turbulent Central America and Caribbean today."[11]

"The U.S. basically won on the treaties," commented Mario Galindo, a lawyer who led the local opposition to their ratification in Panama. "In fact, the new treaties make us more subservient to the Americans than ever. The 1903 treaties at least pretended Panama was sovereign. The 1977 treaties give the U.S. the right to intervene here without even asking permission."[12]

The Neutrality Treaty has no termination date. Under its provisions, the United States and Panama both guarantee the neutrality of the canal "in order that both in time of peace and in time of war it shall remain secure and open to peaceful transit by the vessels of all nations on terms of entire equality." Attached to the treaty was the DiConcini Condition stating that "if the Canal is closed, or its operations are interfered with, [the United States and Panama shall each] have the right to take such steps as each deems necessary. . . including the use of military force in the Republic of Panama, to reopen the Canal or restore the operations of the Canal."

General Wallace Nutting, Commander of the U.S. Southern Command, based in Panama, told a group of businessmen in Panama that the defense of the Panama Canal didn't stop at its banks. He said that the military aid to El Salvador was part of the task of maintaining the present and future security of the sea route through the Canal. Nutting's remarks have alarmed Panamanians concerned that their country will be a staging ground for a U.S. counter-insurgency war in Central America.[13]

The right of permanent intervention, said General Brown of the Joint Chiefs of Staff, could mean "defending the Canal even against Panama," if the U.S considers the neutrality of the Canal threatened.[14]

The Pentagon's Southern Command is the most important gathering of U.S. military strength in Latin America. The Panama Canal Treaty of 1977 allows 9,000 to 12,000 U.S. troops to remain at Panama bases through the year 2000. Also remaining in Panama are the following U.S. installations: the Interamerican Military Network, the Interamerican Telecommunication Network Station and its training schools, the School of Americas for the U.S. Army (USARSA), the Interamerican Air Force Academy (IAAFA), the Small Craft Instruction and Technique Group (SCIATT), the Interamerican Geodesic Survey, and the Permanent Commission for Interamerican Military Communication.[15]

The canal treaties specify that the U.S. military should coordinate its defense of the Canal with the Panamanian National Guard, but the bottom line of the Neutrality Treaty gives the United States the unilateral right to intervene in Panama should cooperation between the two military forces break down or prove inadequate for the defense of U.S. interests.

POLITICS

The process of popular reformism in government that began in 1968 with the ascent to power of General Omar Torrijos has died. It was dying even before the July 1981 airplane crash that killed Torrijos. In the late 1970s, Torrijos and the ruling party, Partido Revolucionario Democratico (PRD) started edging away from their alliance with progressive sectors of the population. His early reformist programs had given Torrijos a strong base among workers, *campesinos*, and students, but the government started to swing back into the fold of the bourgeoisie after having gained a firm hold on the country. In 1978, Phillip Butcher, Secretary General of the Confederation of the Workers of the Republic of Panama, said, "In 1972, there was more unity between the government and the workers because the government had not yet established good relations with the capitalist class. So it needed support from the working class to stay in power. The bosses are now on good terms with the government and have imposed their terms on the workers."[16]

Torrijos became Panama's Supreme Commander after a 1968 National Guard coup that sent the oligarchy packing from the national political scene. The oligarchy, derisively called the *Rabiblancos* (white-tailed birds), comprised the *Veinte Familias* (twenty families) who had been intermarrying and concentrating economic power since before the turn of the century. According to the Life World Library (1964), the "*Rabiblancos* constitute less than one percent of Panama's population, but they own half of all the land not owned by the government. They own the banks, the breweries, the newspapers, the radio, the television stations, the sugar mills, the coffee plantations, the insurance companies, the construction industry, the luxury shops for tourists. Many represent U.S. companies that do business in Panama. On every board of directors one finds the same names. . . . The Panamanian oligarchs not only dominate the economy of the country; they also dominate its politics."

The political domination was interrupted by the 1968 coup, but the oligarchy retained its wealth. By the late 1970s, the oligarchy had reasserted itself into the nation's political life through the formation of powerful business organizations that had opposed the early Torrijos reforms.

As Supreme Commander, Torrijos had named Dr. Aristides Royo President until the next scheduled elections in 1984. Torrijos remained chief of the National Guard and the acknowledged political power broker in Panama until his death. Royo continued the liberal foreign policy of Torrijos, but after the General's death was unable to resist the mounting pressure from the National Guard for a more prominent role in the country's politics. In July 1982, Royo resigned from office, citing health reasons, and was succeeded by Vice-President Ricardo de la Espriella. Espriella, unlike Royo, had the extensive backing of the National Guard and business interests.[17]

A three-member team, led by Colonel Ruben Dario Paredes, directs the 11,000 members of the security forces. Paredes, a longtime friend of the landowners and cattle ranchers, will likely run for president in 1984. Paredes has criticized Panama's friendly relations with Nicaragua and Cuba. "The moment of great definitions is arriving," said Paredes in an interview with the *Washington Post* about Central American politics, adding that there was no place in Panama for Cuba-style socialism. The resignation of Royo was yet another blow to Nicaragua's Sandinistas who regarded Panama's Royo as one of their few friends in the region.[18]

Colonel Manuel Antonio Noriega, former head of intelligence under Torrijos, may succeed Paredes as head of the National Guard if Paredes runs for the top political office. Noriega was known to maintain links with political radicals for the purpose of surveillance. Another important political figure in Panama is former President Arnulfo Arias (deposed in 1968), a prominent member of the nation's oligarchy and a friend of President Reagan.[19]

Torrijos welded together the PRD from diverse sectors in Panama, and without his leadership, the party broke into factions. The middle class and reformist elements of the PRD have been losing out to the conservatives, led by the publisher of the Panamanian daily, *La Estrella*, Tomas Altamirano Duque, who has close ties with U.S. banking interests.

The era of liberal reforms initiated by Torrijos never directly challenged the economic power of the oligarchy or the system of dependent capitalism. But now, after a decade of populist politics, Panama is firmly back in the hands of the conservative business interests and the oligarchy. Paralleling this rightward shift is the increase of strike activity and popular activism by sectors of the middle class and working class who no longer feel represented in the government.

ECONOMY

International investors see Panama as the bright spot in Central America. Its International Finance Center, the booming free-trade business in Colon, and the Canal Zone have provided Panama with the region's highest per capita income. Panama has a wide-open economy for foreign investment, and investors consider the presence of the U.S. military in the Canal Zone insurance of the country's continuing stability. Although the economy may compare favorably with other Central American nations, it has its own serious problems created in part by its dependency on international trade and investment. The four major weaknesses of Panama's current economy are: its large trade deficit, large public budget deficit, the enormous foreign public and private debt, and high unemployment rate. In 1981, Panama's trade deficit increased from a 1980 deficit of $1,107 million to $1,233 million. In 1981, the United States enjoyed a positive trade balance with Panama of over a half billion dollars.

Its foreign public debt reached the $3 billion mark in 1982. Commenting on its mammoth external debt, the International Monetary Fund (IMF) in 1979 stated that "Panama has arrived at a relationship between indebtedness and national income without precedent in the Western Hemisphere." In the last few years, however, the IMF has praised Panama for its ability to meet its debt payment schedule and for its willingness to abide by the IMF's austerity guidelines. Panama is shelling out $526 million annually to service the foreign debt. This equals 39.5% of the public sector's current annual income.[20] Increased public spending in the 1970s to balance out the decreasing private investment and to fund new government programs is one reason for the tremendous indebtedness. The government has relied on foreign private banks and multilateral funds to cover internal budget deficits. The IMF has successfully prevailed upon Panama to cut back public social services spending, although another public deficit of $270 million is expected for 1982.[21]

The PRD government has backed off from its earlier role as the prime accumulator and distributor of capital in Panama, letting the emphasis of the country's economic structure swing once again back to the private sector. Currently, the economic plan fosters a Hong Kong-type economic development scheme that encourages the economy to attract more foreign capital.[22] Government officials and industry leaders claim the new focus on attracting light assembly industry to Panama will ease the nation's severe unemployment problem. It is estimated that one out of every four workers are unemployed, with the unemployment rate in Colon reaching 35% of the workforce. As workers struggle to keep up with the cost of living and to protect the small gains they made in the government's reformist period, labor is becoming more militant. A frequent complaint of union leaders in Panama is the failure of Canal Zone employers to pay equal wages to U.S. and Panamanian workers.

Panama is vulnerable to world trends in interest rates, trade, and investment. Linked to the United States by the Panama Canal and the country's dollar-based exchange system, Panama is immediately affected by high inflation rates and recessionary trends in the United States. Despite its economic problems, Panama continues to be an attractive place for foreign investment. The 1977 Canal Treaty was accompanied by an economic assistance guarantee by the U.S. Overseas Private Investment Corporation for financing projects in the private sector and up to $200 million in loans and insurance provided by the U.S. Export-Import Bank. Under discussion is the United States/Panama Bilateral Investment Treaty which would create a long-term framework for investment, including guidelines for U.S. investment: preferential treatment for existing U.S. investors; a mechanism for resolving expropriation and nationalization disputes; and a clause guaranteeing unrestricted repatriation of capital.[23]

International Finance Center

"The increasing interrelation of the economy needs new monetary centers characterized by their stability that allows movement in an efficient form of enormous quantities of productive capital that in reality flow around the world," said David Rockefeller about the International Finance Center in Panama City. "Without a doubt, Panama is an ideal place for a new center in the Western Hemisphere."[24]

In 1970, Panama passed its Banking Law which created the ideal conditions for a center of international finance. Bank deposits aren't taxed, there are no reserve requirements for foreign operations nor exchange controls, and there is an income-tax exemption on profits. What really attracts international bankers, though, is that the U.S. dollar is Panama's unit of exchange, meaning that there is no currency devaluation and that the inflation rate matches the U.S. rate.

More than 125 banks, not including branches, from over 30 countries compose the International Finance Center. Bank assets are over $29 billion, giving a feeling of capitalist stability to Panama. But the bulk of the Finance Center's business is offshore and 80% of the transactions cater to the needs of transnational corporations.[25] The Center is now expanding to include insurance companies that specialize in the international reinsurance business.

Panamanians see little of the tremendous banking assets concentrated in their country. Like the Canal, the banking business just passes through Panama, but it has signalled a yet greater subordination of the country to international capital markets.

Agriculture

The United Nations categorizes Panama as a one-commodity country since more than 50% of its export earnings come from bananas. Other important agro-exports are sugar, tobacco, rice, and cattle. Large-scale production began in the 1880s in Panama, and today United Brands operates two-thirds of the nation's banana farms with the balance owned by independent producers under contracts with United Brands. Recently, the company has been selling its banana lands to the government, which then leases the land back to United Brands.[26]

United Brands refused to cooperate with the government when Panama joined the Union of Banana Exporting Countries (UPEB) and its marketing arm, Comunbana. Initially, the company signed an agreement with Comunbana to market its bananas through that organization whenever Comunbana had a cargo ship available. Then in 1981, the Chiriqui Land Company, a subsidiary of United Brands, violated this agreement by refusing to load its bananas on a Comunbana-chartered boat. The government fined the company and charged that United Brands was waging an "unfair and unjustified campaign" against it, including attempts to pressure small producers not to sell to Comunbana. The company's plantations manager in Panama Bobby Walker saw the situation differently. He said that the government taxation and the international marketing organizations like Comunbana are leeching off the company, which bears all the production risks. Comunbana, Walker threatened, "is going to lose [its] behind trying to cash in on the banana trade." He added that United Brands has more capital invested in Panama than any other company. "We employ 10,000 people, 99.8% of them are Panamanians. If that's colonialism, I don't know what their problem is," said Walker.[27]

An important issue for banana workers in Panama is the excessive use of such insecticides and chemicals as Dithane M-45. The Union of the Workers of the Chiriqui Land Company has been pushing for more government regulations on the use of agricultural chemicals.[28]

The agricultural sector as a whole is underdeveloped and unproductive. While it employs 29% of the workforce, it contributes only 14% of the GDP. Currently, Panama imports 30% of its beans, 20-25% of its corn, and 30% of its milk.[29] In 1980, the value of food imports from the U.S. increased 36% over the previous years. The government announced that the development of agriculture including the food processing industry was its number one priority, but there has been little improvement in the local production of food for local consumption. Rather, the agrarian reform programs and projects to assist the small farmers have been cut to reduce the budget deficit.

Industry

Other Central American nations are facing stiff competition from Panama as a location for light assembly industries or *maquiladoras*. Panama has just about everything to make a runaway shop happy: a workforce that receives a 66 cent an hour minimum wage, international finance center, ideal transportation possibilities with the Panama Canal, and an array of incentives offered by the government to new foreign businesses that make the tax advantages and labor costs in Panama better than those in Hong Kong.[30] Until recently, the United States has controlled 90% of the foreign industrial investment in Panama, but that control has diminished in the last several years because of increased Japanese investment. Industry, which accounts for 17% of the GDP, is concentrated in food processing, beverage, metal production, refined sugar, clothing, and furniture manufacturing. The Panama Canal has stunted the development of local industry due to the ready availability of imported consumer goods in the Canal Zone.

Since 1974, the government has taken the lead in industrial development, having established four new sugar mills and a cement plant. The major government initiative was the proposed Cerro Colorado copper mine, but Rio Tinto Zinc, the private partner in the venture, announced its withdrawal from the project in early 1982. Rio Tinto Zinc had purchased the investment from Texas Gulf, but later decided to halt the project because of depressed copper prices and failure to reach agreement with the government. The mine had also met the opposition of the Guaymi Indians who said the project would destroy the environment. Others in Panama objected to the project because the $2 billion undertaking would create an unbearable national foreign debt. Fluor Mining and Minerals was the contractor for the scrapped project.

The government is already heavily indebted to multilateral agencies for money borrowed to construct several hydroelectric plants, which the government hopes will cut down to almost zero its dependence on imported petroleum. Texaco's subsidiary Refineria Panamena operates a 100,000 barrel a day refinery at Las Minas, while Mobil, El Paso, Santa Fe International, and Oceanic Exploration are exploring for oil on the Caribbean coastal shelf.

The latest trans-isthmian project being developed by the United States in Panama is a 78-mile oil pipeline to transport Alaskan crude oil to Gulf Coast and East Coast refiners and distributors. The $250 million pipeline begins at Puerto Armuelles, the present site of an oil transshipment port (financed by Chase Manhattan, Bankers Trust, and First National Bank of Boston) that transfers Alaskan oil from supertankers to smaller vessels that can pass through the Panama Canal. The project is a joint venture with the government's Petroterminal de Panama, Northville Industries of New York, and CBI Industries of Illinois, with the two U.S. partners holding 60% of the equity. The project contractor is Morrison-Knudsen, while Atlantic Richfield, Standard Oil of Ohio, and Exxon will be using the 600,000 barrel-a-day pipeline when completed in late 1982. Although the government will be receiving fees and royalties from the project, it will suffer a loss of tariffs due to decreased traffic through the Canal.

Another thriving part of Panama's industrial sector is the 55,000 "paper" companies that are in Panama to facilitate transfer pricing, tax-free channels for executive salaries and benefits, and other forms of corporate practices designed to avoid taxation and regulation. South Africa uses such companies to circumvent the economic blockade that resulted from its apartheid practices.[31]

Panama's second largest source of revenue is the Colon Free-Trade Zone (CFZ), which is located in Colon near the Atlantic terminal of the Canal. After World War Two, the Panamanian government founded the CFZ based on an original proposal by a vice-president of the National City Bank of New York. A representative of the U.S. Department of Commerce formulated the actual plans for the zone.[32] Since that time, the CFZ has attracted over 1.000 companies and is now the largest free-trade zone in the world next to Hong Kong.[33] In 1981, two-way trade leaped to $4.4 billion, a tenfold increase since 1970. U.S. imports to the CFZ amounted to $260 million, following Japanese imports valued at $551 million.[34]

U.S. firms trading in the CFZ include Coca-Cola, Pfizer, Kodak, Gillette, Goodyear, Firestone, ITT, Colgate-Palmolive, McGraw-Hill, Black and Decker, and Schering-Plough. Corporations locate in the free-trade zone to take advantage of such attractions as exemptions from import duties, preferential income tax rates on exports, and the absence of taxes of any kind on income generated outside Panama. Panama's free convertibility with the dollar and the absence of controls on remittance of dividends and interest payments also attract companies to the free zone. The commercial business of the CFZ is aimed primarily at the Latin American and Caribbean markets, with 7-10% of Latin American sales now moving through the zone.

Concrete walls surround the CFZ, separating it from the harsh realities of Colon. Originating as the starting point of the Panama Railroad, Colon is the most impoverished place in Panama. Over 125 years of international transport and trade have not improved conditions for Colon's residents. Within the walls of the Colon Free-Trade Zone, capitalist representatives from all over the world carry on international trade while outside Panamanians live in a slum city characterized by thievery, prostitution, and dire urban poverty. A Colon taxicab driver said dryly: "Most foreign visitors don't stay here long. They do their business and get out."[35] That's the story of Colon, and it's been the history of Panama.

References for Introductory Statistics

Inter-American Development Bank, *Economic and Social Progress in Latin America, 1980-81*; United Nations, *Monthly Bulletin of Statistics*, April 1982; U.S. Department of Commerce, *Foreign Economic Trends — Panama*, July 1981; U.S. Department of Commerce, *Overseas Business Reports — Market Profiles for Latin America*, May 1981; U.S. Department of State, *Background Notes — Panama*, February 1982.

REFERENCE NOTES

1. Eduardo Galeano, *Open Veins in Latin America*, (New York: Monthly Review Press, 1973).
2. "Panama Canal Treaties," The Committee for the Ratification of the Panama Canal Treaties.
3. Richard F. Nyrop, Editor, *Panama: A Country Study*, (Washington: American University, 1981), p. 18.
4. "Sovereignty for a Land Divided," (Washington: EPICA, 1976), p. 11.
5. Nyrop, p. 198.
6. "Panama: For Whom the Canal Tolls," *NACLA*, September-October 1979, p. 13.
7. *Ibid.*, p. 3.
8. Nyrop, p. 166.
9. *NACLA*, September-October 1979, p. 4.
10. *Ibid.*, p. 9.
11. *Manchester Guardian/Le Monde*, February 22, 1981.
12. *Ibid.*
13. "Military Minds Think Alike," *LARR*, January 29, 1982.
14. *NACLA*, November-December, 1977.
15. Julio Manduley, "Panama: Dependent Capitalism and Beyond," *Latin American Perspectives*, Spring and Summer, 1980, p. 71.
16. *Dialogo Social*, November 1978.
17. Christopher Dickey, "Panama's Chief Quits," *Washington Post*, July 31, 1982.
18. *Ibid.*
19. "Panama: Who Will Fill the Void?," *NACLA*, July-August, 1981, p. 38.
20. "Indebtedness is Growing," *Central America Report*, July 1982, p. 212.
21. "Business Outlook: Panama," *Business Latin America*, April 21, 1982, p. 124.
22. Manduley, p. 64.
23. "Panama Gears Projects Toward Diversified Economic Development," *Business Latin America*, March 3, 1982, p. 71.
24. Juan Jované, "The International Finance Center in Panama," 1976, p. 4, cited in *Dialogo Social*, December 1980, p. 15.
25. Michael Kolbenschlag, "Going for Profits," *Forbes*, March 17, 1980, p. 91.
26. Karen DeYoung, "Gentle Banana Center of Dispute in Central America, *Washington Post*, June 10, 1978.
27. *Ibid.*
28. "Envenenamiento de Trabajadores Bananeros," *Dialogo Social*, April 1981.
29. *Business Latin America*, April 21, 1982, p. 124.
30. "Maquila International," Republic of Panama, 1982.
31. *NACLA*, September-October 1979.
32. Promotional brochure, Colon Free-Trade Zone.
33. *Business Latin America*, June 30, 1982, p. 207.
34. *Ibid.*
35. Interview by Tom Barry, April 1982.

UNITED STATES BUSINESS IN PANAMA*

Abbott Laboratories
  Abbott Overseas; *pharmaceutical
  manufacturing*

Acero Panamá; *steel*

ACF Industries
  Polymer; *plastics and resins
  manufacturing*

Addison-Wesley Publishing
  Fondo Educativo Interamericano;
  educational material publishing

Agromarina de Panamá

Airborne Freight; *freight forwarding*

Allied Artists Pictures Corporation;
  motion picture distribution

Aluminum Company of America (ALCOA)
  Aluminios de Centroamérica
  (ALDECA); *aluminum product
  manufacturing*

American Capitol Insurance; *insurance*

American Express
  American Express International
  Banking; *credit card services*

American Flower Shippers; *flower
  production; LAAD equity*

American Home Products
  Fort Dodge Laboratories;
  veterinary medicine

American Hospital Supply; *hospital
  supplies*

American Life Insurance; *insurance*

AMF
  AMF Panamá

ASARCO; *copper mining*

Atlantic-Richfield
  ARCO Panama Transportation Co.

BankAmerica
  Banco Internacional de Panamá;
  banking
  Financería Bamérica; *banking*

Bankers Trust Company; *banking*

Bata Shoe Company; *footwear*

Beckton, Dickinson & Company; *surgical
  instruments*

Benfield Schools; *correspondence schools*

Bestform Foundations; *underwear
  manufacturing*

Black & Decker Manufacturing
  Black & Decker Interamérica; *electrical
  equipment manufacturing*

Blue Ribbon Meat Company
  Blue Ribbon Products; *sausage
  manufacturing*

The Borden Company
  Alba/Adria
  Borden
  Broex
  Compañía Chiricana de Leche
  Compañía Colombiana de Alimentos
  Lácteos
  Compañía Internacional de Ventas
  Crespan
  Fábrica de Productos Borden
  Frigoríficos de Chaqui
  Gallina Blanca

  Helados Borden; *dairy product
  processing*
  Hendersons; *fish products; ten branches*
  Industrias Internacionales de Plásticos
  Industrias Reunidas
  Istenco
  Pasteruizadora de Valle
  Prolesa
  Materiales Moldeables
  Wilhelm Weber GMBH

Boyd Brothers; *office supplies*

Bristol-Myers
  Brislab
  Bristol Laboratories; *pharmaceuticals*
  Bristol Pharmaceutical Information
  Center

Bullet Construction; *construction*

Cargill; *animal feed processing*

Carnation
  Compañía Panameña de Alimentos
  Lácteos; *dairy product processing*

Castle & Cooke
  Compañía Bananera Antilla; *banana
  production*

CBI Industries
  CBI Industrios; *oil transshipment
  terminal*
  Chicago Bridge & Iron; *petroleum
  pipeline*

CBS
  Distribuidora Panameña Discos;
  record distribution
  Industria de Discos Centroamericanos

*An indented item is a subsidiary, affiliate, or branch of the corporation immediately
above it.

Central Soya
  Central Soya International; *animal feed manufacturing*

Chase Manhattan
  Banco del Comercio
  Chase Manhattan Bank; *six branches*
  Chase International Investment Corporation

Chrysler; *auto industry*

Citicorp
  Citibank; *banking*

Citizen's Insurance Company of America; *insurance*

Coca-Cola
  Coca-Cola Export Company
  Coca-Cola de Panamá Embotelladora; *bottling*

Colgate Palmolive
  Colgate Palmolive Centroamericana
  Kendall; *pharmaceuticals*
  Riviana de Centroamérica; *food processing*

Colpan Motors

Columbia Pictures
  Columbia Pictures of Panamá; *motion picture distribution*

Compañía Universal de Seguros; *insurance*

Consolidated Foods
  Corjan
  Global Finance
  Hanes Panamá

Continental
  Continental Insurance Company; *insurance*

Continental Air Lines
  Hotel El Continental

Continental Group
  Continental Can; *container manufacturing*

Cook Industries; *grain merchandising*

Corporación Agropecuario; *cattle product production; LAAD equity*

Cosméticos; *cosmetics*

Crown Cork & Seal Company
  Crown Cork Centroamericana; *cork manufacturing*

Crown Zellerbach
  Crown Zellerbach Inter-America; *paper product manufacturing*

Crush International
  Compañía Panamericana de Orange Crush; *soft drink industry*

Cummins Engine Company
  Distribuidora Cummins Diesel de Panamá; *heavy equipment sales*

Cutter Laboratories; *chemical product manufacturing*

Dart & Kraft
  Kraftco; *dairy and cheese processing*
  Productos Kraft

Deere & Company
  John Deere; *heavy equipment*

Deloitte, Haskins & Sells; *accounting*

Desarrollo Industrial *private development financing; ADELA equity*

DHL de Panamá

Diamond Shamrock
  Mid-Atlantic Vinyl Supply; *chemical products*

Digital Equipment Corporation
  Digital Equipment Panama

Dow Chemical
  Coral Navigation
  Dow Chemical International
  Dowell Schlumberger; *two branches*
  Dow Química de Centroamérica; *chemical products*
  Lepetit International

Dresser Industries
  Harbison-Walker Refractarios; *high technology equipment*

E.I. Du Pont de Nemours
  Conoco; *petroleum product refining and distribution*

Eastman Kodak
  Panama Kodak Companies; *film distribution*

Eaton
  Cutler-Hammer; *electrical product manufacturing*
  Economic Laboratories; *cleaning material manufacturing*

El Paso; *oil exploration*

Empire Brushes; *brooms and brushes*

Ernst & Whinney

ESB; *accumulators and batteries*

Esmark
  Nutriproducts
  Swift & Company; *meat processing*

Exxon
  Essochem de Centroamérica; *chemical product marketing*
  Exxon Overseas Services; *oil exploration and production*

Firestone Tire & Rubber
Firestone Interamérica· *rubber product manufacturing*

First Boston
Banco de Boston; *banking*

First Chicago
First National Chicago of Panama; *banking*

First Research Corporation; *management and representation services*

Fluor
Fluor Mining & Metals; *mining, engineering, purchasing and management*

Ford, Sosa y Morrice

Foremost-McKesson
Calox Panameña
Foremost Dairies de Panamá; *dairy processing*

Frank B. Hall; *insurance; ADELA equity*

Frederic Harris; *engineering*

H.B. Fuller
Color Centro
Decotinas de Panamá
Fuller Istmena
Kativo Comercial
Kativo de Panamá

Gearhart Industries
Gearhart International South America

General Electric
Utah International; *mining and construction*

General Mills
Danalimientos
General Mills de Panamá
Semolas de Panamá

General Signal; *transportation and energy controls*

General Telephone & Electronics (GTE)
GTE Sylvania; *electrical appliance manufacturing*
General Telephone Directories; *telephone directories*

General Tire & Rubber; *tire manufacturing*

Georgia-Pacific
Aztec Trading Company; *lumber products*

Gerber Products
Productos Gerber de Centroamérica; *baby food processing*

The Gillette Company
Compañía Interamericana Gillette; *razor blade and cosmetic manufacturing*

Gino's Restaurants

Global Pan-Transport

B.F. Goodrich; *auto parts manufacturing*

Goodyear Tire & Rubber Company
Goodyear Export
Goodyear de Panamá
Goodyear Western Hemisphere; *tire and rubber product manufacturing*

Great Northern Nekoosa; *paper product manufacturing*

Greyhound
Armour & Company; *meat processing*

Gulf Oil; *petroleum*

Gulf + Western Industries
Cinema International; *motion picture distribution*
Paramount International Films; *motion picture distribution*

Hang Ten; *clothes manufacturing*

Harbert Construction; *construction and engineering*

H.J. Heinz
Star-Kist International; *food processing*

Hertz
Hertz de Panamá; *auto renting*

Hilton International
Panama Hilton International

Holiday Inn
Holiday Inn Hotel
Posadas de América Central

IBM World Trade Corporation
IBM de Panamá; *business machine distribution*

INA; *insurance*

Industria Panameña de Papel; *paper products*

Insurance Company of the State of Pennsylvania; *reinsurance*

International Business Consultants; *systems consultants*

International Dairy Queen
Dairy Queen; *fast food*

International Executive Service Corporation
Cuerpo Internacional de Servicios Ejecutivos; *business consultants*

International Multifoods
  Fábrico; *prepared feeds*
  Super-Ave; *prepared feeds and hatcheries*

International Proteins
  Abbattoir
  Animal Feeds International
  Empacadora Nacional
  Excellent Products; *fish products*
  Fabricaciones Marinos
  Industrias Marinas; *fishmeal*
  Pescadora
  Pesquera Taboguilla

The Interpublic Group of Companies
  McCann-Erickson Centroamericana; *advertising*

ITT
  ITT de Panamá; *communications equipment and services*

IU International
  Namolco; *sugar production*

Johnson & Johnson International
  Johnson & Johnson Panamá; *cosmetic and toiletry manufacturing*

Jordache Enterprise
  Jordache Jeans; *clothing manufacturing*

Kaiser Cement
  Asian Carriers
  Gypsum Carrier

Kaplan Lazare International
  Interdiam; *diamond wholesale and manufacturing*

Kem Manufacturing
  Kem Centroamericana; *chemical product manufacturing*

Kennametal
  Kennametal International; *mining equipment manufacturing*

Kimberly-Clark
  Kimberly-Clark International; *paper products*

The Kulijian Corporation; *technical consultants*

Lance Industries; *aerosol products manufacturing*

Litton Industries
  Westrex International; *recording equipment*

Lovable; *underwear manufacturing*

Mademoiselle Fashions
  Mademoiselle International; *store*

Marine Midland Banks; *banking*

Marriott
  ATLAPA; *convention center*

MCA
  Universal International Films; *motion picture distribution*

McCormick & Company
  McCormick de Centroamérica; *seasoning and flavoring distribution*

McDermott
  Marine Contractors
  McDermott Overseas
  Oceanic Contractors

McGraw-Edison
  Worthington Pump; *heavy equipment*

McGraw-Hill; *publishing and news gathering*

Measurex
  Measurex International Financial; *computer system manufacturing*

Melo y Compañía; *chicken production; LAAD equity*

Merck & Company
  Merck, Sharp & Dohme; *pharmaceutical manufacturing*

Merrill Lynch & Company
  Merrill Lynch International Bank; *investment brokerage*

MGM Grand Hotels
  Metro-Goldwyn-Mayer; *motion picture distribution*

Miles Laboratories
  Miles; *pharmaceutical manufacturing*
  Miles Laboratories Pan America; *pharmaceutical manufacturing*

Minnesota Mining & Manufacturing
  3M de Panamá; *mining and manufacturing*

Mobil
  Mobil Anpalas
  Mobil Investments
  Mobil Oil Caribe
  Mobil Petroleum Carriers
  Mobil Refining
  Mobil Tankers
  Nocos Tankers

Monsanto
  Monsanto Centroamericano; *chemical and plastic manufacturing*

Moore
  Moore Business Forms de Centroamérica; *business forms*

Morrison-Knudsen
  International Engineering; *engineering and designing*

Morton-Norwich Products
Norwich Pharmaceutical Company of Panama; *pharmaceutical and chemical product manufacturing and sales*

Murphy Oil
Dearborn-Storm Drilling
Deep Submergence Systems
Ocean Contract Services
ODECO Drilling
ODECO-JILD Offshore Exploration
ODECO Nihon
Poseidon Industries
Storm Drilling
Storm International

Mutual of Omaha Insurance
United de Omaha; *insurance*

Nabisco Brands
Distribuidora Pan Americana
Lifesavers; *candy*
Marcos Alimenticos Internacional
Nabisco International; *cracker manufacturing*
Pan American Standard Brands

National Bulk Carriers
Cítricos de Chiriqui

National Car Rental Systems; *auto renting*

National Cash Register (NCR)
Cajas Registradoras Nacional; *business equipment manufacturing*

National Distillers & Chemical; *distilling*

National Union Fire Insurance; *insurance*

Nello L. Teer; *contracting*

New York Brake Company; *hydraulic brakes*

Noranda
Noranda Exploration; *copper exploration*

Northville Industries
Northville Terminal; *oil transshipment*

Norton Lilly
Agencia Naviera Norton Lilly; *shipping*
Norton Lilly & Company Panama

Norton Simon
Avis Rent-A-Car; *auto renting*
Cervecería Nacional; *brewing*
Norton Simon; *paints*

Nova University

Ocean Trucking; *trucking*

Olin
Actinex
Olma
Verdex

Overseas Management Company

Owens-Illinois
Owens-Illinois International

Pan American Life Insurance
Compañía de Seguros; *insurance*

Pan American World Airways
Panameña de Aviación (COPA); *air transportation*

Parker Pen; *pen manufacturing*

Peat, Marwick, Mitchell & Company; *accounting and auditing*

PepsiCo
Compañía Interamericana de Servicios
Navpan
North American Van Lines; *packing and international moving*

Pfizer
Pfizer International; *pharmaceutical and chemical manufacturing and distribution; two branches*

Phelps Dodge International
Alambres y Cables de Panamá; *electrical conductor and cable manufacturing*

Philadelphia National
Primer Banco de Ahorros; *banking*

Philip Morris
Tabacalera Nacional; *tobacco production*

Phillips Petroleum

Phillips-Van Heusen; *shirt manufacturing*

Polaroid
Polaroid Interamerican
Polaroid Intercontinental

Price Waterhouse & Company
Price Waterhouse y Compañía; *accounting and auditing*

Proveedora Marina e Industrial

Rader & Associates
Rader y Asociados; *architecture and engineering*

Ralston Purina
Purina de Panamá; *shrimp production*

Reaseguros Inocap; *reinsurance brokerage*

Republic National Bank; *banking*

Revlon
Armour Panamá
Reiteis International
Revlon Panamá

R.J. Reynolds (Del Monte)
Conservas Panameñas; *food processing*
Federal Transport

Reynolds Metals
   Caribbean Steamship
   Reynolds International

Rohm & Haas
   Rohm & Haas Centroamericana;
      chemical manufacturing

Rowan Companies
   Rowan (Nor-101); *contracting*
   Rowan (Nor-102); *contracting*

Sam P. Wallace
   Sam P. Wallace Panamá; *construction*

Santa Fe Industries
   Santa Fe International; *oil
      exploration*

Schering-Plough
   Schering Corporación de
      Centroamérica; *drug, cosmetic and
      toiletry manufacturing and
      distribution*

SCM
   Fábrica de Pinturas Glidden
   Glidden-Durkee
   Glidden Panamá; *resins and adhesives*

Sears Roebuck & Company; *department
   store*

Security Pacific
   Security Pacific Bank; *banking*

Sel-Rex; *metals and chemicals*

Sherwin-Williams
   Sherwin-Williams de Panamá; *paint*

Siemens Capital; *electrical equipment*

The Signal Companies
   Procon; *construction and engineering*

Singer Manufacturing Company of New
      Jersey; *sewing machine distribution*

Sossa Petroleo; *oil exploration*

Squibb
   Linson International
   Planeta
   Squibb-Mathieson International
   Squibb Middle East
   Squibb Pan American

St. Regis Paper
   St. Regis International; *paper products*

Standard Oil of California
   Chevron Chemical International

Stauffer Chemical
   Compañía Panameña de Industrias
      Químicas; *chemical products*

Sterling Drug
   Sterling International; *paper products*
   Winthrop Products

Syntex; *chemical and pharmaceutical
   products*

Tabacalera Istmeña; *tobacco*

Taylor & Associates
   Taylor & Associates de Costa Rica;
      beef marketing; LAAD equity

TCF
   Twentieth Century Fox Film; *motion
      picture distribution*

Tenneco
   Tenneco International Energy

Texaco
   Panama Exploration
   Refineria Panamá; *refining*
   Texaco Antilles
   Texaco Caribbean
   Texaco Panamá

Texas Instruments
   Geophysical Service International
   Texas Instruments Supply

Textiles de la Chorrera; *textiles*

Touche, Ross & Company International
   Touche, Ross, Bailey & Smart;
      accounting and auditing

Trane; *air conditioning*

Transamerica
   Budget Rent-A-Car

Transway International
   Antroca
   Coordinated Caribbean Transport;
      shipping
   Contabilidad y Servicios
   Gases de Petroleo
   Transporte Tropigas
   Tropigas de Centroamérica
   Tropigas de Chiriqui
   Tropigas de El Salvador
   Tropigas de Nicaragua
   Tropigas de Panamá

Union Carbide
   Union Carbide Centroamericana;
      electrical appliance manufacturing

United Benefit Life Insurance; *insurance*

United Brands
   Balboa Shipping
   Corona
   Chiriqui Land Company
   Polymer Extrusion
   Productos Plásticos

United States Filter Corporation;
   anti-pollution devices

U.S. Gypsum
   Kaiser Wallboard
   Panama Gypsum

U.S. Steel
  U.S. Steel International; *steel manufacturing*

United Technologies
  Otis Elevator; *elevator distribution and maintenance*

Upjohn; *pharmaceutical manufacturing and distribution*

Vanderbilt
  Vanderbilt Internacional; *designer clothes*

Wang Laboratories
  Wang de Panamá (CPEC)

Warner Communications
  Warner Brothers Pictures; *motion picture distribution*

Warner Lambert International
  Parke Davis Interamerican Corporation; *pharmaceuticals*

Wells Fargo Bank
  Banco Continental; *banking*

Weyerhaeuser
  Timber Trading: *wood products*
  Weyerhaeuser; *paper products*

White Motor
  White Motor International

Williams Brothers; *contracting*

Wright Contracting; *contracting*

Xerox
  Panama Services & Development
  Xerox de Panamá; *business machine distribution and services*

REFERENCES

Directory of American Firms Operating in Foreign Countries, 1979; *Directory of Corporate Affiliations*, 1982; Dun & Bradstreet, "Principal International Businesses," 1982; *Export/Import Markets*, 1982; *Foreign Index to the Directory of Corporate Affiliations*, 1981; *Million Dollar Directory*, 1982; *Moody's*, 1981; *Rand McNally International Bankers Directory*, 1982; 10-K Reports, 1981; *World Directory of Multinational Enterprises*, 1980.

ADELA, Annual Report, 1981; *Agribusiness in the Americas*, 1980; American Chamber of Commerce and Industry of Panama, "American Firms, Subsidiaries and Affiliates Operating in Panama," Bank of London, "Quarterly Economic Review Annual Supplement," 1981; BankAmerica, "Bank of America Worldwide Facilities," May 1981; Donald Castillo Rivas, *Acumulacion de Capital y Empresas Transnacionales en Centroamerica*, 1980; Guia de Informacion Para Centroamerica, Panama, Miami y San Andres Isla, 1981-1982; Latin American Agribusiness Development Corporation (LAAD), Annual Reports, 1976-1981; *Latin American Weekly Review*, August 7, 1981; *Mergers & Acquisitions*, Spring 1982; Overseas Private Investment Corporation (OPIC), Annual Reports, 1978-1981; United States Department of Commerce, "Foreign Economic Trends — Panama," July 1981; Zona Libre de Colon, Institucion Autonoma, "Lista de Usuarios Establecidos en la Zona Libre de Colon."

HONDURAS

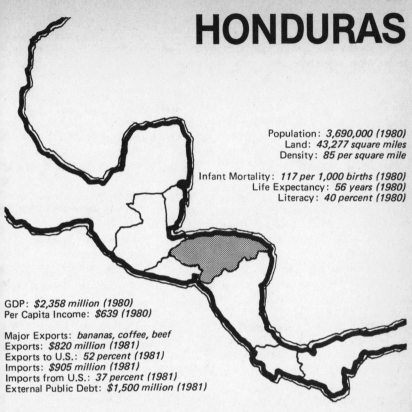

Population: *3,690,000 (1980)*
Land: *43,277 square miles*
Density: *85 per square mile*

Infant Mortality: *117 per 1,000 births (1980)*
Life Expectancy: *56 years (1980)*
Literacy: *40 percent (1980)*

GDP: *$2,358 million (1980)*
Per Capita Income: *$639 (1980)*

Major Exports: *bananas, coffee, beef*
Exports: *$820 million (1981)*
Exports to U.S.: *52 percent (1981)*
Imports: *$905 million (1981)*
Imports from U.S.: *37 percent (1981)*
External Public Debt: *$1,500 million (1981)*

The pervasive control by United Brands and Castle & Cooke over the country's economy has made Honduras the prototype of a Banana Republic. Government bribery, military coups, and corruption are political traditions in this second poorest country in the Western Hemisphere (after Haiti). Long ignored by everyone but the fruit companies, Honduras has recently been thrust into a central role in the U.S. strategy to keep the region firmly under U.S. control. President Julio Suazo Cordova echoed earlier statements of the State Department during a July 1982 trip to Washington. He said that Honduras, "due to its geo-political situation, is of fundamental strategic importance in pacifying the region and stabilizing democratic, economic and social progress in Central America."[1]

Honduras shares a common colonial history with the rest of Central America. Upon arriving in Honduras in the 16th century, the Spanish conquered the then fading Mayan empire based in Copan and established Honduras as part of its large colony of Guatemala. In 1821, the region gained its independence from Spain. When the short-lived Federal Republic of Central America disbanded in 1838, Honduras became its own nation.

Honduras in 1867 obtained four British loans totalling six million pounds to build its first railroad. William Krehm, a reporter for *Time* magazine, wrote "The money [for the railroad] stuck to the fingers of politicians and bankers, and to top it all, Honduras made the grievous mistake of paying the contractor by the mile. . . . [T]he debts contracted, with accumulated interest, amounted to $125 million in 1916, and proved a millstone around the neck of the tiny land."[2]

At the turn of the century, U.S. financiers assumed the servicing of European debts under a plan formulated by President Taft whereby the debts would be guaranteed by a U.S. customs receivership. This creditor/debtor type of arrangement placed the U.S. in a perfect position to manipulate Honduran politics to its own ends.

Honduras missed the Central American coffee boom of the late 19th century, but its rich Atlantic coast did attract the U.S. banana companies that would later become Standard Fruit and United Fruit. The two corporations found Honduras weak and decentralized without the necessary infrastructure for their operations. Installing and then removing Honduran governments became the standard mode of operation for the banana companies. As United Fruit's Samuel ("Sam the Banana Man") Zemurray said, "In Honduras, a mule costs more than a deputy." In 1931, United Fruit and Standard Fruit helped place dictator Tiburcio Carias Andino in power. During the next 16 years of martial law, Carias fashioned the central institutions and infrastructure that made Honduras a modern state.[3]

A transitional epoch for Honduras began in the 1950s when new forces started to challenge the traditional balance of power maintained by the large landowners and the banana companies. A new bourgeoisie began to emerge, and the workers and peasants started to speak out and organize.

A successful strike in 1954 by the banana workers of United Fruit sparked widespread organizing for the first time among the country's other workers. By the end of the decade, the *campesinos*, encouraged by the Catholic Church, also organized to demand agrarian reform and better wages.[4] The *New York Times* called "the awakening and mobilization of the peasantry the most important social phenomenon in Honduras since independence from Spain in 1821."[5] The struggle of the *campesinos* in the last 20 years has focused on having the country's 1962 and 1975 agrarian reform laws enforced. In Honduras, half of the farms under three acres occupy less than five percent of the land, while 1.5% of large farms occupy almost 50% of the total land.[6] The government, careful not to anger the coffee growers and the ranchers, has never vigorously enforced the provisions of the land reform. As a result, the *campesino* movement became more militant and by the mid-1970s was resorting to land takeovers.

The demand for land by the *campesinos* met head-on with the demands for more land by the expanding cattle industry in Honduras. One of the most conservative elements in the Honduran agricultural sector, the National Federation of Farmers and Ranchers, charged that the agrarian reform "attacked private property, the democratic system, liberty, and individuality."[7] But the *campesinos* said that the country's Agrarian Reform Law offered too little and that even its small promises weren't kept. An ex-Minister of Finance reported in March 1982 that ten percent of the population receives 80% of the gross national product and only five percent of the population controls 60% of the land. Responding to a recent government estimate that complete land reform may take 150 years to accomplish, Efrain Diaz Caleas, the director of the Federation of Agrarian Cooperatives said: "It is unpardonable that [the government] tells us that 150 years are needed to carry out agrarian reform. How can that be? Hunger is spreading in the countryside, and the people cannot wait that long. . . ."[8]

How long does Honduras have before it explodes into violent repression and revolution like its neighbors? The U.S. government lauds Honduras as an "oasis of peace" in Central America, and the State Department cites the heavy turnout of the 1982 presidential election as evidence that the Hondurans will keep their peace. But given the degenerating economic conditions, the spreading war, and the increasing polarization of Honduran politics, the peace that Hondurans have is likely the calm before the storm.

POLITICS

In 1982, a civilian government entered office, but it is the military — armed and trained by the United States — that has the power behind the democratic trappings in Honduras. According to an editorial in *El Tiempo*, the liberal daily newspaper in San Pedro Sula, Honduras has a "two-headed government, of which the military head is the more effective."[9] Both leading parties, the Liberal and the National parties, are right-wing and have close links to the military. The seven-member military council known as the "Iron Circle," chose as the Commander-in-Chief Colonel Gustavo Alvarez. This decision, reached soon after the 1982 elections, had the full support of President Suazo Cordova and the U.S. Embassy.

As the former head of the feared special police force, Alvarez organized raids against suspected sympathizers of both the Sandinistas and the Salvadoran guerillas. He is known for his role in the repression of banana workers and death squad operations against leftists. Alvarez considers all Salvadoran refugees in Honduras to be subversives. In a nationally televised address in July 1982, Alvarez expressed open admiration for Argentine methods of law and order and also declared open war on El Salvador's guerillas. Referring to the situation in El Salvador, Alvarez said it is "not a war with a physical frontier, but a war in which the frontier is our liberty, our democracy, our Christian faith, and our social harmony."[10] Alvarez has said that his country "would be in agreement with U.S. intervention in Central America because we now confront an armed aggression from the Soviet Union via Cuba."[11] Interviewed by Joseph Collins of the Institute for Food and Development Policy, Alvarez said his favorite reading was *Geopolitica* by Augusto Pinochet of Chile. He also recalled that while training at Fort Bragg, he especially enjoyed watching ABC's *Wide World of Sports*.

Although revolutionary opposition is building in Honduras, it has been reformist peasant and workers unions that constitute the main opposition. Allied with the union movement, the Honduran Christian Democratic Party is among the most radical on the continent. Another important part of the opposition is the People's Revolutionary Union (URP), which has split from the Communist Party to form a wide-based, leftist popular movement. Two armed opposition organizations also operate in Honduras: the Popular Liberation Movement (MPL) or *Cinchoneros* and the Popular Revolutionary Forces (FPR). In April 1982, the MPL machine-gunned the offices of the U.S. Embassy, the Agency for International Development, and the U.S. Information Services. The FPR has circulated a manifesto asserting that "imperialist intervention against Central America is on the march and has the total and unconditional support of the present government and armed forces of Honduras."[12]

In addition to the "Iron Circle" or military council of Honduras, there are several death squads which are responsible for a rising number of dead and mutilated bodies found along roadsides. One such death squad is the Movimiento Anti-Communista Hondureno (MACHO).

The United States has promoted Honduras as a base for counterrevolution against the Sandinistas in Nicaragua and the guerilla forces in El Salvador and Guatemala — countries all sharing a border with Honduras. Between 1971 and 1980, the United States trained 2,259 Honduran military personnel; and from 1976 to 1980, nearly 100 Honduran officers attended the Commander and General Staff courses at the U.S. Army School of the Americas in the Panama Canal Zone.[13] The shift toward U.S. direct military involvement became evident in 1981 when Green Berets dressed in camouflage were seen patrolling the Honduran border with El Salvador.[14] In March 1982, approximately 100 U.S. military personnel were stationed in the country. They were "training the Honduran military in such technical areas as helicopter maintenance, air base security, patrol boat maintenance, and communications."[15]

"This dump is the center of the world now," U.S. Army Captain Michael Sheehan told *New York Times* reporter Raymond Bonner in August 1981. President Reagan has doubled the military aid to Honduras in 1981 and increased the 1983 budget by another $5 million. Former Ambassador to El Salvador Robert White, in a July 1982 article in the *New York Times Magazine*, wrote: "The Reagan fixation with military solutions to political, economic and social problems is being felt in Honduras. . . . [which] today is alive with U.S. military uniforms: Green Berets advising on counterinsurgency at the Salvadoran border; Air Force officials flying obscure missions in U.S. helicopters on loan to Honduras; Spanish-speaking Army personnel 'inspecting' the border with Nicaragua. Honduran troops have even begun fighting the guerillas in El Salvador."[16]

Hondurans have prided themselves on their tranquility and the lack of bloodshed in their country, but these traditions are threatened by the increase of militarization due in part to pressure from the United States. Washington regards Honduras as its strongest ally in what it calls the Iron Triangle — El Salvador, Guatemala, and Honduras. A Western diplomat, however, told the *New York Times*: "This place is too vulnerable and disorganized to play the role it is being assigned in Washington. You're pushing Honduras into the line of fire. You can't destabilize Nicaragua any more from here without also destabilizing Honduras."[17]

ECONOMY

The Honduran economy is in ruins. "Only God can save us," lamented the president of the national business organization COHEP. Imports are up, while exports are down. Inflation and unemployment are rising rapidly, while foreign exchange revenues continue to drain from the Treasury. The Gross Domestic Product (GDP) is at a standstill, capital is fleeing the country, and the international debt is skyrocketing. In the late 1970s, the GDP was progressing at 7-8% annually, but in 1981 the national economy dropped 0.4%.

"Produce more, export more, consume less, and spend less" were the orders from the Liberal Party government of Roberto Suazo Cordova. Spending less and consuming less is the only choice for most Hondurans who face a 64% combined unemployment and under-employment rate.[18] In 1981, with its debt rising and reserves dwindling, Honduras accepted an Emergency Economic Plan by the International Monetary Fund (IMF). The IMF's austerity program for Honduras required the government to decrease imports, increase exports, keep capital in the country, and stimulate production of basic grains. The IMF promised that this program would reduce inflation and keep the currency stable, while fattening the public coffers and attracting foreign loan money.

After a year of these austerity measures, the economy remained stagnant with little hope for improvement. Instead of halting the economic downturn, the IMF measures heightened political and social tension. The government fired 3,000 public employees under the austerity program in early 1981, and has been unable to stop the growing militancy of its own workers. While workers and *campesinos* in Honduras say they are the primary victims of the IMF programs, business people have also criticized the IMF emergency steps. A ten percent import tax has terminated any lingering hopes of a beneficial common market trade between Honduras and the other Central American nations that reacted with their own tariffs on Honduran goods. Though it collects a bit more from import taxes, Honduras is now paying more for the imports it needs to operate its industries.

Honduras is also paying a high food import bill to supply the staple food it isn't producing on its own land. Inflation in the United States translates directly into the high import bill for Honduras which receives 37% of its imports from the U.S. A hefty 60% of Honduran imports are capital goods, raw materials, and intermediate goods — items that Honduras needs to maintain its own industrial and agricultural production.

Further weakening the small capital base in Honduras, capital is fleeing at a quickening ·pace. It's estimated that between $500-$600 million in capital has quietly left Honduras from 1979 through 1981.[19] Private investment tumbled 14% in 1981. Little money is available for local credit, slowing down local business and forcing the business community to turn to U.S. private banks for investment capital. Private banks are looking warily at Honduras, however, after the bankruptcy of the country's second largest bank which owes $24 million in unsecured loans to foreign creditors. More bad news is the rate of inflation in Honduras, which is over 52%. Workers all over the country are consequently demanding cost-of-living raises, but even if the government was inclined to grant the raises, it would be hard pressed to do so. The budget deficit is expected to exceed $200 million at the end of 1982. As of March 1982, Honduras' international reserves had fallen to a negative $18 million.[20]

Since 1979, the public sector has been increasing its investment, which is 30% of the GDP. Public works projects include a new port at La Castilla, expansion of the country's telecommunications network, and the El Cajon hydroelectric plant. Although the government has increased public spending, it hasn't raised income to offset the increase. Business taxes remain low.[21]

The traditional political economy in Honduras is conservative, pro-business, and pro-foreign investment. The military and business elite represented by both the National and Liberal parties is unlikely to change this short-sighted orientation.

Agriculture

Agriculture is the mainstay of the Honduran economy, but most Hondurans don't have enough to eat. Life expectancy and malnutrition are the worst in the region — in some areas as many as nine out of ten children are malnourished. Nowhere else in Central America is the lack of proper nourishment so noticeable as in the rural areas of Honduras. Children stand outside dirt homes with bloated stomachs, and the *campesinos* stare lifelessly as travelers pass through their towns. Agriculture employs 60% of the population and accounts for 27% of the nation's GDP. In 1981, agricultural production declined 1.6% with no improvement expected in coming years.[22] Leading export crops are coffee, bananas, meat, and lumber, which accounted for 63% of the nation's exports in 1980.[23] Agriculture is geared toward the U.S. market which buys 60% of its agricultural products. In 1980, Honduras imported $51 million in food from the United States, up 61% from 1979. That same year its exports to the United States only increased three percent. The U.S. sells wheat and wheat flour, corn, grease and tallow, vegetable waxes and products, soybean cake and meal, and vegetables to Honduras.[24]

In 1981, the U.S. Embassy in Tegucigalpa wrote: "Investment has been slack in the basic grains sector for several years due to better incentives for export crops, such as prices and credit. . . ."[25] In its drive for increased export earnings, the government has encouraged farmers to produce more for the foreign market rather than to meet the needs of its own citizens.

Asked what the major U.S. firms in Honduras were, the commercial attache in the U.S. Embassy in Tegucigalpa said: "There are only two to speak of: United Fruit and Standard. They have their hands into just about everything in this country."[26] There are other U.S. corporations in Honduras, but it is hard to exaggerate the power of these two corporations over the country. Everything else is small potatoes when compared with the size, diversity, and muscle of United Fruit (United Brands) and Standard Fruit (Castle & Cooke). No longer just banana companies, they have diversified into pineapples, African palm, cattle, and vegetables for the winter market in the United States.

United Brands

In the 1920s, United Fruit obtained generous franchises in the Tela and Trujillo regions of the Atlantic coast. United Fruit made an agreement with the government to build a railroad from the north coast to the capital in exchange for land and tax exemptions. For each kilometer of railroad built, the companies would receive 550 to 1,100 acres. The mileage laid, however, was little more than what was strictly necessary for the operation of the banana industry, so that it ran through the coastal agricultural lands and never reached the capital of Tegucigalpa.[27]

An example of the company's attitude about doing business in Honduras is a letter written in 1920 by United Fruit's H.V. Rolston to the company's lawyer in Honduras. He instructed the lawyer to:

> "obtain rigid contracts of such a nature that no one can compete against us, not even in the distant future, so that any enterprise that could establish and develop itself must be under our control and must adapt itself to our established principles. . . . [T]he wind must blow only on our sails and the water must only wet our keel . . . . We must obtain concessions, privileges, franchises, repeal of custom duties, freedom from all public liens, burdens, and all those taxes and obligations which restrict our profits and those of our associates. We must erect a privileged situation in order to impose our commercial philosophy and our economic defense."[28]

The power of *El Pulpo* (the octopus) was challenged for the first time when in 1954 thousands of banana workers won a 69-day strike. Not only did they win this first agricultural strike in Honduran history, but they won official recognition by the state that workers had a formal right to organize. The 1954 strike set the stage for the creation of other peasant and worker unions. The companies reacted in several ways. By 1959, 20,000 banana plantation workers had lost their jobs.[29] Because of mechanization, the companies were able to increase production while decreasing the number of workers. Between 1950-1954, the banana productivity per worker in Honduras was 552 boxes, and twenty years later it was 2,131 boxes per worker.[30] In addition, United Fruit's strategy included infiltration of the union by members associated with the Inter-American Regional Organization of Labor (ORIT) and the American Institute for Free Labor Development (AIFLD), after the founding of AIFLD in 1962. Both organizations are associated with the AFL-CIO in the United States. AIFLD trains union members in programs that stress anti-communism and organizing limited to wage demands.

A United Fruit employee recalled: "After the strike, the AFL-CIO, the U.S. Embassy, and ORIT fell on us like a plague, offering us scholarships to 'study in Puerto Rico,' and getting us all kinds of favors from our employers .... The U.S. consuls overwhelmed us with visas.... the greatest interest in these scholarship students is to be found on the north coast, land of the Banana Companies.... Not only do these companies grant their permission for these workers to spend months on leave, but they are favored with the choicest jobs and are placed, very 'democratically' as union leaders, when they return...."[31]

In 1979, progressive workers won back leadership of the union on United Brands' banana plantations and led the first major labor initiative since the 1954 strike. In late 1980, when the union directed a strike in protest of the company's use of harmful pesticides, union leaders received death threats and were fired from their jobs. In this repressive atmosphere, the ORIT-affiliated Confederation of Honduran Workers took over in 1981, making it once again a company union.[32]

Castle & Cooke

In Honduras, Castle & Cooke has as many divisions and subsidiaries as most local firms have employees. The company's Dole bananas corner 40% of the U.S. market and approximately 25% of Dole bananas come from Honduras. Each year, its subsidiary Standard Fruit and Steamship transports 20 million forty-pound boxes of bananas from Honduras.[33]

In 1899, the Vacarro brothers came to Honduras from New Orleans to begin their banana operation by buying up local producers and by building railroads and other infrastructure projects around La Ceiba. The Vacarro brothers established Banco Atlantida as well as factories to produce beer, alcohol, and shoes. In 1926, their operation became the Standard Fruit and Steamship Company. Standard Fruit is lord and master over the La Ceiba area of north-eastern Honduras, which until fifteen years ago wasn't connected by good roads to the country's capital of Tegucigalpa. The company has enjoyed a reputation slightly better than its notorious competitor, United Fruit, but Standard's role in repressing a workers' cooperative in Las Isletas has undermined any good public relations it had previously managed to create in Honduras.

After Hurricane Fifi destroyed 5,000 acres of Standard Fruit land in 1975, the company demanded several million dollars from the government to rebuild the plantation. When the government refused, Standard fired over 700 workers who later led the occupation of the plantation and began the Las Isletas cooperative.

In just two years, the cooperative brought production up to levels equalling Standard Fruit in both quality and quantity. One cooperative member explained: "We wanted to show the multinational companies and the entire world that we didn't need the companies to cultivate bananas. And that's what we've done."[34] Standard Fruit saw Las Isletas cooperative as a threat not only because it showed workers that they themselves could produce bananas without the company, but also because Las Isletas cooperative had begun to market its bananas through the state agency COHBANA rather than through Standard Fruit.

In February 1977, the military arrived at Las Isletas in Standard Fruit's railroad cars. They forced new elections and seized the co-op's officers who were held illegally in jail without bail for 18 months. A few weeks after the military intervention, the U.S. ambassador visited the remote cooperative and praised the members' "rejection of totalitarianism."[35] Shortly thereafter, the military arrested over 200 union members and leaders on Standard Fruit's plantations near Las Isletas.

After the Las Isletas incident, the daily newspaper *El Tiempo* published evidence that Standard Fruit had made "special payments" to Colonel Gustavo Alvarez (in 1982 named Commander-in-Chief), the leader of the military battalion which had intervened at the cooperative and union. In a 1976 U.S. Securities Exchange Commission investigation, Castle & Cooke admitted that between 1971 and 1975, the company made $1.2 million in payments to government officials in foreign countries "for security purposes." The company added that it had made private payments specifically to police for protection in emergency situations such as occurred "during an unruly labor strike."

Against tremendous odds, the progressives of Las Isletas cooperative regained control in 1979, but the government proceeded to siphon the profits out of the cooperative. In 1981, the military again invaded Las Isletas, bringing a violent and final end to the cooperative. *Latin America Regional Report* noted that the history of Las Isletas "illustrates the virtual impossibility of attempts at minor agrarian reforms without radical changes in the government and the military."[36]

Industry

Next to Belize, Honduras has the least industrial production of any Central American nation. Manufacturing accounts for 15% of the GDP and is concentrated in textiles, food processing, pharmaceuticals, and beauty aids. The purpose of the Central American Common Market (CACM), founded in the early 1960s, was to equalize development and investment among its member nations. But from the start the CACM brought millions of dollars into Central America with little regard for regional balance of development. Honduras did gain some industry, but most was controlled by U.S. companies, and its level of industrial development was nowhere near that of Guatemala or El Salvador. Honduras entered the 1970s facing a $20 million deficit to the CACM.[37]

Because the Industrial Incentive Law in Honduras offers tax exemptions and duty-free importation of materials and equipment to labor-intensive export industries, the textile assembly industry is booming in San Pedro Sula and Puerto Cortes. A dozen U.S. corporations have taken advantage of the Cortes Free Zone where Honduran women assemble bras, men's underwear, boots, and baseballs for export. The zone gives the U.S. corporations a tax free license to import materials for assembly that are then exported back to the United States. U.S. corporations also find the low wage scale and the unorganized work force good reasons for doing business in Honduras.

Representing a new trend in foreign investment in Central America, Inrecorp is a New Orleans export finance and sales group. Inrecorp says that it is proving that U.S. firms eager to do business in the region can easily establish joint venture operations that are profitable for both the United States and Central American business partners. Inrecorp's investments in Honduras include Mariscos del Caribe (MARCASA) which in its first year accounted for 26% of Honduran seafood exports, Casa Comercial Munson which distributes Mack trucks, and Compania de Cafe Creole. Inrecorp's Executive Vice-President Norma Castillo said: "Our ability to coordinate the activities of the investment and sales arm of the Group has been a critical factor in our growth and profitability. A coffee producer is not simply a supplier for Compania de Cafe. He is also a customer for the export sale of fertilizer and insecticides as well as a Mack truck to move his coffee — all with financing arranged by the export sales section."[38] Inrecorp has three divisions: Inrecorp Ltd., a real estate firm; Inrecorp Financial, which arranges export financing with emphasis on Central and South America as well as syndicating loans to Latin American governments and banks; and Nordford, the import-export division representing both U.S. manufacturers and Latin American buyers. Inrecorp Group has offices or representatives in Guatemala, Honduras, Nicaragua, and El Salvador.

For the last few years, the Honduran government and Texaco, which owns the country's only refinery, have been battling over the available supply and price of petroleum and petroleum products in Honduras. In September 1981, the company stopped refining operations, claiming that government price controls made business "uneconomical." Texaco's refinery at Puerto Cortes contains the nation's only facilities for refining crude oil and for storing petroleum. Six times during 1981, the closures of Texaco's refinery caused severe fuel shortages in Honduras, at times paralyzing up to 95% of urban transport.

Since arriving in Honduras 15 years ago, Texaco has enjoyed the benefits of the Law of Exemption for new industry. The law exempted the company from taxes for only the first five years of its presence in the country, but Texaco has managed to extend the exemption into the present. The Honduran government has lost an estimated $1.5 billion in the last ten years from Texaco's tax exemptions.[39] Attempting to end Texaco's monopoly control over oil refining in Honduras, the government has offered Texaco $11 million for the refinery, but Texaco refused and made a counter offer of $37 million. Mexico and Venezuela have proposed that they sell Honduras 6,000 barrels of oil daily at a 30% discount to cut down on its fuel bill. But Texaco refused to refine the Mexican oil, claiming that the crude oil is too heavy. Symbolizing Yankee imperialism in Honduras, Texaco has been the target of several bombings in 1981 and 1982.

Like the agricultural sector, most Honduran industries are in the hands of U.S. firms. At first the banana companies resisted the move toward industrialization in Honduras, fearing a new economic sector would threaten their traditional power base. But the companies later decided to take advantage of the regional market, and both are now major industrial companies in Honduras. Castle & Cooke manufactures soap, plastic products, cans, cardboard boxes, wooden containers, and cement. It also produces and bottles soft drinks and beer and has interests in a variety of food processing operations. United Brands has similar interests in food processing companies and several manufacturing firms. Although no longer a Banana Republic, Honduras is still dominated by the two companies that shaped its history.

References for Introductory Statistics

Business America , March 8, 1982; *Business Latin America*, July 7, 1982; Inter-American Development Bank, *Economic and Social Progress in Latin America 1980-81*; *Latin America Regional Report*; United Nations, *Monthly Bulletin of Statistics*, April 1982; U.S. Department of Commerce, *Overseas Business Reports — Market Profiles for Latin America*, May 1981.

REFERENCE NOTES

1. *Central America Report*, July 23, 1982, p. 220.
2. Steve Volk, "Honduras: On the Border of War," *NACLA*, November-December 1981, p. 3.
3. *NACLA*, November-December 1981, p. 7.
4. James Morris and Marta Sanchez Soler, "Factores de Poder en la Evolución del Campesino Hondureño," *Estudios Sociales Centroamericanos*, January-April, 1977.
5. *New York Times*, November 30, 1975.
6. *Mesoamerica*, June 1982.
7. *LARR*, April 11, 1975.
8. *Mesoamerica*, March 1982, p. 10.
9. *Ibid.*
10. *LARR*, July 23, 1982, p. 8.
11. *Barricada*, April 2, 1982.
12. *Central America Report*, April 30, 1982, p. 126.
13. Michael T. Klare and Cynthia Arnson, *Supplying Repression: U.S. Support for Authoritarian Regimes Abroad*, (Washington: Institute for Policy Studies, 1981).
14. Raymond Bonner, *New York Times*, August 9, 1981.
15. Cynthia Arnson, "Background Information on Honduras and El Salvador," Institute for Policy Studies, 1981, p. 1.
16. Robert White, "Central America: The Problem That Won't Go Away," *New York Times Magazine*, July 18, 1982, pp. 21-28.
17. Alan Riding, "United States is Looking to Honduras to Hold the Line," *New York Times*, April 20, 1982.
18. "Business Outlook: Honduras," *Business Latin America*, June 16, 1982, p. 188.
19. "Honduras," *Foreign Economic Trends*, August 1981.
20. *Business Latin America*, June 16, 1982.
21. *Ibid.*
22. *Ibid.*
23. *Foreign Economic Trends*, August 1981, p. 9.
24. "U.S. Farm Exports Gain in Central America," *Foreign Agriculture*, October 1981, p. 21.
25. *Foreign Economic Trends*, August 1981.
26. Interview by Tom Barry, April 1982.
27. *NACLA*, November-December 1981, p. 4.
28. Written in 1920 and first published in 1949. Published in its entirety in *Cuadernos Americanos*, Mexico, March 1954.
29. *Mesoamerica*, June 1982.
30. Daniel Slutzky and Esther Alonso, *Empresas Transnacionales y Agricultura: El Caso del Enclave Bananero en Honduras*, (Tegucigalpa: Editorial Universitaria, 1982), p. 33.
31. Alberto Ruiz, "Agentes Patronales en el Movimiento Obrero Hondureño," *Octubre* (Tegucigalpa), November 2, 1957, p. 2.
32. "Banana Companies Oust the Left," *LARR*, October 23, 1981, p. 7.
33. Joseph Collins, "Trouble in Honduras," *Food Monitor*, September-October 1979, p. 11.
34. *Ibid.*
35. *Ibid.*
36. "The Ruin of Las Isletas," *LARR*, February 13, 1981.
37. *Mesoamerica*, June 1982.
38. *International*, New Orleans, November 2, 1982, p. 48.
39. *Mesoamerica*, March 1982.

UNITED STATES BUSINESS IN HONDURAS*

Abbott Laboratories
   Abbott Laboratorios; *pharmaceutical manufacturing*

ACF Industries
   Polymer; *plastic and resin manufacturing*

Agencia Guilbert; *importer and agency representative*

Agencia Rhinehart; *U.S. and foreign firm representative*

Agrodinámica Holding Company
   Industria Ganadera de Honduras
   Oriente Industrial
   Ranchos de Choluteca
   Repastadora de Oriente

Air Florida; *air transportation*

Airlift International; *air cargo carrier*

Alberti International
   Caribbean Products; *shrimp processing*
   Empacadora Alus; *beef processing and slaughterhouse*
   Empacadora Cortes; *food processing*
   Rancho Lorenzo, *meat processing*

Alberto Culver
   Alberto Culver Centroamericana; *cosmetic and hair preparation manufacturing and distribution*

Alimentos Marinos Hondureños; *shrimp and lobster packing plant*

Allied Corporation
   Texgas Gases Nacionales; *water heaters*

Amapala Marine; *yacht building*

AMAX
   Rosario Resources; *silver, lead and zinc mining*

Amed International
   Amedicor; *medical supplies*

American Biltrate Rubber Company
   Compañía Hulera Sula; *rubber product manufacturing*

American Express; *credit card services*

American Home Products
   Fort Dodge Laboratories; *veterinary medicine*

American International Group
   American International Underwriters; *insurance*
   Hanover Insurance; *insurance*

Anthony's Key; *resort*

Araca Petroleum; *oil exploration*

Arthur Young & Company; *accounting*

Baby Togs
   Novelty Honduras; *children's clothes manufacturing*

BankAmerica
   Almacenes de Deposito; *banking*
   Bank of America; *five branches*
   Credomatic de Honduras; *Master Charge credit card services*

Bayman Club; *resort*

Beatrice Foods
   Chitos de Honduras; *food processing*

Bell Western
   Compañía Minera Bell Western de Honduras

Bemis
   Compañía de Sacos Centroamericana; *burlap and cotton sack manufacturing*
   Fábrica Textile Bemis Handal; *cotton thread and fabric manufacturing*
   Bemis Bijao de Honduras; *paper bag manufacturing and wholesale*

Boise Cascade; *lumber products*

Bufete Gutierrez Falla

Calmaquip, Ingenieros de Honduras; *commission agents for hotel and hospital equipment*

Camiones y Equipos de Sula

Cargill
   Alimentos Concentrados (ALCON); *animal feed processing*
   Centrocom; *poultry production*
   Fanalco; *animal feed manufacturing*

Caribbean Corporation; *boat building*

Caribbean Lumber Company
   Industria Madera del Norte; *wood products*
   Industria Maderera del Occidente; *lumber mill*

Casa Comercial Mathews; *construction machinery*

Casa Comercial Munson; *Mack truck distribution*

*An indented item is a subsidiary, affiliate, or branch of the corporation immediately above it.

Castle & Cooke
  Aceros Industriales
  Banco del Comercio
  Cervecería Hondureña; *beer and soft
    drinks; four branches*
  Cervecería Tegucigalpa
  Compañía Agrícola Industrial Ceibeña;
    vegetable oil processing; LAAD equity
  Compañía Bananera Antillana
  Dole Pineapple of Honduras
  Enlatadora del Campo
  Envases Industriales de Honduras;
    metal container manufacturing
  Fábrica de Manteca y Jabón Atlántida;
    oil, margarine and soap
  Frutera Hondureña
  Industria Aceitera Hondureña; *cotton
    seed oil processing*
  Manufacturera de Carton; *paper box
    manufacturing*
  Nacional Inmobiliaria
  Plásticos; *plastic material
    manufacturing*
  Semillas Mejoradas
  Servicios Agrícoias
  Servicios de Investigaciones Areas
  Standard Fruit; *fruit production*
  Standard Fruit and Steamship

Cat Ketch; *boat manufacturing*

Central American Cigar Company; *cigar
  manufacturing*

Cerritos de Honduras; *mining*

Chamco
  Chamco Construction; *road
    construction*

Champion International
  Danli Industrial; *paper products*
  Maya Lumber; *lumber mill*

Charles P. Evans; *sawmill*

Chase Manhattan
  Banco Atlántida; *banking; 38 branches*
  Inversiones Atlántida

Citicorp
  Banco de Honduras; *banking; five
    branches*

Clark Equipment
  Atlas Eléctrica; *refrigeration equipment
    and supplies*

Colgate Palmolive
  Colgate Palmolive Centroamérica;
    toothpaste and soap manufacturing
  Colgate Palmolive West Indies; *dentifrice
    and soap distribution*

Construction Aggregates; *construction*

CPC International
  Alimentos de Istmo; *corn starch and
    vegetable oil processing*

Crescent Construction; *construction*

Crescent Corset; *textile manufacturing*

Crown Cork & Seal
  Crown Cork Centroamericana; *cork
    manufacturing*

Dibrell Brothers
  Exportadora de Tabaco de Honduras;
    tobacco production

Diners Club
  Diners Club de Honduras; *credit card
    services*

Distribuidora Industrial; *electrical
    component distribution*

Eaton
  Cutler-Hammer; *electrical control
    panel and box manufacturing*

El Paso
  El Paso Mining & Exploitation; *mining*

Electronicos Diversificados Hondureños;
    electronic parts manufacturing

Exxon
  Esso Standard Oil
  Essochem de Centroamérica; *chemical
    product marketing*

Fábrica Industrial de Alimentos de
    Honduras; *condiment processing*

Fábrica de Resortes "El Tecolote"; *auto
    and truck spring manufacturing*

First Boston
  Compañía de Credito; *banking*

Foremost-McKesson
  Famosa; *ice cream and condensed milk
    production*

H.B. Fuller
  Adhesivos Industriales
  Aerosoles de Centroamérica
  Comercial Kioskos de Pintura
  Comercial Punto de Viniles
  Kativo Comercial
  Kativo de Honduras; *paint and varnish
    manufacturing and wholesale*
  Kioskos de Pinturas
  Pinturas Surekote
  Punto de Viniles

General Mills
  Aqua Finca de Camarones

General Telephone & Electronics (GTE)
  GTE Sylvania; *electric houseware
    manufacturing*

Granja Mareana; *hog farm*

Gulf+Western Oil
  Petroleos de Atlántida; *petroleum
    exploration*

Hacienda Corbano

Halliburton
  Brown & Root; *contracting*

Harold McKay; *lumber and timber consultant*

Harrison & Associates; *gold and silver mining*

Hemphill Schools; *school*

Hershey Foods
  Hummingbird-Hershey; *cocoa*

Holiday Inn

Hon-Bra; *bra manufacturing*

Honduras Oil & Water Drilling Industry (HOWDI); *oil and water drilling and mineral exploration*

Hotel Honduras Maya

Hybur; *shrimp and lobster packing for export*

IBM World Trade Corporation
  IBM de Honduras; *business equipment distribution*

Imesa; *liquor import and export*

Impex; *merchandise import and export*

Imported Brands; *liquor import and export*

Industrial Electric Service; *electrical appliance sales and service*

INRECORP Group
  Compañía de Café Creole
  Mariscos del Caribe (MARCASA); *seafood*

International Executive Service; *business consultants*

International Wood Products; *wood components; LAAD equity*

The Interpublic Group of Companies
  McCann-Erickson Centroamericana; *advertising agency*

Kem Manufacturing
  Kem Centroamericana; *chemical product manufacturing and sales*

Leche y Derivados (LEYDE); *food processing; LAAD equity*

Líneas Aéreas Nacionales; *LAAD equity*

Lloyd
  Lloyd Petroleum; *oil exploration*

Louisiana Land & Exploration
  LLE Petroleum; *mining*

The Lovable Company
  Lovable de Honduras; *women's clothes manufacturing*

Maderera Subirana; *sawmill*

Manufacturas Electrónicas (MANEHSA); *electrical repairs*

Manufacturera Cortez; *men's underwear manufacturing*

Mejores Alimentos de Honduras; *food processing; LAAD equity*

Mendieta, Fortin, Lagos y Asociados

Meridian Engineering; *construction*

Merriam & Merriam

MILISI; *shoe import and export*

Milson Magee Lumber; *logging and sawmill operations*

Mineral International
  Mayan Minerals; *mining*

Mobil
  Mobil Exploration Honduras; *petroleum exploration*
  Mobil Oil; *petroleum*

Mohawk Industries
  Compañía Cabos Caribe; *broomsticks*

National Car Rental Systems; *auto renting*

Nello L. Teer; *contracting*

Norton Simon
  Max Factor & Company; *cosmetic distribution*

Occidental Petroleum
  Occidental de Honduras; *oil exploration*

Olivia Tobacco Company de Honduras

Palmeto Bay Resort

Pan American Life Insurance
  Compañía de Seguros Panamerican; *insurance*

Pan American World Airways; *air transportation*

Parker-Hannifin; *auto part manufacturing*

Parker Tobacco

Paul Laeton; *flavoring and fragrance exporting*

Peat, Marwick, Mitchell & Company; *accounting and auditing*

Pesquería del Caribe; *fish processing*

Phelps Dodge
  Electroconductores de Honduras (ECOHSA); *electrical conductor manufacturing*

Pieltro; *caiman and crocodile farm*

Plantas del Caribe; *plant production and exporting*

Plantas Lindas

Plata; *industrial equipment representative*

POLCO; *flavoring and fragrance exporting*

Port Royal; *marine services and yacht building*

Port Royal Farms; *retirement and vacation community*

Price Waterhouse & Company; *accounting and auditing*

Procesadora de Mariscos y Peces de Honduras (PROMAHO); *fish*

Productos Consolidados; *plaster, paint, and chalk manufacturing and distribution*

Productos Industriales de Madera; *lumber mill*

Reef House; *resort*

Remington Business Systems
Máquinas de Escribir Remington; *typewriters*

REPCO; *wood production*

Rey Café; *coffee production*

R.J. Reynolds (Del Monte)
Banana Development Corporation of Costa Rica (BANDECO); *farm management*
Conservas del Campo; *food processing*

RI-DO; *importing and exporting*

Roatan Developments
Roatan Lodge; *tourist resort*

Robinson Lumber & Export; *lumber*

Rodin Warehouse & Ramirez Cold Storage
Empacadora del Norte; *food processing*

Sale City; *clothes manufacturing*

Sanco, S.; *industrial goods import and export*

SCM
Glidden de Honduras

Sea Farms; *technical assistance in shrimp cultivation*

Seahawk Oil International; *oil exploration*

Sears Roebuck & Company
Sears Roebuck; *department store*

Seatrain Lines; *shipping*

Selmont Oil
Petroleos de Honduras; *petroleum exploration*

Shell Oil; *oil exploration and distribution*

Shrimp Culture; *shrimp farm*

Siemens; *electrical equipment*

The Signal Companies
Signal Exploration; *oil exploration*
Signal Oil & Gas; *oil exploration*

Singer Manufacturing Company of New Jersey
Singer Commercial Sula; *electrical appliance distribution*

Spyglass Hill; *resort*

Standard Oil of California
Compañía Petrolera Chevron; *oil products*

The Stanley Works
Stanley Centroamericana; *machete manufacturing*

Star Commercial Refrigeration; *refrigeration equipment distribution*

Sterling Drug
Sterling Products International; *pharmaceutical product manufacturing*

Stokely-Van Camp; *pineapple production*

Sunrise Fashions
Jozmin; *clothing*

Tabor International

Terminales de Cortes; *custom brokerage and freight transport*

TESTCO; *swimming pool and purification system distribution*

Texaco
Estación del Servicio Texaco
Refinería Texaco de Honduras; *petroleum refining*
Texaco Caribbean; *service station*

Textiles Red Point de Honduras

Textiles Rio Lindo; *cotton cloth manufacturing; ADELA equity*

Theonett & Company
Theonett Centroamericana; *soft drink concentrate manufacturing*

Timex
Relojes Timex; *watch distribution*

Transamerica
Budget Rent-A-Car; *auto renting*

Transcarga; *freight transport*

Transway International
Coordinated Caribbean Transport (CCT); *ocean transport*
Tropical Gas (TROPIGAS); *gas and equipment distribution*

Union Oil
  Union Oil Company de Honduras;
    oil drilling and exploration

United Brands
  Caribbean Enterprises
  Compañía Agrícola de Rio Tinto; *food
    production*
  Empresa Hondureña de Vapores
  Fábrica de Aceites de Palma
  Fábrica de Cajas de Carton
  Frigorífica Hondureña
  Numar de Honduras; *vegetable oil
    processing*
  Polymer; *rubber and plastics*
  Productos Acuáticos Terrestres
    (PATSA)
  Servicio de Investigación Agrícola
    Tropical (SIATSA)
  Tela Railroad; *fruit production, cattle
    production and slaughter*
  TRT Telecommunications
  Unimar; *palm oil*

United Marketing

United States Tobacco
  Tabacos de Honduras; *tobacco products
    and smokers accessories*

United Technologies
  Compañía Otis Elevator; *elevator sales*

Villa Utila; *restaurant*

Viveros Industriales

Warnaco
  Warner's de Honduras; *clothes
    manufacturing*

Webster International

Welsh Energía y Petroleos

William Itaimes; *sawmill*

Woodscraft

Worth de Honduras;
  baseball manufacturing

Xerox
  Xerox de Honduras; *business machine
    distribution and services*

YU-HWA; *clothes manufacturing*

REFERENCES

Directory of American Firms Operating in Foreign Countries, 1979; *Directory of Corporate Affiliations*, 1982; Dun & Bradstreet, "Principal International Businesses," 1982; *Export/Import Markets*, 1982; *Foreign Index to the Directory of Corporate Affiliations*, 1981; *Million Dollar Directory*, 1982; *Moody's*, 1981; *Rand McNally International Bankers Directory*, 1982; 10-K Reports, 1981; *World Directory of Multinational Enterprises*, 1980.

ADELA, Annual Report, 1981; *Agribusiness in the Americas*, 1980; BankAmerica, "Bank of America Worldwide Facilities," May 1981; Donald Castillo Rivas, *Acumulacion de Capital y Empresas Transnacionales en Centroamerica*, 1980; Guia de Information Para Centroamerica, Panama, Miami y San Andres Isla, 1981-1982; Roger Isaula, *Las Transnacionales y el Derecho*, 1981; Latin American Agribusiness Development Corporation (LAAD), Annual Reports, 1976-1981; *Mergers & Acquisitions*, Spring 1982; Overseas Private Investment Corporation (OPIC), Annual Reports, 1978-1981; Unidad de Promocion, Zona Libre de Puerto Cortes, "Empresas que Operan Bajo el Regimen de Zona Libre," 1982; United States Embassy in Honduras, "American Firms, Subsidiaries, and Affiliates," 1982; United States Embassy in Honduras, "U.S. Businessmen List," 1981.

EL SALVADOR

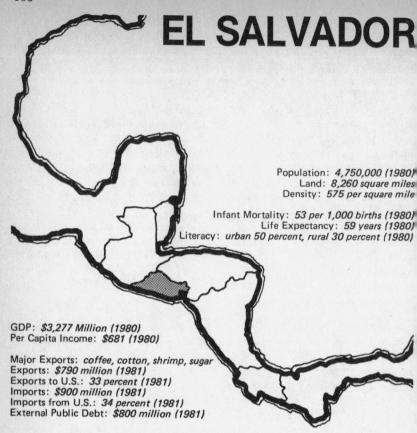

Population: *4,750,000 (1980)*
Land: *8,260 square miles*
Density: *575 per square mile*

Infant Mortality: *53 per 1,000 births (1980)*
Life Expectancy: *59 years (1980)*
Literacy: *urban 50 percent, rural 30 percent (1980)*

GDP: *$3,277 Million (1980)*
Per Capita Income: *$681 (1980)*

Major Exports: *coffee, cotton, shrimp, sugar*
Exports: *$790 million (1981)*
Exports to U.S.: *33 percent (1981)*
Imports: *$900 million (1981)*
Imports from U.S.: *34 percent (1981)*
External Public Debt: *$800 million (1981)*

The Reagan Administration has vowed to draw the line in El Salvador against leftist advances in Central America. The administration claims the "decisive battle for the Western Hemisphere" is being fought in this tiny country. But the flood of U.S. military and economic aid to the government of El Salvador has yet to stop the opposition forces, and war continues to ravage the country.

Outside powers have interfered in El Salvador for the last four centuries. Pedro de Alvarado and his conquistadors invaded the area in 1524, but it took the Spanish over 20 years to crush the Indian resistance. Historians estimate that the Indian population declined 80% in the first century after the conquest. In 1821, El Salvador gained its independence from Spain after three centuries of colonial rule. The short-lived Federal Republic of Central America encouraged the confiscation of Indian communal lands to increase the land available to the rising oligarchy. Indigo and cocoa were the first major export crops, but coffee became the leading crop by the mid-century. These three export crops linked El Salvador to European markets. Outside control increased in El Salvador with the amount of foreign investment and financing after the turn of the century. El Salvador didn't have bananas, but its gold and silver did appeal to foreign investors. British and U.S. capital developed the nation's first roads, electricity plants, and communications network to facilitate the exportation of minerals and coffee.

U.S. adventurer Minor Keith built railroads in Costa Rica, Guatemala, and El Salvador. By 1929, the Salvadoran and Guatemalan lines were joined, enabling Salvadoran coffee to reach the U.S. east coast ten days faster. In a self-serving financial deal, Keith negotiated long-term loans in 1923 between American banking interests and El Salvador amounting to $16.5 million. The loans paid off the debts of Keith and the British railway companies in El Salvador and funded several public works projects in San Salvador. The terms of the 1923 loan provided that in case of default the U.S. bankers and the State Department would manage the country's international trade through a customs receivership.[1]

The presence of the U.S. military in the region backed the growing U.S. economic influence in El Salvador. The United States overtook Britain as the main foreign power in El Salvador, providing most of El Salvador's capital and also acting as arbitrator of regional disputes. An engineer from the United States served as arbitrator between El Salvador and Guatemala in a 1936 border dispute.

Coffee was the foundation of both the country's economy and the national oligarchy, often called the Fourteen Families. In 1931, historian David Browning wrote that, "Coffee was king . . . . It produced 95.5% of export earnings, paid the country's taxes, proportioned funds for central and local governments, financed the construction of roads, ports, and railroads, created permanent or seasonal employment for one part of the population and made the fortunes of a few."[2] The Life World Library in 1964 described the Salvadoran oligarchy as a mixture of old families and immigrants. "Their fortunes are based on coffee, cotton — and politics. . . By and large they are extremely progressive in business. The *Catorce Grande* also live the lives of men of wealth. They have lavish homes in town and imposing estates in the country. They work in fancy, air-conditioned offices and drive to work in flashy sports cars." Older families of the oligarchy — Regalado, Palomo, Escalon, Menendez — prided themselves on their direct Spanish ancestry. Also included as later members of the country's elite were the wealthy immigrant families of Hill, Parker, Sol, De Sola, and D'Aubuisson.[3]

The country's economy and history have reflected the state of the world coffee market. The Depression of 1929 in the United States caused the coffee market to drop to an all-time low. The oligarchy acquired more land during this period and reduced the subsistence-level wages of coffee workers. In 1932, Farabundo Marti, with *campesino* and labor organizations, mounted a widespread rebellion against the country's oligarchy and military. The Salvadoran military crushed the uprising and massacred 30,000 Salvadorans, or 4% of the population. The United States did not actively intervene during the conflict, but stationed war ships off the coast. Since the rebellion, the oligarchy has relied on the military to run the government. The military has usually controlled the presidency and ministries of defense, interior, and labor, while the oligarchy has kept tight hold on the country's economic policy.[4]

The dip in coffee prices in the 1930s also caused the oligarchy to diversify into cotton production. The expansion of the cotton plantations pushed more *campesinos* off their land and many into the cities. During the late 1940s coffee prices bounced back and export revenues quadrupled. The government increased taxes and channeled the money into infrastructure projects like a large hydroelectric plant on the Lempa River. The World Bank supplied $12.5 million in loan money for the dam and power plant, which was constructed by a North Carolina firm.[5] *Fortune* magazine said, "El Salvador must have more electric power; Rio Lempa would meet the need. The establishment of light industries and the expansion of old ones waited on it."[6] U.S. investor interest in El Salvador soon picked up, particularly in three areas: 1) processing of cotton, coffee, and vegetable oil, 2) consumer goods such as paints, drugs, and shoes, and 3) services like hotels and stores. Among the U.S. companies that came to El Salvador in the 1950s were: Genesco (shoes), Intercontinental Hotels, Toyo Spinning Company (textiles), P.V.O. Corporation (vegetable oils), ABC (television), Sears Roebuck and Company, Sterling Drugs, and Sherwin-Williams. U.S. investment in El Salvador skyrocketed with the opening of the Central American Common Market (CACM). El Salvador and Guatemala, the more industrialized Central American nations, attracted more U.S. capital than the less industrialized nations like Nicaragua and Honduras. Calculations by Marc Herold of the University of New Hampshire show that over half of all foreign investments in El Salvador during the 20th century were made in the 1960s.[7]

A new wave of political opposition in El Salvador began in the 1960s. The Christian Democratic Party (PDC) formed in 1962 with initial support from the professional and bourgeois sectors which were created by the new industrialization and the expansion of the country's economy. The Christian Democrats, as the only viable political opposition to the oligarchy, also gained support from some *campesino* and worker groups. Also emerging during this period were a number of *campesino* unions that protested the oligarchic control of land in El Salvador.

Between 1961 and 1975 the number of landless peasants increased from 11% to 40% of the rural population.[8] And while the manufacturing sector expanded 24% in the 1960s, manufacturing jobs only increased 6%. The conditions of landlessness, unemployment, poverty, and the increased population density persuaded many *campesinos* to emigrate to neighboring Honduras. By 1965, as many as 350,000 Salvadorans were living in the sparsely-populated country, and at least 30% of the banana workers in Honduras were Salvadoran.[9] At the same time, the drive of capitalist agriculture and ranching in Honduras was forcing that country's *campesinos* off their land. The Honduran economic and military elite blamed the Salvadorans for Honduran problems, and tensions increased between the neighboring countries. In 1969, Honduras started deporting Salvadorans. The uneven industrial development of El Salvador and Honduras also added to mounting tension since the promises of balanced regional development of the early CACM proposals had fallen flat and most industrial activity had located in El Salvador and Guatemala. By 1968, El Salvador contributed 23.8% of the regional manufacturing while Honduras contributed only 7.7%.[10] Honduras' trade deficit with El Salvador grew steadily, and the merchants in Honduras responded with a campaign to boycott Salvadoran goods. A typical piece of boycott propaganda stated: "Compatriot, join the boycott: do not consume products made in El Salvador. Here are some of them: Mirasol margarine, Adoc shoes, La Estrella fabric. . . . You know other Salvadoran products in addition to these, refrain from buying them."[11]

On July 14, 1969, war broke out between the two countries when the Salvadoran air force bombed Tegucigalpa, followed the next day by an invasion of the Salvadoran army and national guard. The war lasted less than a week, but it took 3,000 lives. It served both governments by uniting the populace around nationalistic slogans and obstructing the worker and peasant movements.

Before the war, the emigration of Salvadorans to Honduras was an escape valve for the building political pressure in El Salvador. With that release gone and more landless peasants back in the country, the friction increased between the oligarchy and the workers and peasants. Salvadorans created mass organizations of students, workers, women, *campesinos*, and church members to defend their rights and to stand up to the dictatorship. Although the hierarchy of the Catholic Church was an ally of the military and oligarchy, the priests and nuns working on the parish level helped create mass organizations. In reaction to the ecclesiastical activism, a death squad called the White Warriors Union circulated flyers with the slogan, "Be a Patriot, Kill a Priest!"[12] The mass movements strengthened steadily, and by the mid-1970s the government was responding regularly with violence. In 1975, students in Santa Ana occupied the local campus to protest the government's expenditure of $3.1 million to stage the Miss Universe pageant in El Salvador. When students in San Salvador held a march in solidarity with the Santa Ana students, the National Guard opened fire. Scores of students were wounded and killed, and 24 disappeared. Government and right-wing violence has since become an everyday occurrence in El Salvador. It was only with the assassination of Monsignor Oscar Romero and the deaths of the four American churchwomen that the daily terror of El Salvador started receiving international attention.

The army and death squads have murdered over 34,000 civilians in the past two and a half years, yet the leading causes of death in El Salvador are still malnutrition and painful gastrointestinal diseases caused by poor sanitation. Of the total deaths of natural causes in rural El Salvador, 47% are of children under age five who starve to death. In 1982, 80% of the U.S. economic aid to El Salvador went for government operations, infrastructure projects and aid to the private sector; only 20% went to the country's needy.[13]

POLITICS

The year of the Sandinista victory in Nicaragua was also the year that politics started heating up in El Salvador. In October 1979, a group of reform-minded junior officers ousted General Carlos Humberto Romero. The officers feared that the military government of El Salvador would face the same fate as the Somoza regime in Nicaragua if something wasn't done to gain popular support. The new junta government included three civilians and promised to initiate a series of reforms that would halt military repression and improve the nation's economy. The older, hard-line military officers permitted superficial changes, but maintained control of the actual power and decision-making in the government. Holding military power were Colonel Jose Garcia as Minister of Defense and junta member Colonel Jaime Abdul Gutierrez. Both Garcia and Gutierrez were former officials of ANTEL, the state telecommunications agency. One of the new civilian junta members, Mario Antonio Andino, had been associated with a subsidiary of Phelps Dodge, which was a major supplier of cable wire to ANTEL.[14] Civilian junta member Guillermo Ungo said he soon realized that the real power behind the government remained with the military High Command. The junta could not stop the right-wing terror and military violence because, as Ungo explained, "the army still views as the principal enemy not the oligarchy but the organizations of the left."[15] On January 3, 1980, Ungo resigned along with the other civilian member of the junta, Ramon Mayorga.

The second junta formed on January 10, but lasted only until the beginning of March. Two Christian Democrats became members of the short-lived junta. Since its formation in the early 1960s, the Christian Democrat Party (PDC) had been vying for national political power. In 1972, the military stole the presidential election from PDC presidential candidate Napoleon Duarte through a fraudulent vote count. The Christian Democrats in 1980 saw their chance to gain power by cooperating with the military in the junta government. Many PDC members abhorred the idea of joining hands with the military and eventually they split from the party's conservative leadership. Some rank and file of the PDC moved directly to the popular opposition movement which was then beginning to form broad coalitions. When the opposition staged a massive demonstration of 80,000 people in the streets of San Salvador on January 22, 1980, the military killed more than 20 of the demonstrators. On March 3, Christian Democrat Hector Dada resigned from the junta, saying, "We have not been able to stop the repression, and those committing acts of repression . . . go unpunished . . . the chances for producing reforms with the support of the people are receding beyond reach."[16]

PDC leader Napoleon Duarte then took Dada's place in what became the third junta government. The United States moved quickly to support Duarte in the hope both of thwarting a right-wing coup and of keeping a moderate political base alive in El Salvador. The new U.S. ambassador, Robert White, arrived in El Salvador in early March and attempted to construct a center-left coalition, but it was too late. Violence by the military and the death squads was increasing and only the old-guard conservative faction of the PDC would associate with the military. Major Roberto D'Aubuisson, who had close links with the White Warriors Union death squad, founded a new right-wing group called the National Broad Front (FAN) to lead the oligarchy's offensive against both the popular opposition and the reform government. D'Aubuisson and members of FAN publicly threatened Archbishop Oscar Romero in February 1980 for Romero's criticism of military repression. On March 24, 1980, right-wing sharpshooters assassinated Archbishop Romero who only the week before had asked President Carter to stop military aid to the junta. Romero's death was the catalyst for the creation in April 1980 of the popular opposition coalition called the Democratic Revolutionary Front (FDR). Virtually all the opposition groups in the country, including political parties, mass organizations, unions, and peasant groups, compose the FDR. Ambassador White said later that the FDR is supported by over 80% of the Salvadoran people. The FDR is now the diplomatic representative of the guerilla forces of the Farabundo Marti National Liberation Front (FMLN). The guerilla armies of the FMLN were formed in the early 1970s by disillusioned members of political parties who saw the need for armed struggle. The FMLN is a coalition of four "political-military organizations" and the Communist Party of El Salvador. Its member groups orient the work of their respective mass organizations and trade unions and direct the military struggle through the Unified Revolutionary Directorate (DRU), the FMLN's central command. They identify themselves variously as Marxist, Marxist-Leninist, and Marxist-influenced. Their combined armies are estimated to be from 5-7,000 with 20-25,000 members in people's militias.[17]

On December 2, 1980, the country's security forces killed four U.S. churchwomen who were doing relief work for the growing number of refugees within El Salvador. The United States temporarily suspended military and economic aid to El Salvador. A new junta formed on December 13, 1980, and the United States resumed its aid in January 1980. Duarte became the country's president, and Gutierrez was named vice-president and commander-in-chief. This fourth junta lasted until March 28, 1982, when D'Aubuisson gained political power. Duarte was more of a public relations agent than a true president. He talked about land reform, democracy, and the need to stop extremist violence, but the military held the real power. In March 1982, the United States staged national elections to demonstrate the viability of the government. The FDR stated that their participation would signify unilateral disarmament, and they boycotted the elections.

The March 1982 elections gave birth to a new "government of national unity." D'Aubuisson as a candidate promised to abolish the agrarian reform and to unleash the security forces on the opposition. He became the president of the National Assembly, and the United States in concert with the military prevailed upon D'Aubuisson to accept Alvarado Magana as the country's provisional president. The Reagan Administration thought that Magana could provide a dignified, centrist image to the new government. Magana, a scion of the country's oligarchy, was a wealthy lawyer who had studied economics at the University of Chicago. For 17 years he had directed the Salvadoran Mortgage Bank and maintained good relations with the military and oligarchy.

The triumph of D'Aubuisson and the appointment of General Guillermo Garcia as Minister of Defense put the most conservative political and military elements in El Salvador firmly in power. It signalled the end of the reform effort that the younger officers had set off in October 1979. The conservative sector which gained power in March 1982 represented, according to NACLA, "the most ruthless, explicitly fascist and corrupt elements of the military, precisely those which the U.S. policymakers have tried to urge the Salvadoran government and military leaders to control."[18]

The Carter Administration believed it could divert the revolutionary movement in El Salvador by forming a civilian/military coalition apart from the oligarchy. It speculated that by redistributing some of the oligarchy's power and wealth a new reform government could gain popular support. But the reforms were half-hearted and came too late. The United States had overestimated the potential for a liberal, bourgeois government. By the end of Carter's term, human rights and reforms became secondary considerations for the United States as the guerilla forces advanced.

The Reagan victory was a sign to the hard-line military and the oligarchy that the days of dabbling in liberal reforms were over. They heard presidential candidate Reagan say that "in El Salvador, Marxist totalitarian revolutionaries, supported by Havana and Moscow, are preventing the construction of a democratic government."[19]

Though the U.S. government was not happy with the turn to the right in El Salvador's government, the business community in El Salvador was. The National Association for Private Enterprise and the Federation for Small Business complained that the former government's mismanagement of the economy — nationalization of the banks, increased state control of the foreign commerce, and the agrarian reform — was responsible for deteriorating economic conditions. Unlike Nicaragua, where the business community joined the opposition, both the local business sector and the oligarchy are supporting a right-wing, fight-to-the-finish solution in their country. The FDR has recognized that it can't depend on the bourgeoisie in El Salvador for any support in their fight against the oligarchy and the military. It is a class war they are fighting, and they intend to establish a democratic society controlled by the masses of workers and *campesinos*.

Reagan's appointment for ambassador to El Salvador was Deane R. Hinton, who was the mission director for the Agency for International Development (AID) in Guatemala from 1967-69, the years when AID funded a "model police program" for counterinsurgency. He was AID mission director in Chile during the CIA's anti-Allende campaign.[20] Shortly after becoming ambassador, Hinton told the American Chamber of Commerce in El Salvador that the future of the country "is in your hands," noting that ". . . your organization symbolizes and reinforces the tight bonds of friendship and commerce which unite the people of El Salvador and the U.S." The Reagan Administration has described the war in El Salvador as a "textbook case of Communist aggression." It has demonstrated that it is ready to put U.S. money and guns behind any government, no matter its human rights violations, as long as it stands a chance of defeating the popular opposition.

U.S. Military Involvement

Recent military history in El Salvador begins with the 1931 military coup of Maximiliano Hernandez Martinez, whose reign as dictator coincided with the reigns of Ubico in Guatemala (1931-1944), Carias Andino in Honduras (1931-1949), and Somoza Garcia in Nicaragua. Hernandez Martinez put down the 1932 uprising in El Salvador with a brutality that Salvadorans will never forget. Poet Roque Dalton wrote: "We all were born half dead in 1932. We have survived, but half alive . . . ."

The United States gave the long line of military dictatorships of El Salvador full diplomatic support, and after World War Two started providing military aid and police training to El Salvador. From Fiscal Year 1950 to 1980, the United States provided El Salvador with $16,840,000 in military aid.[21] This aid came under three programs: Foreign Military Sales (FMS), Military Assistance Program (MAP), and International Military Education and Training (IMET). During those thirty years, the United States trained 2,113 members of the Salvadoran military.[22] Training courses included Urban Counterinsurgency, Military Intelligence, Basic Combat and Counterinsurgency, and Basic Officer Preparation. Chronicling the direct U.S. military presence in El Salvador, former U.S. Ambassador Murat W. Williams (1961 to 1964) said, "In 1948, we sent our first military mission to El Salvador a group from the United States Air Force. By 1961 . . . we had both a large army mission and air force mission. In fact, there were more men in the air force than El Salvador had either pilots or planes."[23]

The Office of Public Safety program (OPS), under the sponsorship of the Agency for International Development (AID), was a military-related program designed to "develop the managerial and operational skills and effectiveness of [Salvadoran] police forces." Between 1957 and the program's termination in 1974, OPS spent a total of $2.1 million to train 448 Salvadoran police, and provide arms, communication equipment, transport vehicles, and riot control equipment.[24] Graduates of OPS training, some schooled at the International Police Academy in Washington, occupied key positions in the Salvadoran security establishment, U.S.-trained officials held the top posts in the treasury police, the intelligence division of the national police, the customs police, and immigration, as well as the second and third in command in other security agencies. The OPS program revamped the police school in El Salvador, prepared a standard text for the treasury police, and trained and equipped special riot control units. OPS created a bomb-handling squad within the national police which was responsible for investigating terrorist activities, and it installed a teletype system that linked El Salvador and other Central American countries. When the U.S. Congress terminated the OPS program in 1974, U.S. AID analysts concluded that ". . . the National Police . . . has advanced from a nondescript, barracks-bound group of poorly trained men to a well-disciplined, well-trained, and respected uniformed corps. It has good riot control capability, good investigative capability, good records, and fair communications and mobility. It handles routine law enforcement well."[25]

Direct military aid to El Salvador increased dramatically in 1980, when President Carter pressed Congress to authorize $5.7 million in emergency military aid to El Salvador. Carter insisted that the request was for nonlethal equipment, but the *New York Times* reported that the aid package also included "combat-related equipment that stretches the definition of 'nonlethal' beyond credibility."[26]

Later in 1980 the United States initiated the training of several hundred Salvadoran military officers at its Panama Canal counterinsurgency training programs. In addition to government aid, the Commerce Department licensed the export of $8,000 worth of nonmilitary shotguns and spare parts to that country in 1980.

In 1982, 52% of all the U.S. military aid sent to Latin America was sent to El Salvador. Total military aid from Fiscal Year 1981 through 1983 amounts to almost $200 million, eleven times the amount of aid sent to El Salvador from 1950 to 1980.[27]

Hundreds of millions of dollars in U.S. military aid and training has accomplished what is at best a stalemate with the FMLN forces. But the U.S. government still seems determined to pursue this "decisive battle for Central America."

ECONOMY

El Salvador's only growth sectors are foreign aid and counterinsurgency. Export earnings dropped $170 million in 1981, and the Gross Domestic Product dropped 9.5%. Annual per capita income was down to $540, a drop of $240 from 1975. [28] U.S. economic and military aid has poured into El Salvador to hold up the staggering economy and to stave off military defeat by the opposition forces. Between 1980 and 1982, the United States gave a total of $609 million to the government of El Salvador.[29] In 1982, the war cost almost a million dollars a day; and while the soldiers could count on their $200 monthly salary, public service workers were not being paid regularly and the combined unemployment/underemployment rate rose to 60%. The gross disparity in income is the prime reason for the Salvadoran conflict. Less than two percent of the five million people receive about 50% of the country's income.[30]

In 1982, the United States gave $260 million in military and economic aid to El Salvador. It seems, though, that sending aid to El Salvador only encourages more capital to leave the country. From 1979 to 1981, over $1.5 billion in capital fled El Salvador. Commenting on this boomerang effect, former U.S. Ambassador to El Salvador Robert White said, "It has been estimated that for each dollar in economic assistance that the United States provides El Salvador, five dollars are exported out of the country by the economic and military elites."[31] It is not necessarily the U.S. aid itself that is leaving the country but this U.S. support, by propping up the economy, allows other capital to flee El Salvador.

U.S. direct investment in El Salvador accounts for approximately 56% of total foreign investment in the country.[32] In 1980, U.S. direct investment recorded by the U.S. Department of Commerce amounted to $103 million.[33] Direct investment hardly reflects the importance of U.S. capital in the Salvadoran economy, since it doesn't include the crucial role U.S. banks play in financing coffee and cotton production in El Salvador. Citibank, a leading agribusiness bank in El Salvador, has financial connections with three non-financial firms doing business in El Salvador: Kimberly-Clark, Phelps Dodge, and Monsanto.[34]

Most foreign or U.S. investors in El Salvador are not optimistic about new investment in the country, but they intend to keep their existing investment as long as possible. *Business Latin America* reported that U.S. corporate executives, when asked what they envision in the event of a guerilla victory, responded overwhelmingly that they would have a "conciliatory approach to doing business with 'the new bunch'."[35]

U.S. and multilateral aid has served to keep the country from going bankrupt and to make strategic repairs of war damages. In April 1982, the Inter-American Development Bank (IDB) and the International Monetary Fund (IMF) proposed a $279 million program of new loans to El Salvador. The program included one $20 million loan, which the Center for International Policy in Washington called "one of the most frankly political loans in IDB's history." The loan is for the reconstruction of Puente de Oro, a bridge over the Lempa River that was blown up by guerillas in 1981 and was one of their chief military targets.[36]

Credit for Salvadoran businesses and farms has been severely limited by the scarce deposits in national banks. To remedy that situation, the Reagan Administration has formulated a $77 million private sector support program in 1982 to provide credit, loans, and subsidies to private interests.

Tourism has predictably declined because of the war, but in 1982 the Reagan Administration reported an improvement in the human rights situation in El Salvador. Upon a request from the Tourism Institute of El Salvador, the State Department lifted its travel warning for El Salvador. "This is a curious decision," commented *Central America Report*, "for just this week guerillas blew up electricity installations leaving most of San Salvador without power for hours. And military authorities admit that transport in one third of the western part of the country is paralyzed . . . ." The Tourism Institute is so interested in attracting tourists to its beautiful but bloody country, that it is negotiating for the franchise on the 1983 Miss Universe Contest.[37]

While the war certainly has dampened the investment climate, there are still some daily business opportunities that are not being missed. *Mesoamerica* reported that to boost their funeral business, a group of undertakers searches the dumps every morning where tortured and mutilated bodies are commonly thrown. All bodies not destroyed beyond identity are taken back to the funeral parlors as a new and macabre commodity in a desperate economy.[38]

Agriculture

"The whole foundation of the nation's social progress depends on the sale of that wonderful bean without which no American Breakfast is a success," noted a State Department Bulletin in 1952. Coffee, which supplies more than half of El Salvador's export earnings, is certainly the foundation of the country's economy, but the wonderful bean has hardly contributed to social progress. Rather, the unequal distribution of land and power of the coffee growers has stifled social progress and is responsible for the desperate poverty of the country's rural population. Over a third of El Salvador's land is used for three export crops: coffee, cotton, and sugar. The introduction of capitalistic, mechanized agriculture practices such as intensive use of fertilizer has given large landowners the methods and the incentives to expand their land ownership and crop production, thus forcing yet more of the rural population onto an ever diminishing portion of the nation's total land area. In a country where 60% of the population is engaged in agriculture, a mere 1.9% of the population owns 57% of the land, while only 21.9% of arable land is distributed among 91% of the population.[39]

The country's elite controls virtually all the prime agricultural land – the middle volcanic slopes, the interim basins and river valleys, and the coastal plain – while the poor majority crowd onto the nation's least fertile land. A study by the Organization of American States found that 77% of El Salvador's land area suffers from accelerated erosion, in part the result of skewed land ownership patterns that force the *campesino* population to work the same barren land year after year. El Salvador is one of the most environmentally devastated countries in the Western Hemisphere. The tropical deciduous forests once covered 90% of the country but have been totally destroyed by centuries of clearance for grazing, plantations, mining, charcoal manufacture, and intensive land cultivation.[40]

While the *campesinos* struggle to survive on barren hills, the nation's coffee oligarchy makes its fortunes from the sale of coffee beans to the U.S. companies like Procter & Gamble and General Foods. Most *campesinos*, both those with and without land, must find work as wage laborers on the coffee and cotton plantations during the four to six month growing seasons. Those who do find jobs receive only one to two dollars a day. The coffee beans leave El Salvador for the United States and so do the coffee profits. The coffee growers generally put their money in Miami banks, thereby continually reducing the amount of capital available for credit in their own country. Business hasn't been very good lately as coffee exports dropped 25% in 1981 and are expected to drop another 30% in 1982.[41] The war and tightening of credit in El Salvador have also affected cotton production, which dropped 45% from 1979-1982.[42]

Agrarian Reform

Introduced in March 1980, the agrarian reform program and a bank nationalization plan came too late to prevent the political polarization of the country. At that time, the State Department reasoned that the right-wing repression supported by the oligarchy was counterproductive since it was driving a large sector of the population into revolutionary organizations.

The first phase of the program didn't go to the heart of El Salvador's land distribution inequity since over 60% of the plots affected were pastures, mountainous land, or forests, and not prime agricultural land. Also undermining the effectiveness of the first phase was the advance notification given to the oligarchy, which gave them time to parcel out their larger landholdings among family members.

Phase II, which would have nationalized landholdings between 247 and 1,235 acres, was vetoed in April 1982 in one of the first acts of the new National Assembly. The oligarchy vigorously opposed Phase II since coffee lands were its main targets. Phase III, the AFL-CIO-backed Land to the Tiller Program, was suspended in May 1982 by the National Assembly. Phase III proposed the distribution of 17-acre parcels of land to peasant sharecroppers. Phase III would have affected 31.2% of the land and distributed 150,000 acres. President Magana said that the government was suspending Phase III "to stimulate greater agricultural production."[43] The small part (5%) of the Phase III program that doesn't affect lands used for agro-export production will not be affected by the suspension.

Supported and largely designed by the United States, the entire land reform program backfired. Instead of creating a base of support for the government, it increased political tension in El Salvador. Landowners, outraged by the agrarian reform, increased their backing of the death squads and right-wing factions of the military. During the initial stage of the agrarian reform, government security forces and the death squads attacked peasant leaders. In 1982 congressional hearings on aid to El Salvador, Representative Clarence Long commented on the killings of the recipients of agrarian reform land. He said, "You have roughly one out of 14 farmers who has been thrown off his land, murdered, tortured, done in a most public way to frighten them. That is certainly not very reassuring to the tiller of the soil . . . ." Long questioned the U.S. government's continued certification of aid to El Salvador given that "not a single permanent title has been given, and that large numbers of people . . . have been thrown off their lands."[44]

A successful, though temporary, aspect of the agrarian reform was to polish the image of the Salvadoran government in the eyes of the American public. An AID study of the program concluded that even the Salvadoran administrators of the agrarian reform program in El Salvador regarded it as a "symbolic measure which was proposed because it would look good to American politicians and not necessarily because it would be beneficial or significant in the Salvadoran context."[45] As an ironic last touch to the agrarian reform program, the House Foreign Affairs Committee in July 1982 authorized $20 million to compensate the property owners whose land was confiscated under the controversial land reform program.[46]

Industry

El Salvador is by no means an industrialized nation, but it has been in the forefront of Central America's industrialization and has received a disproportionately high amount of the region's foreign industrial development capital. Industry contributes only half as much to the country's GDP as does agriculture. More than half of the foreign investment in El Salvador, however, has gone to the industrial sector. With the possible exception of the brewing and cement industries, foreign capital dominates all major industries in El Salvador.

Most industries established between 1959 and 1975 produced items for the Central American Common Market (CACM). As the regional market began to contract in the late 1960s, the Salvadoran government, encouraged by the United States, opened the San Bartolo Free-Trade Zone and promoted the country as a center for assembly industries known as *maquiladoras*. In 1974, it officially entered the race to attract the world's runaway shops with the introduction of its Export Promotion Law. Features of the law included: a total exemption on imports of machinery, equipment, and spare parts; a ten-year holiday from income and capital taxes; unrestricted repatriation of profits to the home country; investment guarantees against expropriation; and a specialized recruiting agency for labor. Runaway firms came from all parts of the world to El Salvador. The year that Dataram closed down its operation in Malaysia it established a plant in El Salvador; Texas Instruments shut one plant in Curacao and the same year moved to El Salvador; and both Beckman and AVX Corporation previously had plants in Ireland before they chose to expand in El Salvador. Other firms attracted to the San Bartolo free zone in the 1970s were Bourns, Form-O-Uth, Eagle International, Delka, and MANEXPO.

Textile firms locating in El Salvador to assemble material for the U.S. market have taken advantage of a U.S. tariff regulation that allows apparel components to be shipped from the United States, then sent back as assembled finished clothing with duty paid only on the value added, namely the labor of the Salvadorans. The growth of *maquiladoras* resulted in the doubling of

U.S. apparel imports from El Salvador between 1975 and 1978.

The government of El Salvador advertised lavishly in the U.S. media. "El Salvador is right next door," read an ad in the *New York Times*, "For example, Salvador plant sites are closer to California markets than are New England sites, and producers in El Salvador are nearer to New York markets than are California manufacturers."[48] And in addition to this accessibility, the beautiful climate, and the country's "stable, democratic government," El Salvador said that its two million workers would labor for wages that were one-tenth of the average rate in the United States. One promotional advertisement quoted a U.S. executive who said, "I have never, repeat never — and I've travelled all over — seen such wonderful people . . . . My only fear is that we will spoil the *Salvadorenos*."[49]

In 1980, as the political violence mounted, U.S. businesses started leaving El Salvador. The American Chamber of Commerce in El Salvador reported that 12 corporations had left by August 1981. About 90 corporations, however, decided to stick it out in El Salvador. Some like Dataram established back-up plants in other countries or have cut back production. While the businesses may stay, all the U.S. managers have moved, leaving local management to take care of business until things settle down. One company executive told *Business Latin America* that for safety reasons company executives rarely visit El Salvador. Salvadorans manage the plants and telex vital information about company operations each week to the firm's U.S. headquarters. An executive of AVX Ceramics said, "We missed less production in El Salvador because of that country's problems than we did in our plant in South Carolina because of snow."[50]

Other factories that were more closely tied to the local economic structure, however, have shut down. The guerillas, knowing that there never will be a final victory as long as the economy keeps functioning, have regularly attacked the country's economic infrastructure. As part of the war effort, the United States has rushed economic aid to El Salvador to repair the damaged power plants, roads, and bridges. The FDR/FMLN forces have said that they are ready to negotiate an end to the war but that they are also prepared to fight a prolonged war. Given the commitment and the growing strength of the guerillas and the opposition movement, the question then is just how long the economy and the military of El Salvador can hold out and just how much the United States is prepared to do to keep the unpopular government alive.

References for Introductory Statistics

Business America, March 8, 1982; *Business Latin America*, July 7, 1982; Inter-American Development Bank, *Economic and Social Progress in Latin America, 1980-81*; *Latin America Regional Report*; United Nations, *Monthly Bulletin of Statistics*, April 1982; U.S. Department of State, *Background Notes — El Salvador*, February 1981.

194

REFERENCE NOTES

1. Marc Herold, "From Riches to 'Rags': Finanzkapital in El Salvador, 1900-1980," Unpublished manuscript, University of New Hampshire, 1980), p. 12.
2. David Browning, *El Salvador: La Tierra y El Hombre*, (San Salvador: Ministerio de Educacion, 1975), p. 365.
3. Cynthia Arnson, *El Salvador: A Revolution Confronts the United States* (Washington: Institute for Policy Studies, 1982), p. 7.
4. Jenny Pearce, *Under the Eagle* (London: Latin American Bureau, 1982), p. 210.
5. Herold, p. 17.
6. *Fortune,* June 1950, p. 73.
7. Herold, p. 21.
8. Arnson, p. 7.
9. *Latin American Perspectives*, Issues 25 and 26, (Spring and Summer 1980), p. 129.
10. Susanne Jonas and David Tobis, Editors, *Guatemala*, (Berkeley and New York: NACLA, 1974), p. 99.
11. J. Waiselfisz, "El Comercio Exterior, El Mercado Comun y La Industrializacion en Relacion al Conflicto," p. 202, cited in *La Guerra Inutil* by M.V. Carias and D. Slutsky (San Jose: EDUCA, 1971).
12. Penny Lernoux, *Cry of the People,* (Garden City, NY: Doubleday, 1980), p. 76.
13. John Eisendrath and Jim Morrell, "Arming El Salvador," *International Policy Report,* Center for International Policy, August 1982.
14. Pearce, p. 221.
15. Arnson, p. 45.
16. *Ibid.*, p. 49.
17. *NACLA*, March-April 1982, p. 28.
18. *Ibid.*, pp. 21, 22.
19. Arnson, p. 63.
20. *NACLA*, January-February 1982, p. 12.
21. *Foreign Military Sales and Military Assistance Facts as of September 1981,* (Washington: Dept. of Defense, 1982).
22. *Congressional Presentation: Security Assistance Programs Fiscal Year 1982* (Washington: Dept. of Defense, 1981).
23. *New York Times,* April 17, 1980, cited in "U.S. Military Involvement in El Salvador 1947-1980," (San Francisco: Casa El Salvador), p. 11.
24. Cynthia Arnson, "Background Information on the Security Forces in El Salvador and U.S. Military Assistance," *Resource*, Institute for Policy Studies, March 1980, p. 7.
25. *Ibid.*
26. Thomas Conrad and Cynthia Arnson, "The Aid for El Salvador is Called Nonlethal," *New York Times*, June 15, 1980.
27. *Congressional Presentation: Security Assistance Programs Fiscal Year 1983*, (Washington: Dept. of Defense, 1982).
28. *Latin America Weekly Report*, March 5, 1982, p. 7.
29. *Central America Report*, March 21, 1982.
30. *New York Times*, November 22, 1981.
31. Hearing before the Subcommittee on Foreign Operations and Related Agencies of the Committee of Appropriations, House of Representatives, May 19, 1982 (Washington: Government Printing Office, 1982), p. 124.
32. Herold, Table 8.
33. U.S. Dept. of Commerce, International Investment Division, telephone interview with Obie Whichard, May 1982; *U.S. Direct Investment Abroad 1977*, (Washington: U.S. Dept. of Commerce, April 1981).
34. Herold, p. 23.
35. *Business Latin America*, March 17, 1982, p. 84.
36. International Policy Report, August 1982.
37. *Central America Report*, June 1982, pp. 168, 122.
38. *Mesoamerica*, June 1982, p. 4.
39. *Resource*, March 1980, p. 2.
40. Erick Eckholm, *Losing Ground*, (New York: Norton for Worldwatch Institute, 1976), p. 167.
41. *Latin America Weekly Report*, March 5, 1982, p. 7.
42. *Central America Report*, February 26, 1982.

43. *Mesoamerica*, June 1982, p. 5.
44. Subcommittee on Foreign Operations, May 20, 1982, p. 212.
45. *Wall Street Journal*, February 6, 1981.
46. *Washington Report on the Hemisphere*, Council on Hemispheric Affairs, August 10, 1982, p. 8.
47. Herold, p. 22.
48. *New York Times*, January 28, 1972.
49. *New York Times*, May 2, 1976.
50. "U.S. Plants Humming Along," *Business Week*, April 13, 1981, p. 60.

UNITED STATES BUSINESS IN EL SALVADOR*

Abbott Laboratories
  Abbott; *pharmaceutical manufacturing*

Aluminum Company of America (ALCOA)
  Aluminios de Centroamérica (ALDECA); *non-ferrous metal industry*

AMAX
  New York & El Salvador Mining ; *gold and silver mining*

American Life Insurance; *insurance*

Arnold Enterprises

ATSA Export Import; *exporting and importing*

AVX Ceramics; *electronic ceramic capacitor manufacturing*

Baldwin United
  Compañía de Alumbrado Eléctrico de San Salvador (CAESS)

BankAmerica
  Bank of America National Trust & Savings Association; *banking*

Bemis
  Bemis de El Salvador; *paper products*

Blindaje Internacional

Bourns
  Bourns International; *electronics*

Bristol-Myers
  Compañía Bristol-Myers de Centroamérica; *toiletries and pharmaceuticals*

Cargill
  Adria; *animal feeds and poultry production*

Cigarrería Morazan; *cigarette manufacturing*

Citicorp
  Citibank; *banking*

Coca Cola
  Tenco; *instant coffee processing*

COMCA Internacional

Commerce Group
  San Sabastian Gold Mines: *mining*

Conductores Eléctricos de Centroamérica

Corporación Industrial Centroamericana; *steel manufacturing; ADELA equity*

Crown Zellerbach
  Signa; *paper products*

Curtis Industrial; *cosmetics and toiletries*

F.A. Dalton y Compañía

Dataram
  Dataram International; *electronics manufacturing*

Delka; *medical equipment manufacturing*

Eaton
  Cutler-Hammer Centroamericana; *electrical equipment manufacturing*

Exitomotivación

EXPON

*An indented item is a subsidiary, affiliate, or branch of the corporation immediately above it.

Exxon
  Esso Standard Oil; *oil exploration and petroleum product distribution*
  Essochem de Centroamérica; *marketing of chemical products*
  Refinería Petrolera Acajutla; *oil refinery*
  West Indies Oil

Foremost-McKesson
  Corporación Bonima
  Empresas Lácteas Foremost; *dairy processing*

FORM-O-UTH; *brassieres*

H.B. Fuller
  Kativo de El Salvador; *toiletries*

General Telephone & Electronics (GTE)
  GTE Sylvania; *electric equipment manufacturing*

Goodyear Tire and Rubber

Hyatt
  Hotel Presidente Hyatt

IBM World Trade Corporation; *business machines*

Implementos Agriícolas Centroamericanos; *agricultural equipment; ADELA equity*

Impresora la Union; *commercial printing; ADELA equity*

International Basic Economy Corporation (IBEC)
  Automercados de Centroamérica

The Interpublic Group of Companies
  McCann-Erickson Centroamericana; *advertising*

Inversiones Consolidadas de El Salvador

ITT
  Hotel El Salvador Sheraton
  ITT de Centroamérica; *telephone and telegraph systems*

Johnson and Johnson; *cosmetics and toiletries*

Kay Electronics; *electrical component manufacturing*

Kem Manufacturing
  Kem Centroamericana; *chemical product manufacturing and distribution*

Kimberly-Clark
  Kimberly-Clark de Centroamérica; *toilet paper and sanitary napkins*

Lenox
  Lenox de Centroamérica; *jewelry, crystal, plastic and ceramic dinnerware manufacturing*

Levi Strauss
  Centro Industrial de Ropa; *clothes*

Maidenform
  Confecciones de El Salvador; *bra manufacturing*

MANEXPO; *servicing and trading*

Mario Sulit

McCormick & Company
  McCormick de Centroamérica; *food processing*

McDonald's
  McDonald Servipronto de El Salvador; *fast food*

Minnesota Mining and Manufacturing
  3M Interamericana

Monsanto
  Monsanto Centroamericano; *chemical manufacturing*

Moore
  Moore Business Forms de Centroamérica
  Moore Comercial

Nabisco Brands
  Pan American Standard Brands; *food processing*

National Cash Register (NCR)
  Cajas Registradoras Nacional; *office machine manufacturing*

Nixon; *textile and plastic manufacturing*

Pan American Life Insurance; *insurance*

Pan American World Airways; *air transportation*

Pavos; *poultry production*

Peat, Marwick, Mitchell & Company; *accounting*

Phelps Dodge
  Cables Eléctricos de Centroamérica; *electric cables*
  Phelps Dodge de Centroamérica; *electrical equipment*

Price Waterhouse & Company; *auditing*

Procesadora Agricola Salvadorena; *grain production; LAAD equity*

Quality Foods de Centroamérica; *frozen foods; LAAD equity*

Quinonez Hermanos; *food processing; LAAD equity*

Richardson-Vicks; *air transportation*

Rohm & Haas
  Rohm & Haas de Centroamérica; *chemicals*

Rorer Group
Rorer de Centroamérica;
*pharmaceutical preparations and
chemicals*

Sam P. Wallace
Sam P. Wallace El Salvador;
construction

Sears Roebuck and Company
Sears Roebuck y Compañía;
department store

La Seguridad Salvadoreña

Sheller-Globe
Fábrica Superior de Centroamérica;
auto parts and electrical equipment

Sherwin-Williams
Sherwin-Williams de Centroamérica;
paint distribution

Singer Manufacturing Company of New
Jersey
Singer Importadora de Máquinas;
distribution of electric appliances

Standard Oil of California
Compañía Petrolera Chevron;
petroleum products

Sterling Drug
Droguería Centroamericana;
*pharmaceutical manufacturing and
distribution*

TACA International Airlines; *air
transportation*

Tejidos Industriales (TISA)

Terson
La Ballena; *seafood*

Texaco
Texaco Caribbean

Texas Instruments
Texas Instruments El Salvador;
electronic parts manufacturing

Transway International
Coordinated Caribbean Transport
(CCT); *shipping*

United Air Lines
Hotel Camino Real

Xerox
Xerox de El Salvador; *business machine
distribution and servicing*

REFERENCES

Because of political turmoil in El Salvador, many foreign investors have been pulling out. Therefore only the most up-to-date sources were used.

ADELA, Annual Report, 1981; Latin American Agribusiness Development Corporation (LAAD), Annual Reports, 1976-1981; Multinational Enterprise Data Base, Marc Herold, University of New Hampshire; Overseas Private Investment Corporation (OPIC), Annual Reports, 1978-1981; United States Embassy in El Salvador, "U.S. Investors, Local Branches of U.S. Firms, Licensees, and Franchises," 1981.

COSTA RICA

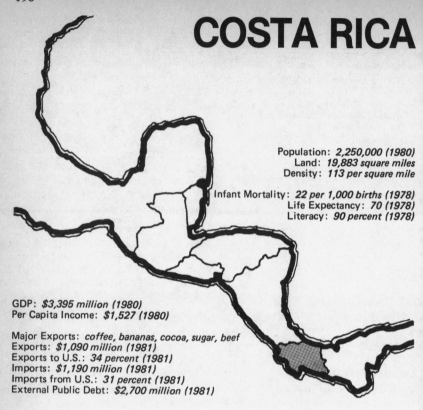

Population: *2,250,000 (1980)*
Land: *19,883 square miles*
Density: *113 per square mile*

Infant Mortality: *22 per 1,000 births (1978)*
Life Expectancy: *70 (1978)*
Literacy: *90 percent (1978)*

GDP: *$3,395 million (1980)*
Per Capita Income: *$1,527 (1980)*

Major Exports: *coffee, bananas, cocoa, sugar, beef*
Exports: *$1,090 million (1981)*
Exports to U.S.: *34 percent (1981)*
Imports: *$1,190 million (1981)*
Imports from U.S.: *31 percent (1981)*
External Public Debt: *$2,700 million (1981)*

Costa Rica is an exception in this region of repressive military dictatorships and entrenched poverty. Costa Rica's high literacy rate, relatively large middle class, regularly-held elections, and absence of an army are traditions not commonly held by its neighbors. But the country's reputation as a stable democracy is now wavering in the face of the worsening regional situation and Costa Rica's own escalating economic crisis.

Christopher Columbus came upon Costa Rica on his fourth and final voyage to the New World, but the Spanish colonizers failed to find the wealth for which they were searching. Costa Rica had neither gold nor a large exploitable Indian population for plantation labor. The European settlers who did eventually settle in Costa Rica established subsistence farms rather than the expansive, labor-intensive haciendas like those in Guatemala.

This quiet existence continued until the mid-1800s when farmers found that production of the coffee bean was a profitable use for the country's fertile central mesa. With the advent of coffee production in Costa Rica came the increased concentration of land ownership. By the turn of the century, 5% of the coffee growers produced more than 50% of the coffee.[1] Despite this increasing concentration, the heritage of small farmers has set Costa Rica apart from other Central American countries and contributed to its democratic traditions. Another factor is that since 1880 public education has been available to most Costa Ricans. The consequent high national literacy has created a middle class of professionals and white collar workers.

"In most Latin American countries," wrote John P. Bell in *Crisis in Costa Rica*, "the middle class was a mere extension of landowning oligarchy, allying itself with it against . . . the lower class. Costa Rica's middle class has been strong and numerous and it has possessed a sense of identity distinct from the oligarchy. . . ."

In 1871, the construction of the country's first railroad introduced banana production to Costa Rica. Minor Keith, later a founder of United Fruit, brought in mostly Black workers from Louisiana and the Caribbean islands to build the first part of his International Railways of Central America. Five thousand workers died from tropical diseases and accidents to bring to life Keith's dream of a banana railroad.[2]

Costa Rica is really two countries: the rich, central mesa which produces coffee, and the hot, impoverished Atlantic coastal plain that is banana land. Because the companies didn't need roads to the country's capital, the two regions weren't connected by highway. The Atlantic region, as the domain of the banana companies, was more closely tied to Miami and New Orleans than to San Jose.

The labor movement in Costa Rica grew out of the struggles of the banana workers who associated with the publicly-communist Bloque de Obreros y Campesinos. The Bloque, later called Vanguardia Popular, met with great success among the oppressed banana workers and soon became the leading representative of progressive forces in Costa Rica.

In 1942, Jose Figueres Ferrer leaped into the public consciousness where he has stayed ever since. In a radio speech, he denounced President Calderon Garcia for, among other things, seeking the alliance of Vanguardia to strengthen the base of Calderon's National Republican Party. Calderon reacted to Figueres' speech by exiling him, which made "Don Pepe" a public martyr and a hero to many middle class Costa Ricans.[3]

Figueres, who shared the anti-communist fervor of the U.S., mounted what was later called the Revolution of 1948 against the National Republicans who had stayed in power despite questionable election results in 1948. Figueres counted on significant support from the United States, which was concerned about the growing power of Vanguardia. When it became clear that the government's own forces were unable to repel Figueres and his followers, the government requested assistance from Vanguardia, which summoned up its membership and its supporters to defend the capital of San Jose.

Moving in on this critical situation was Nicaragua's feared dictator Somoza, whose troops occupied a northern Costa Rican village, stating the intention to stay until the communist threat was removed from Costa Rica. For a week before Figueres' final move, the U.S. ambassador to Costa Rica visited him seven different times. On April 17, 1948, the U.S. government delivered a message to the Costa Rican government that U.S. military forces were on standby in the Panama Canal Zone, ready to come to San Jose to end communist control of Costa Rica. Figueres, with this powerful backing, threatened to march into San Jose against Vanguardia. But the government called off the Vanguardia forces and arranged for negotiations, and the resulting pact recognized Figueres' troops as victorious. Vanguardia's role in the negotiations brought about the inclusion of one of the seven points in the pact which stated that "the social rights and guarantees of all employees and workers [will] be respected and extended."[4]

"Don Pepe" Figueres, who has served three times as president of Costa Rica, is the patriarch of the National Liberation Party (PLN), which has been in power frequently and is in power now. Still one of the country's most important politicians and national leaders, Figueres has lived in the U.S., speaks fluent English, and frequently jokes that he is "first Catalan, second gringo, and third Costa Rican." Figueres, who was good friends with Richard Nixon and Allen Dulles, admits to having had connections with the CIA.[5]

Since 1948, Figueres has promoted his mixed economy philosophy of interaction between private and public sectors. An unabashed admirer of the United States and its way of life and business, Figueres is largely responsible for encouraging the foreign tastes and consumer habits of the Costa Rican middle class.

The golden days of Costa Rica are approaching an end. The PLN administration, which took office in May 1982, has inherited a bankrupt country with the third highest inflation rate in Latin America.

POLITICS

When returning from a stormy trip through South America in 1968, Nelson Rockefeller stopped in Costa Rica before going home. Not having to face the throngs of rock-throwing crowds that he encountered elsewhere, Rockefeller called Costa Rica "the perfect jewel of a country."

Costa Rica is becoming ever more precious to the United States as guerilla warfare threatens to overrun El Salvador and Guatemala. Costa Rica has always been a good ally, but now the United States seems willing to pay a higher sum for its loyalty. The Reagan Administration has discussed an economic recovery package with the PLN government of Luis Alberto Monge in return for its acquiescence to the dictates of U.S. foreign policy.

Signs that Costa Rica was willing to drop its liberal foreign policy as an expendable luxury began appearing toward the end of the Rodrigo Carazo Administration (1978-82). President Carazo expelled the Cuban ambassador and signed an OAS resolution supporting the 1982 elections in El Salvador. Immediately after a visit to Costa Rica by Assistant Secretary of State Thomas Enders in early 1982, Costa Rica joined the Central American Democratic Community (CDC). The four country organization – Costa Rica, El Salvador, Guatemala, and Honduras – aims to isolate Nicaragua and to give credibility to Central American support of U.S. policies in the region. The United States lifted a two-year ban on Costa Rican tuna shortly after it joined the CDC as an apparent reward for Costa Rica's new behavior.

The Monge government is pinning its hopes on the United States to rescue the country from its economic nightmare. Indeed, the only solution to Costa Rica's financial condition, other than a radical restructuring of its economy, may be the adoption of a rich guardian angel like the United States.

In past years, economic aid to Costa Rica has been a pittance compared to aid offered several Latin American dictatorships. In 1981, the United States delayed offers of increased economic aid until Costa Rica agreed to sign and abide by a new austerity agreement with the International Monetary Fund (IMF).

With the Reagan Administration's concern about the spreading crisis in Central America, Costa Rica can be sure of increasing aid. According to the Agency for International Development (AID), "Costa Rica's continued well-being is vital as a stabilizing influence in the region and is therefore critical to long-term U.S. interests in the region."[6]

The United States pressured Costa Rica to abide by the austerity measures, including cutbacks in the public sector. The 1983 AID budget stated that the austerity measures will cause a dramatic jump in unemployment to as high as 19% of the workforce by 1985. "A contraction of economic activities and a rise in unemployment of these magnitudes will result in sharp cuts in the national budget and in the public sector service programs and create the possibility of growing social unrest."[7]

Former Vice President Jose Miguel Alfaro charged that the U.S. Ambassador to the United Nations Jeane Kirkpatrick told Costa Rican officials in 1981 that they shouldn't expect to receive any U.S. assistance until they agreed to build an army.[8] In 1983, the U.S. will spend $150,000 in military aid to train 103 members of Costa Rica's security forces, up from $50,000 the previous year.[9]

Alfonso Carro, Minister of Government under the current administration of Monge, said that the "fundamental threat here is external," referring to Costa Rica's neighbor, Nicaragua, but that "in the cellars of Costa Rican society there are very dangerous elements." He said he was impressed with the judgement of a former public security minister who told him, "This country is completely unaware of the forces operating beneath the surface. . .completely unaware, really, of the volcano below."[10] President Monge, when in Washington to seek economic aid, also met with the Israeli Prime Minister Menachem Begin. The two leaders discussed the possibility of Israeli assistance in building up the Costa Rican security forces; the funds would originate in the United States, but would be channeled through Israel.[11]

Monge and the PLN leadership are concerned about the possibility of disruptions within Costa Rica. As Jose Figueres said in a 1981 interview: "We'll soon have hunger and widespread unemployment, and our large middle class won't stand for that."[12] It's been the working class, however, not the middle class, that has reacted most strongly to the economic squeeze. A joint statement from Costa Rica's two central labor bodies in late 1981 condemned the "intervention of the International Monetary Fund" and called for tough measures to control prices and for increases in the salaries of private and public sector workers.

The Costa Rican government has clamped down harder on strikers and political dissenters. The Civil Guard in 1980 fired into striking banana workers threatening to "do the same if other strikers stir up trouble." The government said that the banana strike was "another outbreak of labor unrest directed by Moscow."[13] Despite the harsh official response, strike activity is on the rise: between 1972 and 1979, there were 110 strikes; however, in 1980 alone, 63 strikes occurred.[14]

Most Costa Ricans take pride in the absence of an army, but with official and U.S. pressure, the militarization of Costa Rica might take place. A first step in such a process is the new 500 member Organismo de Investigacion (OIJ), a counter-insurgency force that was used in 1981 to combat Costa Rica's still-born guerilla organization called the Frente Armado Centroamericano.[15] With the increase of official counter-insurgency efforts, the rightist Movimiento Costa Rica Libre, which has connections with Guatemalan death squads, has also gained strength.

As the Central American maelstrom spreads, Costa Rica may shed its democratic trappings in favor of a more authoritarian approach to internal and regional crises. *Business Week* reported common rumors of a political shake-up in Costa Rica,[16] and Jose Figueres has suggested an emergency government that dissolves the legislature and exercises full legislative and executive powers.[17]

ECONOMY

Costa Rica is bankrupt. Twenty years of relative economic prosperity have ended, and Costa Ricans are now feeling themselves and their country slipping into the same desperate economic circumstances of other Central American countries.

The economic statistics are truly staggering. A $2.9 billion foreign debt (June 1982) weighs down the economy, which had a negative growth rate in 1981. Until 1970, Costa Rica had not been bothered much by inflation or unemployment, but in 1982 the country confronted a 100% inflation rate and a combined unemployment and underemployment rate of 22%. The immediate cause of the debt crisis is the drop in the value of its coffee exports, while its imports become steadily more expensive. The value received from 1980 exports, for example, could only buy 76% of the imports that it could in 1977.[18] In 1980, imports cost $565 million more than the amount Costa

Rica received for all of its exports that year. Other factors that precipitated the current crisis were higher oil prices, higher official interest rates, and imported inflation.

The economic crisis in Costa Rica had been brewing under the facade of a comparatively high standard of living. For two decades, the country had experienced a chronic trade and budget deficit that was softened only by foreign borrowing. But the inevitable happened in May 1981, when the government had to sell off all its gold reserves, and in September 1981 announced that it could neither pay the principal nor the interest on its foreign debt. Costa Rica barely had enough foreign currency to pay for the essential imports of food, medicine, and petroleum. And the IMF refused to deliver a $340 million loan because Costa Rica had failed to meet the conditions of that loan. Costa Rica had nowhere to turn and had to put its economic future in the hands of foreign banks.

Representatives of the multilateral banks and 148 private banks met in New York and Miami to decide what could be done about Costa Rica. By June 1982, the country was on its way to accept a new debt repayment schedule which requires a number of harsh austerity measures. Due to the urgency of its debt problem, Costa Rica agreed to the demands of the bankers and the IMF. Without what is called the IMF's "certificate of good housekeeping," it is virtually impossible for a capitalist country to secure loans from foreign private banks or other multilateral lending agencies.

The IMF demands include dramatic cuts in the nation's public spending, a freeze on wages, an end to price support for basic items, and rate increases for the public utilities. Scheduled increases for 1982 have already been put into effect: a 70% hike in electricity and telephone charges, a 90% increase for water, and 44% for fuel. Social security taxes will also be rising. These increases are hitting a population which in the last three years suffered a 40% drop in real wages. As in other IMF agreements, the money to balance the budget and settle the debt comes from the sector of the population that can least afford it.

Commenting on the IMF's stringent measures, Ronald G. Hellman of the Center for Inter-American Relations in New York said: "If the people are required to sacrifice too much in a too short time, both the nation's social fabric and its democratic traditions will weaken."[19]

Costa Rica has balked at other IMF austerity plans because of its commitment to provide good educational and health services to its citizens. Former President Carazo said, "Instead of helping us get fair prices, the IMF has asked us to spend less on everything without considering what this would mean to the population."[20] In Costa Rica 28% of the budget had been spent on education, resulting in an over 90% literacy rate. About 75% of the population has phones and electricity through Costa Rica's government-owned utility; 90% are eligible for government-sponsored health care; and 20% are employed by the public sector, representing 35% of all salaries.

The Monge Administration is hoping for a degree of leniency from the

United States and the multilateral banks because of Costa Rica's strategic political position. But the commercial banks, which hold $1.1 billion of the foreign debt, aren't as concerned about the exigencies of the geo-political situation: Bank of America, Continental Illinois, Citibank, and Chase Manhattan just want their money back. They have even threatened an attachment order on the assets of the national Central Bank of Costa Rica.

Foreign private banks also hold over $1 billion in private debt within Costa Rica. The country's business sector complains that loans procured three years ago were at the rate of 8.6 *colones* to a dollar and now the exchange rate has jumped to over 50 *colones* to a dollar (July 1982).

Agriculture

Costa Rica is a fertile country capable of producing almost any crop, but lately it hasn't been growing enough to feed its own citizens. Costa Ricans are growing resentful about the country's agricultural system that produces ornamental flowers and strawberries for the United States yet can't provide them with corn and beans. In 1980, food imports from the United States increased 64% in value over 1979, while the value of Costa Rica's agricultural exports to the United States declined 16%. Costa Rica in 1980 had to import over 68,000 tons of corn from the U.S. for internal consumption.[21]

The government has oriented its credit and promotion programs to large farmers who produce for the export market which results in a lack of available credit for small farmers who grow for the local market. The World Bank and especially the Inter-American Development Bank (IDB) also foster this imbalance by concentrating their agricultural lending in export production projects, which will bring in the foreign revenue needed to pay off the country's ever-increasing international debt. The imbalance in food production is the result of a trend that has been building for some 150 years in Costa Rica. First came coffee production, then bananas, and after World War Two, sugar cane and the cattle industry took yet more land away from production for the internal market. The latest trend in this race to increase export earnings is a boom in the non-traditional U.S. market for vegetables and flowers from Central America.

Three U.S. corporations control banana production in Costa Rica: United Brands, Castle & Cooke, and R.J. Reynolds. R.J. Reynolds' Del Monte, the latecomer to Costa Rica, bought out the West Indies Company of Miami to establish its base of banana production, but in the last few years, it has been switching to pineapples. Del Monte also operates the Del Campo fruit and vegetable canning business in San Jose. United Brands has been diversifying into African palm production in Costa Rica for the manufacture of edible oil products marketed by its Numar subsidiary in San Jose. Coffee production has become increasingly concentrated. Costa Rica's reputation for having a large class of small farmers is dying a slow but sure death. An exhaustive study of land ownership found that 73% of Costa Rica's rural population are now a landless people who work on large farms and ranches for the equivalent of less than $2.00 a day.[22]

The booming cattle industry has been clearing Costa Rican forests at the rate of more than 10,000 acres a year. The forest reserve diminished from 71% of total area in 1955 to a dismal 15% in 1981.[23] The cattle industry, which produces almost exclusively for the U.S. market, uses 3.1 million acres in Costa Rica.[24] The expanding cattle industry not only takes land that could otherwise be used for local food production, but it is also taking beef out of financial reach for Costa Ricans, since local prices now match U.S. prices. According to the Costa Rican Planning Office, "The system of quotas utilized by the U.S. for beef imports has given rise in recent years to considerable increases in the price of beef and beef by-products domestically."[25]

Recognizing the problem of the drop in local food production, the Monge government has promised a "Back to the Land" program. At the same time, however, the government is catering to the demands of the IMF which encourages agro-exports as a way of balancing the trade deficit.

Not only do people from the U.S. eat bananas and beef from Costa Rica, but they also buy its land. Over 20,000 U.S. citizens live in Costa Rica, enjoying the beautiful setting, the cheap land, and the low cost of living. North Americans living in Costa Rica can import duty-free cars and furniture while Costa Ricans pay a 300% import tax on imported automobiles.

"Our country is up for sale in American newspapers and magazines," said former President of Congress Alfonso Carro Zunica. "Land prices have shot up tenfold in five years because of speculation. There has been a drop in agricultural production because foreigners have chased peasant farmers off their land."[26]

Industry

In the last twenty years, Costa Rica has become a semi-industrialized country — yet industry in Costa Rica is commonly owned by United States corporations. Industrialization has, according to former President of Costa Rica Balmorcich Francisco Orlich (1965), "put the economic sovereignty [of Costa Rica] into a foreign context, in which decisions are made in accordance with the expansion of foreign enterprise and not the needs of Costa Rica, nor of the Central American regional economic whole."[27]

The largest U.S. industries in Costa Rica include Firestone, Coca-Cola, and United Brands (through its subsidiaries Polymer and Numar). Foreign industry is finding Costa Rica more and more attractive because of devaluation of the *colon*. "Costa Rican labor costs are now among the lowest in Latin America," stated *Latin America Regional Report*. "Manufacturers who have been able to build markets in North America or Europe are placed to do extremely well. Government statistics show Costa Ricans working in the clothing industry for around 50% of their counterparts in Taiwan."[28]

The success of free trade zones in Hong Kong and neighboring Panama has encouraged Costa Rica to open two free trade zones of its own in 1982. The corporations locating in these zones are offered duty free import of raw materials, components, machinery, and packaging material. In addition, they offer a 100% exemption from income taxes for the first five years and 50% for the following ten years.

Protecting local industry and promoting production of goods for the internal market are not among the priorities that the U.S. has for Costa Rica. A report by the Overseas Private Investment Corporation (OPIC) stated: "It is our belief that through application [of the Export Promotion Law], Costa Rica can move from the development stage which emphasizes a protected domestic market into a stage in which the national economy can prove its efficiency and the quality of its products in international competition."[29]

The government-sponsored Costa Rican Development Corporation (CODESA) administers the Export Promotion Law. The president of this promotional organization and development bank is Richard Beck, also the president of Atlas Electrica, an affiliate of the Clark Equipment Corporation from the U.S. President of the Costa Rican Chamber of Industries is Walter Kissling, the chief executive of Kativo Industries, owned by H.B. Fuller.

Local industry is facing hard times in Costa Rica because of the lack of foreign currency and slackening product demand in Central America. A University of Costa Rica study found that at the end of 1981, 34% of medium and large industries in Costa Rica had 30 to 180 days remaining before bankruptcy.[30] Industry is encouraged by the likelihood that the government will sell some public industries to the private sector because of pressure from the IMF.

Industrialization has only furthered the economic orientation commonly known as *desarrollo hacia afuera* or development for the outside. During the heyday of the common market in the 1960s, foreign investment increased over 3500% in Costa Rica; and 75% of it comes from the United States.[31]

The multilateral agencies hold much of the blame for the imbalance of trade caused by industrialization. Over 70% of IDB's current funding to Costa Rica goes to road and energy projects which provide increased opportunities for U.S. exports.[32] IDB's $50.4 million loan to the Arenal hydroelectric project is one example of an infrastructure project eroding the national trade position. The contract for the Arenal loan requires that most of the technical assistance and equipment be supplied by an IDB member, thereby insuring the contractors and the technology that aid would come mostly from the U.S.[33] Such projects continue *desarrollo hacia afuera* by creating new markets for U.S. exports.

"Costa Rica is not a country," said Jose Figueres. "It is a pilot project. It is an experiment."[34] Costa Rica isn't an independent nation, but an appendage of the international capitalist system, and a case study of how that system keeps Third World nations underdeveloped and dependent.

References for Introductory Statistics

Business America, March 8, 1982; *Business Latin America*, July 7, 1982; Inter-American Development Bank, *Economic and Social Progress in Latin America 1980-81; Latin America Regional Report;* United Nations, *Monthly Bulletin of Statistics*, April 1982; U.S. Department of Commerce, *Overseas Business Reports — Market Profiles for Latin America*, May 1981.

REFERENCE NOTES

1. John P. Bell, *Crisis in Costa Rica*, (University of Texas Press, 1971), p. 6.
2. Thomas McCann, *United Fruit: Tragedy of an American Company*, (Crown, 1976).
3. Bell, p. 37.
4. Bell, p. 151.
5. Alan Riding, "For Rudderless Costa Rica, a Quixotic Rescue Effort," *New York Times*, January 12, 1981.
6. "Congressional Presentation: Fiscal Year 1983," Agency for International Development, p. 77.
7. Foreign Assistance and Related Programs, Congressional Appropriations, 1983.
8. "Monge Whistles in the Dark," *LARR*, July 9, 1982, p. 6.
9. Foreign Assistance and Related Programs, Congressional Appropriations, 1983.
10. Christopher Dickey, "Costa Rica's Idyll Ending," *Washington Post*, April 28, 1982.
11. *LARR*, July 9, 1982, p. 6.
12. *New York Times*, January 12, 1982.
13. *LARR*, June 6, 1980.
14. "Workers Walk Out," *Central American Report*, July 1981.
15. *LARR*, September 18, 1981.
16. "Why Democracy is Tottering in Costa Rica," *Business Week*, February 23, 1981, p. 60.
17. *New York Times*, January 12, 1982.
18. Helio Fallas, *Economic Crisis in Costa Rica*, (Editorial Nueva Decada, San Jose:1981).
19. Ronald G. Hellman, "How to Help — and Hurt — Costa Rica," *Los Angeles Times*, May 12, 1982.
20. *Mesoamerica*, March 1982.
21. "U.S. Farm Exports Gain in Central America," *Foreign Agriculture*, October 1981, p. 21.
22. "Origins of the Crisis," *A Shift in the Wind*, No. 13, (The Hunger Project, 1982), p. 5.
23. *Ibid*.
24. *Quarterly Economic Review, 1981 Annual Supplement*, The Economist Intelligence Unit Ltd.
25. OFIPLAN, Government of Costa Rica, 1968.
26. Alan Riding, "Americans Pose Costa Rica Issue," *New York Times*, February 23, 1975.
27. J. Edward Taylor, "Peripheral Capitalism and Rural-Urban Migration: A Study of Population Movements in Costa Rica," *Latin American Perspectives*, Issues 25 and 26, (Spring and Summer, 1980).
28. "Carazo Era Limps to a Close," *LARR*, September 18, 1981.
29. Overseas Private Investment Corporation (OPIC) Report on Costa Rica.
30. Shirley Christian, "Costa Rica Starving for Dollars to Pay Creditors," *Miami Herald*, February 16, 1982.
31. R. Peter DeWitt, "The IDB and Policy Making in Costa Rica," *The Journal of Developing Areas*, October 1980.
32. *Ibid*.
33. *Ibid*.
34. *New York Times*, January 12, 1982.

UNITED STATES BUSINESS IN COSTA RICA*

ABA Industries; *metal machine parts manufacturing*

ABC
Televisora de Costa Rica; *radio and television broadcasting*

ACF Industries
Polymer; *plastic and resin manufacturing*

Allegheny International
All State Welding Alloys de Centroamérica

Allied
Allied Chemical International
Atico

Agrodinamica Holding Company
Ganadera Industrial (GISA); *cattle production*

American Cyanamid
Cyanamid Inter-American; *medical and chemical product manufacturing and distribution*

American Flower; *flower growing and exporting; LAAD equity*

American Home Products
Anakol de Costa Rica
Laboratorios Veterinarios Crespo; *veterinary medicine*

American Mushroom
American Mushroom Corporation Costa Rica; *fruit, vegetable, and mushroom processing and export*

American Realty; *real estate brokerage*

American Standard
Industria Cerámica Costarricense; *sanitary fixtures and accessory manufacturing*

American Tropical Hardwoods

Amindus

Arrow Beef
Pecuaria Costarricense

Bache, Halsey, Stuart, Shields
BONA; *investments and brokerage firm*

H.J. Baker
Bakerbro Centroamericano

BankAmerica
Bank of America; *banking; two branches*
Credomatic International; *Master Charge credit card services*
Development Credit
Financería América

Bartlett-Collins
Industrias Bartlett-Collins de Costa Rica; *glass manufacturing*
Textiles Flex

Beatrice Foods
Hacienda la Rosita; *food processing*

Bendix
United Geophysical; *auto and aerospace electronics product manufacturing*

Bienville Export; *coffee processing*

Boise Cascade
Industria Nacional de Papel; *lumber*

The Borden Company
Figoríficos de Puntarenas; *fish processing*
Henderson; *fishing*
Peseuig Mariscos; *fishing*

Boudet, James L.; *orange and lime production*

Bristol-Myers
Empresas Bristol de Costa Rica; *toiletries*

Burroughs
Burroughs de Centroamérica; *business equipment and sales*

Campbell Air Survey
Servicio Nacional de Helicópteros

Castle & Cooke
Compañía Financiera de Costa Rica
Dole; *fruit production*
Envases Industriales
Standard Fruit
Standard Fruit & Steamship

CBS
Industria de Discos Centroamericanos
Mundo Musical
CBS Columbia

Central American Meats

Central Soya
Central Soya International; *animal feed processing*

*An indented item is a subsidiary, affiliate, or branch of the corporation immediately above it.

Chase Manhattan
  Chase Manhattan Costa Rica
  Desarrollo Agropecuario de Diquis;
    cattle production
  Textilera Tres Rios

Chemetex Fibers
  Olympic Fibre; *yarn manufacturing*

Citicorp ; *banking*

Cities Services
  Cities Service Minerals
  Compañía Minera Annie
  Compañía Minera Eleonor
  Compañía Minera Gabina
  Compañía Minera Joyce
  Compañía Minera Malmisa
  Compañía Minera Praxedes
  Compañía Minera Sandra
  Compañía Minera Ursula
  Compañía Minera Vesta

Clark Equipment
  Atlas Eléctrica; *refrigeration equipment
    and supplies*

Coca-Cola
  Coca-Cola Interamerican; *soft drink
    industry*

Colborn-Dawes

Colgate Palmolive
  Colgate Palmolive; *toothpaste and soap*
  Pozuelo
  Riviana Foods; *food processing*

Collins Foods
  Kentucky Fried Chicken; *restaurant*

Compton Transfer & Storage
  Industria Nacional de Banano

Consolidated Foods
  Manufacturera de Cartago; *clothes
    manufacturing*

Cooper Laboratories
  Laboratorios Cooper de Centroamérica;
    medical equipment

Coopers & Lybrand
  Ceciliano y Compañía; *accounting and
    tax consulting*

Cort Industries
  Compañía del Vestido

Crescent Corset
  Crescent International; *clothes
    manufacturing*

Crown Cork & Seal
  Crown Cork Centroamericana; *cork
    manufacturing*

Crown Zellerbach
  Convertidora Nacional de Papel; *paper
    product manufacturing*

Crush International
  Orange Crush de Costa Rica; *soft drink
    industry*

Damon
  Laboratorios Biológicos Industriales

David Tucker & Garth Kistler

Dawe's Laboratories
  Dawe's Laboratories of Central America

Deloitte, Haskins & Sells; *auditing and
    managerial services*

Dow Chemical
  Dow Química de Centroamérica;
    chemical manufacturing

Dresser Industries
  Harbison-Walker Refractarios; *high
    technology equipment*

E.I. Du Pont de Nemours & Company
  Conoco; *petroleum refining and
    distribution*
  Continental Abonos; *fertilizer mixing*

Eastman Kodak
  Panama Kodak; *film processing*

Eaton
  Cutler-Hammer Centroamericana;
    electrical equipment manufacturing

Ecoland
  Inversiones Nicoya

Embotelladora Tica; *soft drink bottling*

Emerson Electric
  Skil Centroamericana

Empacadora Costarricense Danesa; *meat
    processing; two branches; ADELA
    equity*

Empire Brushes
  Costa Rica Commercial; *brooms and
    brushes*

Exxon
  Esso Standard Oil
  Essochem de Centroamérica
  Exxon; *petroleum refining*

Far West Botanical

Firestone Tire & Rubber
  Industria Firestone de Costa Rica
  Super Servicios; *tires*

First Boston
  Corporación Internacional de Boston
    (CIBSA)
  Financiera de América

First Chicago
First Chicago Costa Rica

First Pennsylvania Bank
Financiera del First Pennsylvania;
banking

Florida Ice & Farm; *brewery*

FMC
FMC International; *technical services
and agricultural chemicals distribution*

Foliage; *plant production; LAAD equity*

Foremost-McKesson
Foremost Industries; *dairy processing*

Frigoríficos Técnicos; *frozen foods;
LAAD equity*

H.B. Fuller
Alfombras Canon
Decontinas de Centroamérica
Kativo Chemical Industries; *paint,
plastics, and resins*
Kativo Commercial
Reichhold de Centroamérica; *plastic
and resin manufacturing*
Syntéticos

General Telephone & Electronics (GTE)
GTE Sylvania; *electric houseware
manufacturing*
General Telephone Directories; *phone
book printing*

Gerber Products
Productos Gerber de Centroamérica;
babyfood processing

B.F. Goodrich
B.F. Goodrich Química de Costa Rica
Recauchadora B.F. Goodrich; *tires*

Goodyear Tire & Rubber
Goodyear Export; *agricultural
production and rubber plantation*

W.R. Grace & Company
Felipe Pozuelo e Hijos; *food processing*

Griffith Laboratories
Laboratorios Griffith de Centroamérica;
food processing

Grolier
Grolier de Centroamérica; *reference
book publishing*

Gulf Oil
Gulf Costa Rica; *petroleum*

Harbour Land & Cattle; *cattle production*

Hearst
King Features Syndicate; *business
services and newspaper cartoons*

Helechos de Costa Rica; *fern farm*

Hemphill Schools; *correspondence schools*

Hershey Foods
Compañía Agrícola Huntro; *cocoa*

Hirsch Fabrics
Hirsch Costa Rica; *clothes
manufacturing*

Hockman Lewis
Equigas de Costa Rica; *gasoline
equipment distribution*

Holiday Inn

Homestake Mining
Minera de los Cerros Negros; *mining*

Honeywell
Honeywell Sistemas de Información;
business equipment sales

Hudson Pulp Paper
Sutil; *paper manufacturing*

Hytronics; *electronic component
manufacturing*

IBM World Trade Corporation
IBM de Costa Rica; *business machines*

IC Industries
Costa Rican Cocoa Products; *cocoa
and chocolate processing*

Ingenio La Garita

International Executive Service; *consulting
services*

International Flavors & Fragrances
International Flavors & Fragrances
Centroamericana

International Paper
Papel Internacional Costa Rica

The Interpublic Group of Companies
McCann-Erickson Centroamericana;
advertising

Intrópica

ITT
ITT de Costa Rica; *business equipment*

IU International
Cariblanco; *sugar production*

Johns-Manville
Ricalit; *asbestos and cement sheet
manufacturing*

Johnson & Johnson International
Químicas Ortho; *chemicals*

S.C. Johnson & Son (Johnson Wax)
S.C. Johnson de Centroamérica;
household products

Joseph J. Master; *ornamental plants*

Joseph E. Seagram & Sons
Destiladora Conveco; *liquor distilling*
Seagrams de Costa Rica; *liquor*

Kaiser Aluminum & Chemical

Kaiser Industries
Auto-Técnica; *automotive parts and supplies*

Kem Manufacturing
Kem Centroamericana; *chemical product manufacturing and sales*

Latin American Development Enterprise (LADESA)
Acropolis Centroamericana
Latin American Development Enterprises

Lear Siegler; *industrial equipment*

Lee B. Teacher

Loctite
Permatex de Centroamérica; *industrial machinery and adhesive manufacturing*

Loews
Loews Hotels

Longyear
E.J. Longyear; *diamond drills*
Longyear Centroamericana

The Lovable Company
Celebrity; *clothes manufacturing*

Management Assistance
MAI de Costa Rica; *business equipment manufacturing*

Manhattan Industries
Barzuma Hermanos; *clothes manufacturing*

Maquinaria Tractores; *tractor sales*

Maricultura; *shrimp farm*

Marine Midland Banks
Almacenadora
Crece; *import-export development*

McDonald's
McDonald's Costa Rica; *fast food*

The Mennen Company
Industrial Hible; *toiletries*
Mennen de Costa Rica; *toiletries*

Merck & Company
Merck, Sharp & Dohme; *pharmaceutical manufacturing and distribution*

Miles Laboratories
Miles Chemicals Overseas de Costa Rica
Miles de Costa Rica; *pharmaceutical product manufacturing*

Minnesota Mining & Manufacturing
3M Centroamericana

Monsanto
Monsanto de Costa Rica; *chemicals*

Motores Americanos; *AMC auto dealer*

Motorola
Electronica Nacional
Motorola de Centroamérica; *communication components*

Nabisco Brands
Aceitera Centroamericana; *food processing*
Compañía Petrolera California; *petroleum products*
Golden; *food processing*
Pan American Standard Brands; *vegetable oil and fat processing*

Newport Pharmaceuticals International
Newport Pharmaceuticals de Costa Rica

Northern Ventures; *highway and industrial construction project*

Northwest Industries
Microdot; *auto and electrical parts*
Velsicol Costa Rica; *agricultural services*

Norton
Christiansen Diamond Productos de Costa Rica; *diamond bit manufacturing*

Norton Simon
Canada Dry Bottling; *soft drink industry*
Max Factor & Company; *cosmetic distribution*

Occidental Petroleum
International Ore & Fertilizer
Interior Productos Químicos-Agrícolas; *fertilizers*

Osa Productos Forestales

Pan American World Airways; *air transportation*

Peat, Marwick, Mitchell & Company; *international auditing*

PepsiCo
Pepsi Cola; *soft drink industry*
Pizza Hut; *restaurant; four branches*

Pfizer; *pharmaceutical, agricultural and veterinary product manufacturing*

Phelps Dodge
Conducen; *electrical equipment manufacturing*

Philip Morris
Mendiola & Company; *tobacco and liquor manufacturing*
Tabacalera Costarricense; *tobacco*

Phillips Petroleum
Productos Plásticos; *plastic container manufacturing*

Phillips-Van Heusen; *shirt manufacturing*

Playboy International; *hotel and club*

Pollary & Child
Dinámica

Pozuelo Picasso; *wood furniture; LAAD equity*

Price Waterhouse & Company
Price Waterhouse y Compañía; *accounting and auditing*

Projectos Técnica y Ejecución de Costa Rica; *construction management; ADELA equity*

Quaker Oats
Quaker de Costa Rica; *food processing*

Rapistan; *materials handling equipment*

Residencial Los Claveles; *low cost housing project; ADELA equity*

Residencial Los Lagos; *low cost housing project; ADELA equity*

Residencial San Fancisco; *low cost housing project; ADELA equity*

R.J. Reynolds
Banana Development Corporation of Costa Rica (BANDECO); *farm management; three branches*
Bananera del Carmen; *banana production*
Conservas del Campo; *food processing*
Del Monte de Costa Rica
Del Monte Foreign Sales
Monte Libano; *food processing*
Productores Unidos de Banano
Sealand Service; *transportation*
South American Development

Rico Tico Alimentos; *food processing; LAAD equity*

Rio Colorado Drilling
Rio Sabalo; *drilling*

Rohm & Haas
Laboratorios Químicos Industriales
Rogaro Industria Química
Rohm & Hass Centroamericana; *chemicals*

Sam P. Wallace
Sam P. Wallace de Centroamérica; *construction*

Saunders Brothers
Forestal Centroamericana; *forest products*

Schering-Plough
Industrias Arco
Schering Corporación de Centroamérica

SCM
Compañía Agrícola Myristica; *food production*
Holtenman & Compañía; *tire retreading*
Pinturas Centroamericanas Costa Rica (PINTICA)
Plastikart

Scott Paper
Scott Paper Company de Costa Rica; *paper products*

Sears Roebuck & Company; *department store*

Sherwin-Williams
Central de Pinturas; *paint distribution*
Sherwin-Williams de Costa Rica; *paint*

Siemens Capital; *electrical products*

The Signal Companies
Garrett Asociados

Singer Manufacturing Company of New Jersey; *sewing machine distribution*

Skyline
Skyline de Costa Rica; *mobile home manufacturing*

Society
Corporación Costarricense de Financiamento Industrial; *bank holding company*

St. Regis Paper
St. Regis de Costa Rica
Envases Comerciales

Standard Oil of California
Compañía Petrolera Chevron
Químicas Ortho de California

Standard Oil of Ohio
Chocosuela Sulphur; *sulphur exploration and development*
Kennecott Copper

Sterling Drug
Sterling Products International; *pharmaceutical products and cosmetic manufacturing and distribution*

Sugarman Associates; *management services*

Susquehanna
Accesorios Plásticos Centroamericanos; *building materials*

Tandy
Radioshack; *radio-communications equipment*

Tax Planning Company of Costa Rica; *financial consulting*

Taylor & Associates
Empacadora Taylor Associates; *meat processing; LAAD equity*

Tenería GISA; *tannery; LAAD equity*

Texaco
Texaco Caribbean; *petroleum products*

Texas Caribbean Enterprises

Transway International
Coordinated Caribbean Transport
(CCT); *marine and overland
transportation*
Tropigas de Costa Rica; *gas*

Travenol Export
Laboratorios Travenol; *medical
products*

Tropex
Tropec

Union Carbide
Union Carbide Centroamericana;
electrical apparatus manufacturing

Uniroyal; *chemical sales*

United Brands
Compañía Bananera Atlántica (COBAL)
Compañía Bananera de Costa Rica;
banana and palm production
Mundimar
Numar de Costa Rica; *vegetable oil
products*
Polymer de Costa Rica; *plastic
manufacturing and distribution*
Polymer United
Proyecto Agro-Industrial de Sixaola
(PAIS); *agricultural projects
development*
Sistemas Electrónicos de Datos y
Ciencias Administrativos (SEDCA);
data preparation
Transporte Internacional Gash
Unimar; *marketing*

U.S. Gypsum; *mining and exploration*

United Technologies
Compañía Otis Elevator; *elevator sales
and maintenance*

Universal Food Products
Universal Food Products International;
food processing

Vaughan

Warnaco
Warner's de Costa Rica; *clothes
manufacturing*

West Chemical Products
West Chemical Products Costa Rica

Wheelabrator-Frye
Sinclair & Valentine de
Centroamérica; *chemical product
manufacturing*

Xerox
Copicentro Costa Rica; *business
equipment*
Xerox de Costa Rica; *business
equipment*

Yolanda
Yolanda de Costa Rica

Zapata
Pescamar de Centroamérica; *fishing*
Sardimar

Zinke Smith
Compañía Asfaltica Nacional
Zinke Smith

REFERENCES

Directory of American Firms Operating in Foreign Countries, 1979; *Directory of Corporate Affiliations*, 1982; Dun & Bradstreet, "Principal International Businesses," 1982; *Export/Import Markets*, 1982; *Foreign Index to the Directory of Corporate Affiliations*, 1981; *Million Dollar Directory*, 1982; *Moody's*, 1981; *Rand McNally International Bankers Directory*, 1982; 10-K Reports, 1981; *World Directory of Multinational Enterprises*, 1980.

ADELA, Annual Reports, 1981; *Agribusiness in the Americas*, 1980; American Chamber of Commerce of Costa Rica, "1982 Membership Directory"; BankAmerica, "Bank of America Worldwide Facilities," May 1981; Camera de Industrias de Costa Rica, Directorio Oficial, 1982; Donald Castillo Rivas, *Acumulacion de Capital y Empresas Transnacionales en Centroamerica*, 1980; Guia de Informacion Para Centroamerica, Panama, Miami y San Andres Isla, 1981-1982; Latin American Agribusiness Development Corporation (LAAD), Annual Reports, 1976-1981; *Mergers & Acquisitions*, Spring 1982; Overseas Private Investment Corporation (OPIC), Annual Reports, 1978-1981.

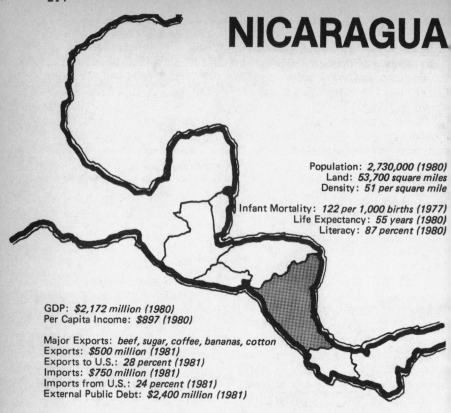

NICARAGUA

Population: *2,730,000 (1980)*
Land: *53,700 square miles*
Density: *51 per square mile*

Infant Mortality: *122 per 1,000 births (1977)*
Life Expectancy: *55 years (1980)*
Literacy: *87 percent (1980)*

GDP: *$2,172 million (1980)*
Per Capita Income: *$897 (1980)*

Major Exports: *beef, sugar, coffee, bananas, cotton*
Exports: *$500 million (1981)*
Exports to U.S.: *28 percent (1981)*
Imports: *$750 million (1981)*
Imports from U.S.: *24 percent (1981)*
External Public Debt: *$2,400 million (1981)*

The oldest family dictatorship in Latin America ended in 1979 when the Sandinista Front for National Liberation (FSLN) overthrew Nicaragua's Anastasio Somoza. Since their triumph on July 19, 1979, Nicaraguans have been trying to build a strong and independent nation, while the United States has been using both direct and indirect means to undermine the Sandinista government.

United States involvement in Nicaragua's internal affairs is a tradition that began in the 1830s when U.S. businessmen started formulating plans to construct an inter-oceanic canal through Nicaragua. In 1837, President Van Buren sent a representative to Nicaragua to negotiate a right-of-way for the proposed canal, but the presidential representative consulted with U.S. businessmen in Nicaragua, not with Nicaraguans. This early canal proposal failed, but shortly afterwards investor Cornelius Vanderbilt had a plan to establish the Accessory Transit Authority (ATA) to finance, build, and operate a canal in Nicaragua. In 1854, after an anti-United States protest attacked the U.S. Foreign Ministry in San Juan del Norte, the U.S. warship *Cayne* shelled that Nicaraguan port.

Vanderbilt's canal plans also failed, but both U.S. business and the U.S.

government retained their interest in Nicaragua. One ambitious U.S. adventurer, William Walker, came to Nicaragua with a band of mercenaries, and declared himself president of Nicaragua in 1856.

By the turn of the century, the proposed canal site shifted to Panama, but the United States continued to meddle in the internal affairs of Nicaragua. In 1912, the U.S. Marines hit the shores of Nicaragua to settle a local political dispute and stayed on intermittently through the next 20 years. In 1927, the U.S. intervened when the U.S.-supported conservative leader was challenged by a liberal revolt. The U.S. occupation army enforced a new political settlement and oversaw new elections in 1928. Finding this dishonorable and imposed peace unsatisfactory, Augusto Cesar Sandino organized an anti-imperialist army of peasants, who had the support of the progressive urban population. The U.S. Marines bombed most of the northern section of Nicaragua, but the U.S. forces couldn't defeat Sandino's Defensive Army of the National Sovereignty.[1]

The Marines finally withdrew in 1932. Popularly known as the "General of Free Men," Sandino had achieved his main objective of chasing the Yankee army out of Nicaragua. Before their departure, the U.S. Marines established the National Guard under the leadership of Anastasio Somoza Garcia, who had lived in the U.S. and was fluent in English. Somoza's first task was clear. Somoza told a council of Nicaraguan officials in February 1934: "I have come from the United States Embassy where I have had a conference with Ambassador Arturo Bliss, who has assured me that the government in Washington supports and recommends the elimination of Augusto Cesar Sandino for considering him a disturber of the peace of the country."[2] Soon thereafter, Sandino accepted a fateful dinner invitation at the Presidential Palace ostensibly to discuss the future of Nicaragua. On his way home after the dinner, Somoza's men assassinated him. General Somoza, having eliminated his main competitor, then ousted President Juan Bautista Sacasa in 1936. With the U.S. blessing, he initiated the longest, most corrupt dictatorship in Latin America.

Twenty years later, Nicaraguan poet Rigoberto Lopez Perez assassinated the Somoza patriarch. State power then transferred to Somoza's eldest son, Luis Somoza Debayle; and upon his death in 1967, his brother Anastasio "Tacho" Somoza Debayle inherited the family dictatorship.

The Life World Library in its book on Central America (1964) reported that the Somoza family "controls about one-tenth of the cultivable land in Nicaragua, and just about everything else worth owning, the country's only airline, one television station, a newspaper, a cement plant, textile mill, several sugar refineries, half a dozen breweries and distilleries, and a Mercedes-Benz agency."

The brutality of the notorious Somoza dictatorship often embarrassed the United States, but the State Department supported him until the very end as the representative of U.S. interests in Central America. Somoza took pride that he was "the only national leader the U.S. could count on to bat 1000% for the U.S. in the United Nations."

The Somoza family was the bully for the U.S. in Central America, directing the CONDECA military forces collaborating with the banana companies to keep other Central American nations in line with U.S. interests. As President Franklin D. Roosevelt said, "Somoza may be a son-of-a-bitch, but he is *our* son-of-a-bitch."[3] With the help of the United States, the National Guard of Nicaragua protected the Somoza dictatorship until the victory of the Sandinistas in 1979. Until that time, the United States had trained 4,693 Nicaraguan soliders, more per capita than any other country in the hemisphere.[4]

POLITICS

The Sandinista Front for National Liberation (FSLN) was founded in July 1961, to carry on the anti-imperialist battle initiated by Augusto Sandino. "The FSLN," noted Commander Carlos Nunez, "is the vanguard of the Nicaraguan people, not only for having defined that the masses were the forces capable of moving history. If yesterday, oriented and directed by their vanguard, they were the motor of the overthrow of the dictatorship, then today, directed by that vanguard, the masses are the motor of the revolution."[5] In July 1979, the FSLN formed the Government Junta of National Reconstruction (JGRN).

Over 40,000 Nicaraguans lost their lives in the two years of fighting before the Sandinista triumph in 1979, but the U.S. Republican Party Platform of 1980 pledged to "roll back" this hard-won victory. President Reagan began the offensive by cutting back on promised economic aid and food shipments, and in 1982 he authorized $19 million for a covert campaign to weaken the JGRN through paramilitary activities.[6]

The United States has also allowed right-wing Nicaraguan organizations to train on U.S. soil for an eventual invasion of Nicaragua. It also doubled military aid in 1982 to the Honduran government, which has let Somocistas raid Nicaragua regularly from Honduran territory. Another part of the U.S. offensive against Nicaragua is its support of anti-Sandinista elements within Nicaragua such as the High Council of Private Enterprise (COSEP), the hierarchy of the Catholic Church, the reactionary newspaper *La Prensa*, and the Permanent Human Rights Commission. Such aid is in keeping with the conservative United States-based Heritage Foundation's recommendation that "appropriately channeled assistance to the democratic institutions in Nicaragua could be far more effective and far less expensive than our currently structured official U.S. aid program."[7]

Nicaragua, though, won't be another Chile or Guatemala, countries where the U.S. engineered coups to remove popular governments. The Sandinista government has educated and armed the Nicaraguan masses, who have the full franchise of the revolution and don't intend to let Nicaragua be taken away from them. Nicaraguans also count on support from the citizens of the United States. As junta member Sergio Ramierz said, "The people of the United

States have become the principal element to stop any aggression against us or intervention in Central America. [Otherwise] people like Haig and Kirkpatrick would have long ago invaded."[8]

ECONOMY

The Sandinistas inherited a devastated economy. According to the United Nations, over 25% of Nicaragua's factories suffered damage to plant and inventory during the insurrection and over 90% closed in its final stages. The war cost Nicaragua $500 million in physical damage, $200 million in lost cotton exports, and $700 million in capital flight, as well as a 25% reduction in cattle herd. Unemployment was 40% at the time of the victory, and inflation was 80%.[9] The Somoza family had plundered the national banks, leaving only $3.5 million in the national treasury and a national debt of $1.6 billion.

After three years of reconstruction, Nicaragua's economy has still not recovered from the war, but there are some hopeful economic indicators. While most of the other Central American nations had negative growth rates in 1981, the Gross Domestic Product (GDP) in Nicaragua rose 8.9% that year. A similar growth rate was expected for 1982 before the May floods, which caused $200 million in losses and set back Nicaragua to the economic position of the immediate postwar period.

Heavy government investment and stringent government regulations on imports have stimulated the economy. By controlling the exchange rate, the government has successfully limited imports, thereby improving the balance of trade and winning the approval of multilateral agencies like the World Bank.

The 1981 economic plan, "An Economic Program of Austerity and Efficiency," proposed a dominant role for the state while welcoming local and foreign private investment at the same time. A March 1981 survey by *Business Latin America* found that there was low investor confidence even though "the economy is still largely in the hands of private industry and farmers." Another survey by *Business Latin America*, in August 1981, concluded that "most multinational corporations receive fair treatment from the Sandinistas."

Although many business people feel they can continue to make a profit in Nicaragua, most have been reluctant to increase their investment, given what they view as the uncertain political direction in Nicaragua. Private investment is below 10% in 1982, with little optimism that it will increase in the near future, despite government incentives for increased production. What frustrates many capitalists is the Decapitalization Law, which encourages company employees to report suspected decapitalization schemes by business owners. The government can confiscate a firm found to be decapitalizing. Decapitalization refers to the deliberate decrease of inventory and sale of equipment and plant in order to liquidate as much investment as possible before shutting down the business and leaving the country. As harsh as the law sounds, *Business Latin America* found in its August 1981 survey that "most executives express little or no fear that expropriations under the Decapitalization Law would extend to their businesses."

The Government of National Reconstruction has enforced the Decapitalization Law when necessary. Sears, Roebuck & Company, for example, was unhappy that its business had slowed down due to the restrictions on luxury imports and began selling its stock in preparation to leave Nicaragua. But before it could divest, the government padlocked the company's doors, declaring the company public property because it had violated the law.

The Sandinistas consider decapitalizing practices part of the destabilization plan the United States has devised against Nicaragua. Junta member Bayardo Arce said: "Those that are trying to sabotage the revolution, that are boycotting it, that are decapitalizing the economy, do so because they are energized, supported and pushed from outside by a power that makes them feel confident. That is imperialist policy."[10]

The Sandinista government announced a new exports promotion plan in 1982 that increased incentives to private investors and guaranteed the private sector an important role in the economy. The government has committed itself to a mixed economy, but as *Business Latin America* suggests, "Continued U.S. opposition to the regime would surely harm any chances of regional rapprochement and resumed trade and investment between the Central American Common Market and the U.S."[11]

Despite the tradition of United States military presence in Nicaragua, the country was never a primary focus of investment activities. The Somoza dictatorship had prevented the growth of an independent bourgeoisie, thereby keeping internal markets small. In the 1960s and 1970s, however, United States investments did increase, as a result of the new Central American Common Market (CACM). At the time of Somoza's fall, 70 major U.S. corporations were operating in Nicaragua. Presently, about 60% of the economy remains in the private sector, including large transnationals such as Exxon, General Mills, H.B. Fuller, Hercules, and American Cyanamid. Exxon's Managua refinery is operating at a level equal to that before the victory, and Hercules, Inc. reports that the deteriorating regional market – not the Nicaraguan market – has hurt its Central American sales.[12]

"In Nicaragua," said junta member Daniel Ortega, "there is the kind of businessman who doesn't flee, who doesn't hide his money, but who invests it and puts it at the service of the revolution."[13]

Public Finance

The United Nations Economic Commission for Latin America (ECLA), stated that the Somoza government "increasingly sought access to international financial support, especially from private sources," as the conflict in Nicaragua became more acute. Towards the end of the Somoza regime, the foreign debt became heavily skewed towards short-term, high-interest loans to support the war.[14] In 1976, Nicaragua faced a foreign debt of $642 million; by 1979, it had more than doubled, reaching $1.6 billion.

Somoza took the money and ran, leaving only $3.5 million in the national treasury. After the victory, the Government Junta of National Reconstruction assured the world banking community that it would honor international debts with the exception of those to Israel and Argentina, countries that had supplied arms to Somoza's National Guard. Multilateral agencies responded favorably and negotiated concessionary terms with the Sandinistas, while the private banks like Citibank and Bank of America were less receptive. Citibank, which has a reputation in other Third World nations for hard bargaining, has been the most inflexible in negotiations for new repayment terms. During the negotiations with Citibank, Alfredo Cesar, then director of Nicaragua's Finance Ministry, said that Citibank was "the type of bank that will try to squeeze the last drop of blood from a pigeon."

The servicing of Nicaragua's accumulated debt is putting severe limits on the revolution. In 1981, 40.1% of its export earnings went to service its external debt and servicing on U.S. loans was still behind. At the end of 1981, the government had to reschedule 93% of its multilateral and commercial loans. The balance of trade deficit shows no signs of improving, with the 1982 account deficit standing at $500 million.[15]

Somoza's greed was a big reason for Nicaragua's huge debt, but like other underdeveloped countries, Nicaragua has been forced to increase its debt because of the falling value of exports and the rising price of imports. In 1960, foreign credit for agriculture financed 43% of production; by 1971, 90%. From 1970-75, the amount borrowed for agricultural production was greater than agricultural export earnings.[16]

Since the Sandinistas took power, the United States has used its influence to obstruct concessionary lending to Nicaragua. It blocked a $40 million Inter-American Development Bank loan which would have revitalized the country's fishing industry. It curtailed insurance and credit from the Overseas Private Investment Corporation and the Export-Import Bank, thereby discouraging new foreign investment and hindering the sales of much needed spare machine parts to Nicaragua.

Cuba and the Soviet Union have given Nicaragua some financial aid and credit, but Mexico, Venezuela, Panama, Argentina, Brazil, France, Sweden, Libya, Holland, West Germany, and the European Economic Community have contributed the overwhelming majority of international assistance to the Sandinista government.

Public spending escalated rapidly after the Sandinistas formed the JGRN, rising from 21% of the GDP in 1980 to 31% in 1981. In 1982, the government faced a half billion shortfall in its administrative budget and launched a strict plan to cut inefficiency and waste. It increased taxes on luxury goods from 30% to 100% and has frozen vacant posts in government enterprises; and to maintain production at this critical time, it has prohibited strikes. Commenting on the government measures and the state of the economy, Nicaragua's largest trade union body, Central Sandinista de Trabajadores (CST), said it has committed itself to guarantee that every worker will "have bread on the table."[17] The Government of National Reconstruction has been successful in increasing what it calls the "social wage" — goods and services that people receive from the government rather than buy in the marketplace.[18]

Industry

Before the revolution, Nicaragua had one of the most wide-open investment policies in Central America, which allowed full profit repatriation and offered attractive tax incentives. The revolution has frightened off some investors, confiscated others, but encouraged those that remained. Industrial production is expected to rise 5% in 1982 after a 9% increase in 1981. Industry, however, is encountering U.S. sponsored sabotage and the regional problems of economic decline in the CACM, lack of foreign exchange, and inadequate credit supply.

The High Council of Private Enterprise (COSEP) and the American Chamber of Commerce in Nicaragua represent the business sector and have often expressed opposition to the Sandinista government. R. Bruce Cuthbertson, regional vice-president of the American Chamber of Commerce in Central America and representative of the Inter-American Builders Association in Nicaragua, believes that Central America is sick. "After more than twenty years of political stability and sustained growth, the area is now suffering from political cancer. . .[which is] a major cause of its economic problems," said Cuthbertson. "The Sandinistas are establishing a Marxist-Leninist dictatorship in Nicaragua."[19]

In reaction to private sector complaints against the Sandinistas, junta member Sergio Ramirez said, "I wish someone would point to another country which, after winning an armed revolution, still has . . . a private sector which not only operates but which receives incentives."[20]

The United States has sent economic aid to COSEP and to unions in Nicaragua affiliated with the AFL-CIO, while cutting off aid to other agencies. In 1981, the U.S. designated 60% of its $75 million in aid to the private sector. Only one half of the other 40% in public development aid made it to Nicaragua before Reagan halted the aid program because Nicaragua was allegedly aiding the Salvadoran guerillas.

The Agency for International Development (AID) in 1982 granted $5 million in aid to COSEP, whose members are the largest capitalists in the country, to initiate a program to expand its base among smaller business people and small farmers. The program competed directly with the government's campaign to win the support of small agricultural producers.[21]

Tensions between COSEP and the Sandinista government climaxed in October 1981 when four COSEP members were arrested for publicizing an open letter that accused the junta of "diverting the revolutionary process" and of "preparing a new genocide." The letter, which was sent to important organizations around the world, was a direct challenge to the Sandinista government's Emergency Decree and an obvious attempt to further destabilize the government. Determined to put an end to U.S. backed destabilization activities, the Government of National Reconstruction jailed the COSEP leaders for four months. After his release, Enrique Dreyfus, president of COSEP, reported that the COSEP leaders were "treated correctly and with no problems." "Willing to start with a clean slate," Dreyfus commented on the law, passed while he was jailed, that provided generous export incentives to private business: "Our release and the new law complement each other. Both were very well received by the private sector."[22]

After the 1979 victory, many commercial and industrial enterprises came under state control. The Industrial Corporation of the People (COIP) oversees the administration of the state productive apparatus. This includes 106 enterprises with state participation, 77 of which the state has majority control. About 35% of the industrial sector is state-operated.[23] According to the national economic plan, these publicly-controlled enterprises will become the base of the transition to a new industrial structure.

In addition to those companies abandoned by Somoza and his followers, the government nationalized the bankrupt insurance and banking industry as well as companies that exploited the country's natural resources.

A focus of anti-Yankee sentiment after the revolution was the Pennwalt caustic chemical plant, which was responsible for the mercury poisoning of Lake Managua and of Pennwalt employees. The Nicaragua Institute of Natural Resources found that the lakeside plant had pumped between two and four tons of mercury into the lake every year for 12 years. The country's new Department of Occupational Safety and Health found that 56 of the 152 workers displayed evidence of mercury contamination.[24] Pennwalt had been aware of the contamination and had installed controls at similar plants in the U.S. The government, now part-owner of the plant with Pennwalt, has insisted on better controls at the Managua plant.

Because of strict import regulations imposed by the new government, some consumer goods manufacturers in Nicaragua are prospering, even with the decline of the Central American Common Market. This increased need within the country for processed foods, toiletries, and pharmaceuticals has kept these import-substitution industries in the black.

The government nationalized gold and silver mines owned by Noranda Mines, Asarco, and Rosario Resources. Nicaragua's Institute of Mining immediately started on a program to improve the working and living conditions of the miners. Despite the departure of most managers and technicians during the insurrection, mining production is keeping up with historic levels. The government is emphasizing public investment in energy development to reduce its oil import bill. Oil currently accounts for one third of the import bill, but the country hopes to achieve self-sufficiency in energy by 1987.

To increase industrial development on the isolated east coast, the Sandinista government has initiated feasibility studies to build a deep water port near

Bluefields. The country's port authority estimates that Nicaragua could save $35 million in annual freight charges if it had an Atlantic port, since 40% of total imports arrive from the Atlantic and need to pass through the Panama Canal to reach the Pacific port at Corinto.

The government has supported the growth of local native handicraft because import restrictions have limited the supply of toys and gifts. With a small investment of $2,000 in loans to artisans for supplies, the government sponsored a huge outdoor artisans' market in Managua before Christmas 1981 at which $2 million worth of items were sold.[25]

The Government of National Reconstruction has admitted an over-emphasis on the public service sector to the detriment of industrial production. The Sandinistas intend to focus more on industrial production, which has suffered from worker-management conflicts and inefficiency in state-operated plants. Although the government has tried to keep the private sector content, it is suspicious of that sector's cooperation in U.S. sponsored destabilization plans. In July 1982, Nicaragua announced that it wouldn't permit COSEP (or the hierarchy of the Catholic Church) to receive $5 million in U.S. aid, charging that the money would be used for destabilization.[26]

It's the government's position that the business community has no right to demand more political power since it was not the bourgeoisie but Nicaragua's lower classes that liberated the country from Somoza. "This is a revolution of the vast majority," said junta member Daniel Ortega, "of the workers and peasants who produce all the country's wealth."[27]

Agriculture

Nicaragua differs politically with other Central American nations, but faces the same economic dependence on a few export crops. And while the value received for these traditional agricultural exports is declining, the cost of necessary imports like farm machinery and petroleum is rapidly increasing. The new government wants to turn around the balance of trade so that it can gain its economic independence. At a farm in Castillo Norte, a sign reads: "In 1977, one tractor cost 33,000 pounds of cotton or 139,400 pounds of sugar, or 9,800 pounds of coffee. In 1981, one tractor cost 47,600 pounds of cotton, 214,300 pounds of sugar, or 24,800 pounds of coffee."[28]

In desperate need for foreign exchange to pay its import bill and decrease its national debt, Nicaragua is encouraging the growth of its agro-export industry; but at the same time, it is planning for food self-sufficiency. Meat, coffee, sugar, cotton, and bananas are the main export crops of Nicaragua. Virtually all of the meat, sugar, and banana exports go directly to U.S. markets.

The Sandinista government has been giving special attention to cotton production. In 1981-82, planted cotton area doubled over 1979, but was still below pre-revolutionary levels. Lack of care during the insurrection caused lower-grade harvests in recent years. The government has encouraged export crop production through price supports, technical assistance, and aid for increased mechanization.[29]

The cattle industry has suffered in Nicaragua due to the contraband cattle trade. Over 79 million pounds of meat were exported in 1979, but a steady loss of cattle across the borders into Honduras and Costa Rica has reduced meat exports to 42 million pounds in 1980.[30] Also affecting the cattle market is the lack of qualified breeding technicians.

Nicaragua has 3,500 banana workers on 17 farms. Before 1979, these workers earned $3 a day and suffered from typhoid, hepatitis, tuberculosis, and pesticide poisoning.[31] About ten years ago, Standard Fruit set up production companies with local landlords to grow and sell bananas to Standard Fruit, a strategy of many large agri-business companies to minimize their risk of nationalization. Agriculture Minister Jaime Wheelock said, "Local owners were proprietors only in the technical sense and could have been expropriated by Standard at any time."

After the victory, Nicaragua joined the Union of Banana Exporting Countries (UPEB) and Comunbana and established an export tax of 50 cents a box. Standard Fruit reacted with sabotage and decapitalization, but the government worked with the company until the two parties reached an agreement in January 1981. The agreement specified that the company would be the sole buyer of the country's banana exports and that the government would buy out the company's investment over a five year period. "From now on," said Wheelock, "the relationship will be between partners, not boss and subordinates."[32]

INRA, the agricultural department, controls about 25% of Nicaragua's cultivated land. The majority of the cotton land is controlled by large producers, but INRA controls the export trade and 50% of the processing facilities. INRA owns 10% of the two million head of cattle, but owns 80% of the slaughterhouses. Only 15% of the coffee land belongs to INRA, while 70% of the processing facilities and all the coffee export trade are in government hands. Most grain and vegetable production comes from small and medium private farmers.[33]

The government has encouraged private producers and processors to remain in Nicaragua. The Nicaraguan Sugar Estates, which has financial ties to Bank of America, is the largest capitalist enterprise in Nicaragua. The company, which employs 10,000 workers in its production, milling, and processing facilities, reports no problems or complaints about the Sandinista government's agricultural programs.

The food import bill is a major problem in Nicaragua; the value in food imported from the United States jumped 227% in 1980.[35] Though agricultural production has been gradually increasing in Nicaragua, local production hasn't been able to meet the sharp jump in demand following the victory. The government is fostering increased production for local consumption through a series of incentives for private farmers such as the increased availability of consumer goods in the countryside in order to supply farmers with something to buy with their increased incomes. According to the Institute for Food Policy and Development, "Unlike many Third World countries, Nicaragua is producing more staple foods — up 15-25% over pre-revolutionary levels. People are eating better." One reason is that "since the victory over Somoza, over 12,000 formerly landless rural families have received land to grow food."[35]

"Unlike land reforms in many other countries," the Institute said, "the pragmatic Nicaraguan reform sets no ceilings on the size of landholdings. Even the very largest landowners can keep their land as long as they obey the laws governing wages and working conditions and do not rent it out." The Institute added, on a general note, that "the vision of many Sandinista leaders is that of a mixed economy in which 50% of the farmland will be independent cooperatives, 30% in private hands, and 20% government."[36]

Beginning its fourth year as the government of Nicaragua, the Sandinista leadership, while expressing continued support for a pluralistic economy, has made clear its commitment to the class nature of the revolution. Tomas Borge told a huge crowd gathered in Managua on May 1, 1982, "This revolution was made to fight the ideological and political contamination of the bourgeoisie and imperialism.... This revolution was made not to affirm the old society but to create a new one."[37]

References for Introductory Statistics

Business America, March 8, 1982; *Business Latin America*, July 7, 1982; Inter-American Development Bank, *Economic and Social Progress in Latin America 1980-81*; *Latin America Regional Report*; *Plain Speaking*, December 31, 1981; United Nations, *Monthly Bulletin of Statistics*, April 1982; U.S. Department of Commerce, *Overseas Business Reports — Market Profiles for Latin America*, May 1981.

REFERENCE NOTES

1. Yvonne Dilling and Philip Wheaton, *Nicaragua: A People's Revolution*, (Washington, DC: EPICA Task Force, 1980), pp. 1-2.
2. John Gerassi, "America's Hit List," *Mother Jones*, June 1981.
3. Penny Lernoux, *Cry of the People*, (Garden City, N.Y.: Doubleday, 1980), p. 81.
4. *Ibid.*
5. *El Brigadista* (Nicaragua, March 1980), cited in *NACLA*, May-June 1980.
6. George Black and Judy Butler, "Target Nicaragua," *NACLA*, January-February 1982, p. 41.
7. Cleto D. Giovanni, "U.S. Policy and the Marxist Threat to Central America," *The Heritage Foundation Backgrounder*, October 15, 1980, pp. 4-5.
8. *Washington Post*, March 10, 1982.
9. George Black, "Challenge of Reconstruction," *Nicaragua* (National Network in Solidarity with the Nicaraguan People), May-June 1982, p. 1.
10. *NACLA*, January-February 1982, p. 41.
11. "Nicaragua Sets Incentives to Demonstrate Support for Mixed Economy," *Business Latin America*, March 10, 1982, p. 77.
12. Interviews by Tom Barry, March 1982.
13. Charlie Roberts, "Nicaragua, the Unfolding Scene," *Multinational Monitor*, March 1980.
14. *Ibid.*
15. "Nicaragua," *Foreign Economic Trends*, November 1981, p. 5.
16. *NACLA*, January-February 1982, p. 41.
17. "Officials Tighten Everyone's Belts," *LARR*, September 10, 1981, p. 2.
18. "Sandinista Economics: Towards a New Nicaragua," *Dollars & Sense*, April 1982.
19. Business Perspectives in Latin America, Sub-Committee on Inter-American Affairs, House Foreign Affairs Committees.
20. Guy Gugliotta, "Sandinistas Extend Hand to Business," *Miami Herald*, February 16, 1982.
21. *NACLA*, January-February 1982, p. 4.
22. *Miami Herald*, February 16, 1982.
23. Information from COIP, March 1982.
24. Annie Street, "U.S. Company Has Poisoned Workers," *Multinational Monitor*, May 1981.
25. *Dollars & Sense*, April 1982.
26. "Nicaragua Stops Aid from the U.S." *Albuquerque Journal*, July 18, 1982, p. A-8.
27. *Barricada*, October 30, 1979, cited in *NACLA*, January-February 1982.
28. "The Revolution Was The Easy Part," *Food First*, 1982.
29. "Business Outlook: Nicaragua,' *Business Latin America*, May 19, 1982, p. 156.
30. *Foreign Economic Trends*, November 1981, p. 5.
31. "Nicaragua: The Banana Agreement," *NACLA*, March-April 1981.
32. *Ibid.*
33. *NACLA*, May-June 1980.
34. "U.S. Farm Exports Gain in Central America," *Foreign Agriculture*, October 1981, p. 20.
35. *Food First*, 1982.
36. *Ibid.*
37. Michael Baumann and Jane Harris, "May Day Marks Deepening Revolution," *Intercontinental Press*, May 10, 1982.

UNITED STATES BUSINESS IN NICARAGUA*

Agentes Internacionales

Agrícola San Enrique; *cattle production;*
LAAD equity

Alfredo Artiles

American Cyanamid
Cyanamid Inter-American;
pharmaceutical, cosmetic, and
veterinary product distribution

American Standard
Industria Cerámica Centroamericana;
sanitary equipment

Arthur Andersen & Company; *accounting*

BankAmerica
Bank of America; *banking*

Beatrice Foods
Química Stahl; *chemicals, leather,*
and plastic

The Borden Company
Química Borden Centroamericana;
chemicals

Bristol-Myers
Bristol-Myers de Centroamérica;
pharmaceutical supplies

Casa Comercial McGregor

Citicorp
Citibank; *banking*

Coca-Cola
Embotelladora Milca; *bottling plant*

Compañía Hotelera de Nicaragua; *hotel;*
ADELA equity

Compañía de Refrigeración Mobile

Coopers & Lybrand
Davila D. y Compañía, Oscar;
accounting

Cosco International
Industrias Unidas de Centroamérica;
flavorings and laxatives
Sabores Cosco de Centroamérica;
flavorings

Cotton States Chemical; *pesticide*
manufacturing and distribution

Cukra Development

Donkin y Arguello

ESB
Acumuladores Centroamericanos;
accumulators and batteries

Exxon
Esso Standard Oil
Essochem de Centroamérica;
chemical distribution

Firestone Tire & Rubber
Industrias Firestone

Fogel Commercial Refrigerator
Fogel de Nicaragua; *refrigeration*
equipment

H.B. Fuller
Distribuidora Comercial
Industrias Kativo de Nicaragua
Mercadeo Industrial

General Mills
Gem-Ina; *flour mill*
Panalimentos

The Gillette Company
Compañía Interamericana; *razor blade*
and cosmetic manufacturing

Hercules
Hercules de Centroamérica; *chemical*
manufacturing

Hokenberg Brothers
Desmotadora de Productores (DEPSA)

Hotel Ticomo

IBM World Trade Corporation; *business*
equipment

The Interpublic Group of Companies
Publicidad McCann-Erickson
Centroamericana; *advertising agency*

Irrigaciones y Perforaciones McGregor

ITR de Nicaragua

Kellwood
Kellwood de Nicaragua

Kem Manufacturing
Kem Centroamericana; *chemical*
product manufacturing and
distribution

Leigh Textile
Grasas y Aceites (GRACSA)

Manufacturera Centroamericana

Más x Menos de Nicaragua; *LAAD equity*

The Mennen Company
Mennen de Nicaragua; *toiletries*

*An indented item is a subsidiary, affiliate, or branch of the corporation immediately
above it.

Miles Laboratories
Miles de Nicaragua; *pharmaceutical manufacturing*

MJB
Café Soluble; *coffee*

Monroe
Hermoso Vigil

Monsanto
Monsanto Agrícola de Nicaragua; *chemical manufacturing*

Moore
Moore Business Forms de Nicaragua

Nabisco Brands
Industrias Nabisco Cristal
Pan American Standard Brands

Nicaragua Química

Pannell Kerr Forster & Company
Mendoza Yescas y Asociados, Armando

Peat, Marwick, Mitchell & Company; *accounting and auditing*

S.F. Pellas
Alf Pellas & Company; *auto parts*
Flor de Cana
Ingenio San Antonio
Nicaragua Sugar Estates

Pennwalt Chemical Corporation
Electroquímica Pennwalt; *caustic soda*

Price Waterhouse & Company; *accounting and auditing*

Productos Sanitarios de Nicaragua; *sanitary products; LAAD equity*

Ralston Purina
Nutrimentos Balanceados (NUBASA); *grain mill*

Sherwin-Williams
Sherwin-Williams de Centroamérica; *paint distribution*

Singer Manufacturing Company of New Jersey
Singer; *electric appliance distribution*

St. Regis Paper
Empaques Multiwall Ultrafort
Envases Industriales Nicaraguenses; *cardboard boxes*

Standard Oil of California
Compañía Petrolera Chevron; *oil exploration*

Stevie Togs
FREDONCO

Tenneco
Fertilizantes Superiores; *fertilizers*

Tennessee Handbags
Doña Cartera

Texaco
Texaco Caribbean; *oil exploration*

Textiles Confeccionados

Thornton, Richard

Transway International
Coordinated Caribbean Transport (CCT)
Tropigas, Division de Nicaragua

United Brands
Aceitera Corona
Polymer de Nicaragua

United Marketing

Van Leer Envases de Centroamérica

Xerox
Xerox de Nicaragua; *business machines*

REFERENCES

During the revolution many foreign investors left Nicaragua. Therefore only the most up-to-date sources were used.

ADELA, Annual Report, 1981; The Industrial Corporation of the People (COIP), March 1982; Latin American Agribusiness Development Corporation (LAAD), Annual Reports, 1976-1981; Overseas Private Investment Corporation (OPIC), Annual Reports, 1978-1981; United States Embassy in Nicaragua, "American Firms with Subsidiaries or Affiliates in Nicaragua," 1982; United States Embassy in Nicaragua, "Firms Operating in Nicaragua with American Capital," 1981.

METHODOLOGY
APPENDIX
INDEX

METHODOLOGY

The listing by country of Central American businesses with U.S. ownership is the most extensive compilation of its kind available. The listing names the branches, affiliates, and subsidiaries of U.S. corporations as well as local businesses that are partially or wholly owned by U.S. citizens. Commodity trading companies and large purchasing and processing companies like Procter & Gamble (Folgers) were not included in the listings. While these companies play an important part in the business activity of Central America, they often do not have direct investment in the region. The work of compiling this listing required trips to each Central American nation by the Resource Center staff and extensive library research in the United States as well as efforts to secure information through correspondence and phone interviews. The on-site work in Central America included visits to the U.S. embassies, the American Chambers of Commerce, and other business organizations. The research in the United States, conducted from May 1982 through August 1982, utilized all the standard business reference sources on U.S. corporations and relied on news sources for the most current information on business activity. Businesses were included only when there was some verification of their presence in a country after 1980. Phone directories, lists from the local chambers of commerce, and U.S. embassy lists were most helpful in providing up-to-date information. Company 10-K reports and annual reports were useful but by no means provided complete information about a company's operations. The annual reports of ADELA, the Overseas Private Investment Corporation (OPIC), and the Latin American Agribusiness Development Corporation (LAAD), were particularly useful in the identification of companies not listed in other sources. The reference journal, *Mergers and Acquisitions*, kept us up to date on who owns whom in the world of transnational corporations. Extensive company listings for Honduras and Belize provided by the U.S. State Department allowed us to include even the smallest U.S.-owned businesses in our lists for those two countries in this book. The lists for the other five countries do not contain as many smaller companies like small hotels and farms. The U.S. embassy lists for Nicaragua and El Salvador were the major references used for those two nations, where information about U.S. business activity becomes dated quickly. The table on page 232 indicates the number of companies by country and category of business.

Number of Companies by Country and by Category
from Resource Center Research

	Food	Finance	Manufacturing	Mineral	Chemical	Pharmaceutical	Service	Agriculture	Sales	Construction	TOTAL
Belize	7	1	2	6	1	1	15	18	4	1	56
Costa Rica	37	25	73	34	19	15	25	27	29	7	291
El Salvador	9	8	29	9	4	7	10	4	14	1	95
Guatemala	36	22	60	31	21	34	43	40	25	12	324
Honduras	30	18	57	34	2	5	33	35	29	8	251
Nicaragua	16	7	16	3	10	5	6	4	15	0	82
Panama	50	37	72	39	13	24	52	15	45	12	359
TOTAL	*185*	*118*	*309*	*156*	*70*	*91*	*184*	*143*	*161*	*41*	*1,458*

APPENDIX

Appendix I. U.S. Direct Investment by Country 1977
(millions $)

All Foreign Affiliates	Number Companies	Total Assets	Total Income	Net Income	Number Employees	U.S. Direct Investment
Belize	11	30	19	3	416	21
Costa Rica	113	426	469	15	22,524	178
El Salvador	67	281	463	32	9,614	79
Guatemala	134	755	735	4	22,904	155
Honduras	60	369	510	30	25,830	157
Nicaragua	70	527	463	32	11,084	108
Panama	266	8,873	2,361	472	23,073	2,442
Central America	*721*	*11,261*	*5,020*	*588*	*115,445*	*3,140*

Source: U.S. Department of Commerce, *U.S. Direct Investment Abroad 1977*, April 1981.

The U.S. Department of Commerce included the U.S. investment in all foreign affiliates where a U.S. owner controlled at least 10% of a corporation or business enterprise. Not included were affiliates having assets, sales or income less than $500,000.

Appendix II.

Dollars and Dictators Chronology 1900-1982

1901   United Fruit is the first transnational corporation to arrive in Guatemala.

1903   Senate of Colombia refuses to permit United States to build a canal through its territory of Panama. President Theodore Roosevelt supports a Panamanian revolt. Panama becomes independent and signs Canal Treaty with United States.

1904   Panama establishes a monetary system based on U.S. dollar.

1905   U.S. troops land in Honduras five times during next 20 years.

1908   U.S. troops land in Panama four times during next ten years.

1911   United States places Nicaragua under a customs receivership and controls Nicaragua's trade revenues for next 38 years.

1912   Over next 20 years U.S. Marines repeatedly occupy Nicaragua.

1914   Panama Canal completed.

1919   Unions from El Salvador, Nicaragua, and Honduras join short-lived Pan-American Federation of Labor which is sponsored by American Federation of Labor.

1920   President Coolidge announces Evart Doctrine to justify U.S. intervention in internal affairs of Latin America in order to protect U.S. foreign holdings.

1921   President Coolidge pressures Guatemala to overthrow President Carlos Herrera, enabling United Fruit to expand.

1926   For seven years, Augusto Sandino, "General of Free Men," leads strong opposition against U.S. Marines' occupation of Nicaragua.

1929   International Railways of Central America, a United Fruit affiliate, connects Guatemalan and Salvadoran railways. IRCA also operates banana railroads in Costa Rica and Honduras.

1929   Great Depression in United States adversely affects all Central American economies.

1931   New dictators Jorge Ubico of Guatemala and Carias Andino of Honduras receive immediate support of U.S. government. In El Salvador dictator Maximiliano Hernandez takes power.

1932   Farabundo Martí leads peasant uprising in El Salvador. U.S. warships stand by during the military massacre of Salvadoran peasants that follows.

1933   President Franklin Roosevelt announces Good Neighbor Policy for Latin America and declares that United States is opposed to armed intervention.

1933   Before U.S. Marines leave Nicaragua, United States sets up National Guard and appoints Somoza Garcia as commander-in-chief.

1945   U.S. government starts to provide credit for purchase of U.S. exports through provisions of Export-Import Bank Act.

1947   U.S.-sponsored Rio Pact stresses cooperation between United States and Latin America against external attack.

1948   An anti-communist revolution led by José Figueres and supported by United States is successful in Costa Rica. Figueres, three-time president of Costa Rica, later admits to his connections with CIA.

1948   President Truman sends first U.S. military training mission to El Salvador.

1948   Organization of American States (OAS) is founded.

1950   U.S. direct investment in Central America totals $313 million.

1951   U.S. Congress passes Mutual Security Act, which makes funds available to strengthen Latin American armies for hemispheric defense.

1951   Inter-American Regional Organization of Workers (ORIT) forms with backing of U.S. Department of State.

1953   Colon Free-Trade Zone in Panama is created from a proposal by a vice-president of National City Bank of New York.

1954   President Eisenhower approves Operation Success which allows CIA to direct coup d'etat in Guatemala.

1954   A successful strike by Honduran banana workers opens way for widespread organizing among other Honduran workers.

1957   President Eisenhower establishes Office of Public Safety (OPS) to train Latin American police.

1958   David Rockefeller initiates U.S. Inter-American Council to promote development of private sector in Latin America.

1959   Inter-American Development Bank forms to channel multilateral grants and loans to Latin America.

1959   Fidel Castro leads guerilla army to victory in Cuba.

1960   U.S. direct investment over last decade more than doubles to a new total of $747 million.

1960   United States uses Guatemala and Nicaragua to stage an invasion of Cuba.

1960   Panama Canal Zone becomes a key center for training in counterinsurgency.

1961   Central American Common Market (CACM) is established. U.S. corporate investment in Central America dramatically increases.

1961   Foreign Assistance Act states that U.S. aid should be used to assist U.S. economy.

1961   Agency for International Development (AID) is established.

1961   President Kennedy creates Alliance for Progress to promote economic development of Latin American countries.

1961   Central American Bank for Economic Integration (BCIE) is formed.

1961	OPS is transferred to AID and program expanded.
1962	National Sandinista Front for Liberation (FSLN) forms in Nicaragua.
1962	U.S.-sponsored Operation Brotherhood, forerunner to CONDECA, stages military exercises with participation by Honduras, Guatemala, Nicaragua, and El Salvador.
1962	American Institute for Free Labor Development (AIFLD) founded to "respond to threat of Castroite infiltration and eventual control of major labor movements within Latin America."
1964	U.S. suppression of Panama's Flag Riots which protest U.S. dominance in Panama leaves 28 dead and over 300 wounded.
1964	United States sponsors formation of CONDECA to coordinate Central American military action against internal subversion.
1964	ADELA forms "to promote economic and social progress in Latin America by encouraging development of the private enterprise sector."
1965	United Brands acquires Numar, a Costa Rican margarine plant. It continues to diversify its ownership along with two other banana companies, Standard Fruit and R.J. Reynolds.
1966	U.S. Special Forces coordinate Operation Guatemala, a counterinsurgency campaign which kills over 8,000 people.
1967	Association of American Chambers of Commerce in Latin America (AACCLA) is established.
1968	Salvadoran Communal Union (UCS) forms with AIFLD's assistance.
1968	General Omar Herrera Torrijos comes to power in Panama.
1969	U.S. government creates Inter-American Foundation to "strengthen the bonds of friendship" between Latin America and United States.
1970	U.S. direct investment over last decade more than doubles to a new total of $1,732 million.
1970	David Rockefeller-led Council of the Americas supersedes Council for Latin America and supports establishment of Panama's International Finance Center.
1970	International Finance Center is established in Panama City.
1970	U.S. corporations form Latin American Agribusiness Development Corporation (LAAD) to promote production of non-traditional exports from Latin America.
1971	Over next four years three separate guerilla organizations form in El Salvador.
1971	Overseas Private Investment Corporation (OPIC) is created to insure and guarantee U.S. investors.
1974	U.S. Congress abolishes OPS upon discovery that police are being trained in torture techniques.
1974	Five Central American countries form Union of Banana Exporting Countries (UPEB) to increase their control in banana market.

1975	In Honduras, United Brands pays a $1.25 million bribe to lower banana tax, and save company $7.5 million in taxes.
1975	Offshore light assembly industries start to locate in Central America because of cheap labor and tax incentives.
1975	Harkin Amendment states foreign assistance won't be sent to governments with gross human rights violations.
1977	Honduran soldiers arrive in Standard Fruit's railroad cars to destroy successful Las Isletas banana cooperative.
1977	Guatemala and El Salvador reject U.S. aid because of human rights attachments.
1977	Comunbana forms as marketing arm of UPEB. In Panama, United Brands refuses to load Comunbana ships and government threatens to nationalize United Brands acreage.
1979	Panama Canal Treaties establish joint United States-Panamanian control over Panama Canal.
1979	President Carter sets up airborne Caribbean Task Force.
1979	Nicaragua's FMLN triumphs over dictator Anastasio Somoza Debayle.
1980	U.S. direct investment over last decade more than doubles to a new total of $4,223 million.
1980	El Salvador's Archbishop Oscar Romero writes a letter to President Carter asking United States to stop military aid to El Salvador. A month later right-wing terrorists murder Romero.
1980	In Guatemala workers win a five year union struggle against Coca-Cola.
1980	Amigos del Pais and Guatemalan Freedom Foundation hire U.S. public relations firms to launch a campaign in United States praising Guatemalan government.
1980	AIFLD sponsors agrarian reform program in El Salvador.
1980	A coalition of over 50 mass organizations join together to form Revolutionary Democratic Front (FDR) in El Salvador.
1980	Farabundo Marti Liberation Front (FMLN) is established as umbrella organization for the five guerilla organizations of El Salvador.
1980	AID funds Caribbean/Central American Action (C/CAA) to promote private sector interest in region.
1980	Four U.S. churchwomen killed by military in El Salvador. United States stops military aid.
1980	Two guerilla organizations come in public view in Honduras.
1981 *Jan*	United States resumes military aid to El Salvador. Reagan bypasses Congress to send additional military aid to El Salvador.
Feb	United States sponsors a peace treaty between El Salvador and Honduras.

March United States suspends aid to Nicaragua claiming that Cuban arms are moving to El Salvador through Nicaragua.

July Panama's Torrijos dies in plane crash.

Aug A team of 21 U.S. military advisors, including four Green Berets, arrives in Honduras.

Aug Americas Society forms as an umbrella organization to coordinate activities of various institutions promoting private sector development in Latin America.

Sept Belize gains independence from United Kingdom.

Nov United States authorizes $19 million to CIA to destabilize Nicaraguan government.

Nov Suazo Cordova becomes president of Honduras and later appoints Colonel Gustavo Alvarez as commander-in-chief.

Dec U.S.-trained Salvadoran Brigade, Atlacatl, is responsible for murdering 1,000 civilians during search and destroy missions.

1982
Jan Reagan Administration begins bringing 1,600 Salvadoran soldiers and officers to United States for training.

Jan President Reagan proposes Caribbean Basin Initiative (CBI) which significantly increases U.S. economic aid to Central America. At same time he also proposes increases in military aid for Central America.

Jan With U.S. prodding, Costa Rica, El Salvador, and Honduras form Central American Democratic Community (CDC) to stimulate private sector development and to provide mutual aid in case of external aggression.

Feb In Guatemala, four main guerilla groups form Guatemalan National Revolutionary United (URNG).

March Military coup d'etat in Guatemala.

March Roberto D'Aubuisson becomes president of National Assembly and Alvarado Magana president of El Salvador.

May Luis Alberto Monge becomes president of Costa Rica, taking place of Rodrigo Carazo.

June General Efrain Rios Montt becomes president and commander-in-chief of Guatemala.

July Aristides Royo exits as president of Panama and former vice president Ricardo de la Espriella enters, marking a move to the right with increasing influence of the National Guard.

Aug UN High Commission on Refugees reports it has 287,000 registered refugees in Mexico and Central America.

Aug Congress passes a revised CBI proposal and additional military aid for Central America increasing fiscal year 1982 economic aid for Central America by $200 million and military aid by $12 million.

APPENDIX III. LAAD INVESTMENTS IN CENTRAL AMERICA
(thousands $)

COMPANY/BUSINESS	Equity	Loan	Total
COSTA RICA — *Current Investments*			
Ganadera Industrial (GISA); cattle	--	410	410
American Flower; cut flower growing	50	337	387
Ingenio Taboga; agriculture	--	750	750
Cañera Las Brisas; agriculture	--	250	250
Sánchez Cortez Hnos.; agriculture	--	750	750
La Rivera; agriculture.	--	250	250
Pozuelo Picasso; wood products.	200	200	400
Taylor & Associates of Costa Rica; food processing	200	251	451
Tenería Gisa; miscellaneous	200	--	200
Frigoríficos Técnicos; miscellaneous	200	--	200
Ganadera Chiamira; cattle	--	200	200
Foliage Incorporated; flowers and ornamental plants.	30	200	230
Rico Tico Alimentos; food processing	50	50	100
Banco de Créditos Agrícola de Cartago; miscellaneous	--	500	500
Banco de Costa Rica; miscellaneous	--	500	500
Ganadera San Jerónimo; cattle	--	350	350
Katojeke; cattle.	--	400	400
Alimentos de Costa Rica; grains.	--	230	230
Hacienda Las Delicias; cattle.	--	700	700
Inversiones Corobicí; cattle	--	600	600
Hacienda La Trampa; cattle	--	600	600
Agropecuaria Milwaukee; cattle.	--	220	220
Liga Agrícola de la Casa; food processing	--	1000	1000
	930	*8,748*	*9,678*
COSTA RICA — *Projected Investments***			
American Flower; cut flower & fern production			$ 200
American Flower; tree nursery			100
Foliage; ornamental plant production			100
Katojeke; cultivation of vegetables & spices			500
Rico Tico; processing of snack foods from coconut			200
Central Agrícola; seed production			600
Conservas del Campo; production of canned fruits and vegetables			1,000
Dos Pinos; milk and milk products processor			500
Cinta Azul; manufacture of pork products.			500
Plumrose; pork processing			750
			$4,450
EL SALVADOR — *Current Investments*			
Pavos; poultry.	--	160	160
Agrícola Salvadoreña; poultry.	--	120	120
Quality Foods de Centroamérica; food processing	240	--	240
Quiñónez Hermanos; food processing	80	320	400
Auto Ahorro; services	--	500	500
Procesadora Agrícola Salvadoreña; grains	200	--	200
Financiera Salvadoreña; services.	--	500	500
Financiera de Desarrollo; services.	--	500	500
Arrocera San Francisco; grains	--	500	500
Granja El Faro; poultry	--	400	400
	520	*3,000*	*3,520*

*Includes cumulative investment of LAAD through February 1981

**Includes LAAD investments projected for 1981-82

COMPANY/BUSINESS	Equity	Loan	Total

EL SALVADOR – *Projected Investments*

	Equity	Loan	Total
Agrícola Salvadoreña; poultry production.			300
Procesadora Salvadoreña; sesame decorticating			400
Cristiani; seed production			300
Arrocera San Francisco; rice production.			500
Mardones; small agricultural equipment manufacture			1,000
Productos Alimenticios; processing of annato and balsam for export.			600
Empresa Cocotera; coconut oil processing.			400
Cooperativa de Colmineras; honey production and export.			200
Cordelera Salvamex; henequen processing for export.			1,000
Cooperativa La Calzada; diversified agricultural cultivation			200
Cooperativa San Isidro; diversified agricultural cultivation			200
Cooperativa Tutulepeque; diversified agricultural cultivation			200
Productores de Bálsamo; balsa wood exporters			100
CLARISA (Cooperative); cotton cloth for export			200
Atarraya; shrimp processing			500
Mariscos; shrimp processing			500
			$6,600

GUATEMALA – *Current Investments*

	Equity	Loan	Total
Horacio Villavicencio y Compañía; cattle	--	255	255
Algodonera Guatemalteca; vegetable oils.	--	750	750
Industrias Tropicales; vegetable oils.	--	200	200
Las Flores; flowers and ornamental plants	--	242	242
Sistemas AQ; services.	--	130	130
Técnica Universal; farm equipment.	--	750	750
Arrocera Los Corrales y Compañía; grains.	–	1,455	1455
Agroquímicas de Guatemala; grains	--	1,000	1000
Industrias Sésamo; grains.	175	375	550
Jardines Mil Flores; flowers & ornamental plants	--	160	160
Promotora Agrícola Básico Ltda.; fruits and vegetables.	--	60	60
Finca Las Fuentes; vegetable oils	--	100	100
Compañía de Distribución Centroamericana (CODICASA); services	78	219	298
Grandel; food processing.	100	60	160
Finca Variedades; vegetable oils.	--	160	160
Remote Sensing Engineering Ltd.; services.	--	80	80
Los Pinos; fruits and vegetables	15	--	15
Alimentos Congelados Montebello, S.A. (ALCOSA); food processing.	--	518	518
Compañía Comercial e Industrial de Supertiendas; services.	110	--	110
Empresa Cucuchan; fruits and vegetables	--	80	80
Ganadería Sta. Lucrecia; vegetable oils.	350	--	350
Asociación de Productores de Aceites Esenciales (APAE); vegetable oils.	--	150	150
Manuel Ralda e Hijos; cattle.	--	200	200
Neil Potter P.; cattle.	--	300	300
Agrícola La Primavera; fruits and vegetables.	--	106	106
Conservas de Centroamérica; food processing	--	400	400
Comercial Agrícola El Escobillo; cattle	--	150	150
Desarrollo Ganadero Chiuihuitán; cattle	--	500	500
Ramiro Castillo y Asociados; services.	--	468	468
Inaflora; flowers and ornamental plants	--	430	430
Hernán Roldán Castañeda; fruits & vegetables.	--	26	26

COMPANY/BUSINESS	Equity	Loan	Total
Agroinversiones; flowers & ornamental plants.	--	125	125
Plantaciones Salamá; fruits and vegetables	--	45	45
Raimundo Riojas; grains	--	500	500
Proyectos Alimenticios; services.	--	81	81
Fomento de Inversiones y Arriendos; services	--	200	200
Fca. Armenia y Anexos; agriculture	--	400	400
Compañía Agrícola Pachonté; vegetable oils.	--	600	600
Alimentos Regia; vegetable oils	--	200	200
Agrorecursos; fruits and vegetables	--	170	170
Internacional de Comercio; services.	200	--	200
Vegetales R y S; fruits and vegetables	--	35	35
Agricultores Productores de Aceites Esenciales (APAESA); vegetable oils	--	200	200
	1,028	*11,880*	*12,909*

GUATEMALA — *Projected Investments*

APAESA; growing of essential oil grasses and oil extraction			800
Promotora Agrícola Básico; cultivation of fruits and vegetables			100
Xelac; cheese products			300
Industrias Sésamo; sesame decorticating			500
To be identified; small machinery manufacturing.			400
Inaflora; ornamental plant cultivation			400
Agro Inversiones; ornamental plant cultivation			200
Finca "Panamá"; tea cultivation (small tea grower program)			600
ALCOSA; frozen food processing.			500
To be determined; new vegetable freezing plant.			500
Finca Armenia; cardamom growing & processing			200
Wilmeth; rice and corn seed production			500
Molinos Modernos; wheat growing and milling			1,000
			$6,000

HONDURAS — *Current Investments*

	Equity	Loan	Total
Compañía Agrícola Industrial (CAICESA); vegetable oils	250	---	250
Fomento Internacional; services.	--	150	150
Astro Agrícola; agriculture	--	750	750
Líneas Aéreas Nacionales; miscellaneous.	50	--	50
International Wood Products; wood products	206	--	206
Mejores Alimentos de Honduras; food processing. . . .	298	157	455
Agrícola de Honduras; fruits & vegetables	--	295	295
Banco La Capitalizadora Hondureña (BANCAHSA); miscellaneous	--	400	400
Empacadora de Carnes Carnilandia; food processing	--	100	100
Banco Financiera Hondureña; miscellaneous	--	500	500
Leche y Derivados (LEYDE); food processing.	275	--	275
Compañía Azucarera Hondureña; agriculture	--	500	500
Fábrica de Muebles Contessa; wood products	--	500	500
Granja Avila; poultry	--	495	495
Pastificios Hondureños; food processing	--	175	175
Industrias Molineras; food processing.	--	850	850
Empacadora Alus; food processing	--	800	800
Probise; cattle	--	200	200
	1,079	*5,872*	*6,951*

HONDURAS — *Projected Investments*

Hermacasa; manufacture of farm tools			200
La Corona; manufacture of small agricultural equipment			500
Leche y Derivados; milk and dairy products.			400

COMPANY/BUSINESS	Equity	Loan	Total
Mejores Alimentos; canned food production			600
Granja Avila; egg production			200
To be determined; grapefruit cultivation.			400
Alcon; processing of corn-based animal feeds			800
COHDEFOR; gum resin processing.			300
CONADI; warehousing.			750
			$4,150

NICARAGUA — *Current Investments*

	Equity	Loan	Total
Empacadora Nicaraguense; cattle	--	300	300
Haciendas Ganaderas; cattle	--	200	200
Más x Menos de Nicaragua; services.	71	--	71
Industrias Almolonca; food processing.	--	340	340
Productos Sanitarios de Nicaragua (PROSAN); miscellaneous	200	225	425
Hielera Sequeira; miscellaneous	--	200	200
Atlantic Coast Chemical (ATCHEMCO); miscellaneous	--	500	500
Agrícola San Enrique; cattle.	400	--	400
Instituto de Fomento Nacional (INFONAC); miscellaneous	--	500	500
Mayorga Hidalgo Compañía; cattle	--	400	400
Mántica Berio; grains	--	300	300
	671	2,965	3,636

NICARAGUA — *Projected Investments*

	Total
ATCHEMCO; production of wood resin, turpentine and pine oil	400
Tip Top; poultry and egg production.	300
Mántica Berio; sesame decorticating	200
Ifrugalasa; canned fruit and vegetable production.	700
Prosan; manufacture of sanitary items from rejected cotton. . .	200
Inpornicsa; hog breeding and pork production	400
Hielera Sequeira; ice production for use by fishermen and market stalls	100
Amolonca; frozen vegetables production.	500
Funde; small loans to small agriculturalists	500
Hercasa; insecticide production	500
	$3,800

PANAMA — *Current Investments*

	Equity	Loan	Total
American Flower Shippers; cut flower growing	50	--	50
Corporación Agropecuario; cattle production	n/a	--	n/a
Taylor & Associates; beef marketing	251	--	251
	301	--	301

PANAMA — *Projected Investments*

	Total
La Castellana; pork processing.	800
Fiduciaria Administrativa; refrigerated warehouse	250
Grupo Hernandez; warehouse	400
Agrícola Industrial; hogs	100
Tesko; rice	315
Punta Los Micos; cattle.	120
Avipecuaria Industrial; boilers.	1,000
Central Agrícola; grain processing.	1,000
	$3,985

Source: ROCAP Agribusiness Employment/Investment Promotion Project Paper: AID/ LAC/P-076, 1981; *LAAD Annual Reports*

Appendix IV. U.S. Military and Economic Aid 1981-83
(thousands $)

TOTAL: $748
Peace Corps: 748

TOTAL: $10,984
ESF: 10,000
Peace Corps: 958
IMET: 26

TOTAL: $1,204
Peace Corps: 1,104
IMET: 100

1981   1982   1983

U.S. Aid to Belize 1981 - 83

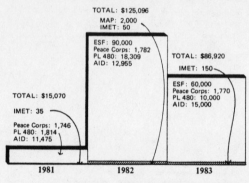

TOTAL: $125,096
MAP: 2,000
IMET: 50
ESF: 90,000
Peace Corps: 1,782
PL 480: 18,309
AID: 12,955

TOTAL: $86,920
IMET: 150
ESF: 60,000
Peace Corps: 1,770
PL 480: 10,000
AID: 15,000

TOTAL: $15,070
IMET: 35
Peace Corps: 1,746
PL 480: 1,814
AID: 11,475

1981   1982   1983

U.S. Aid to Costa Rica 1981 - 83

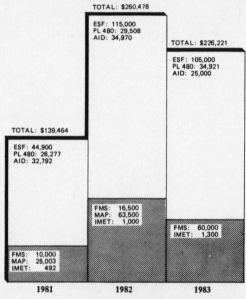

TOTAL: $260,478
ESF: 115,000
PL 480: 29,508
AID: 34,970

TOTAL: $226,221
ESF: 105,000
PL 480: 34,921
AID: 25,000

TOTAL: $139,464
ESF: 44,900
PL 480: 26,277
AID: 32,792

FMS: 16,500
MAP: 63,500
IMET: 1,000

FMS: 60,000
IMET: 1,300

FMS: 10,000
MAP: 25,003
IMET: 492

1981   1982   1983

U.S. Aid to El Salvador 1981 - 83

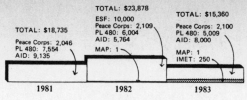

U.S. Aid to Guatemala 1981 - 83

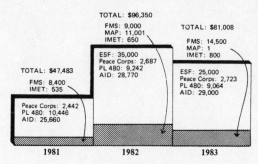

U.S. Aid to Honduras 1981 - 83

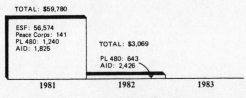

U.S. Aid to Nicaragua 1981 - 83

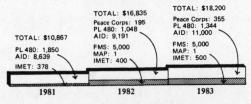

U.S. Aid to Panama 1981 - 83

MILITARY AID:
    FMS — Foreign Military Sales Financing
        Program
    MAP — Military Assistance Program
    IMET — International Military Educa-
        tion and Training Program

ECONOMIC AID:
    ESF — Economic Support Fund
    Peace Corps
    PL 480 — Food for Peace
    AID — Development Assistance

Note: 1983 figures are proposed amounts.

Sources: House of Representatives, *Foreign Assistance and Related Programs Appro-priations for 1983, Part 6,* February 1982; Congressional Quarterly, *Weekly Report,* August 21, 1982.

Appendix V.

Transnationally Speaking . . .

The following is a compilation of what the Resource Center considers to be the most important U.S. corporations in Central America because of the size of their operations and their presence in a number of countries.

	Guatemala	Nicaragua	El Salvador	Costa Rica	Panama	Honduras	Belize
BankAmerica	•	•	•	•	•	•	
Borden	•	•		•	•		
Castle & Cooke				•	•	•	•
Chase Manhattan			•	•	•	•	•
Citicorp	•	•	•	•	•	•	
Coca Cola	•	•	•	•	•		
Colgate Palmolive	•			•	•	•	
Exxon	•	•	•	•	•	•	
Goodyear	•			•	•		
Nabisco (Standard Brands)	•	•	•	•	•		
Pepsico	•			•	•		
R J Reynolds	•			•	•	•	
Standard Oil of California	•	•	•	•	•	•	
Texaco	•	•	•	•	•	•	
United Brands	•	•		•	•	•	

REFERENCES

CDE Stock Ownership Fortune 500 Directory 1981: for stock ownership information. *Forbes,* May 10, 1982: for ranking, assets, or sales when unavailable from *Fortune. Fortune,* May 3, 1982: for ranking, assets, or sales. *Moody's,* 1981: for additional information. *Everybody's Business: An Almanac — the Irreverent Guide to Corporate America* (Harper & Row, 1980): for much of the information in the Top Corporations Section. *Everybody's Business* is an excellent resource for corporate data, history, and current activities.

BANKAMERICA

BankAmerica Center
San Francisco, CA 94104

Assets: $121.6 billion

Rank in Own Industry*
Banking: 1

Brand Names
Bank of America

Top Three Stockholders
BankAmerica
J.P. Morgan
Citicorp

BankAmerica is a huge presence in Central America, particularly in Guatemala where it is the largest private creditor and ranks second only to the government as a source of capital for the agro-export sector. It has received flack from shareholders about its extensive holdings and loans in South Africa, as well as its connections with the military dictatorship in Guatemala. Keith Parker, manager of the Bank of America in Guatemala, has a solution for the country's problems: "What they should do is declare martial law. There, you catch somebody, they go to a military court. Three colonels are sitting there, you're guilty, you're shot. It works very well."

*All ranking from Fortune, May 3, 1982, unless otherwise noted.

BORDEN

277 Park Avenue
New York, NY 10017

Sales: $4.4 billion

National Rank: 85

Rank in Own Industry
Cheese: 2
Dairy industry: 3

Top Three Stockholders
Teledyne
Batterymarch Financial Management
Northwest Bancorporation

Brand Names
Lady Borden Ice Cream
Eagle Condensed Milk
Cracker Jack
Wyler's soup and soft drink mixes
RealLemon
Bama jams, jellies and fruit drinks
Elmer's glue
Lite-line
Mystik Tapes
Krylon spray paints
Sterling office accessories

Borden owns 48 food and dairy plants and 49 chemical facilities overseas, as well as the largest commercial bakery in West Germany and Denmark's Cocio chocolate milk company. 20% of Borden's business is done outside of the U.S. The company is now expanding into oil and natural gas.

CASTLE & COOKE

130 Merchant Street
Honolulu, HI 96813

Sales: $1.8 billion

National Rank (Forbes): 343

Rank in Own Industry
Bananas: 1
Lettuce: 1
Pineapples: 1
Tuna: 3

Brand Names
Bud of California produce
Dole bananas and pineapples
Bumble Bee seafoods
Royal Alaskan seafoods
Pool Sweep swimming pool cleaner

Castle and Cooke were two Christian missionaries who made a fortune in Hawaii and soon expanded their interests throughout the world. The company is prominent in Central America, owning 4800 acres in Costa Rica and 148,000 acres in Honduras. In 1976, it transferred its railroad network in Honduras to the government, which allowed the company to continue operating the railroad and to retain title to all rolling stock.

CHASE MANHATTAN

1 Chase Manhattan Plaza
New York, NY 10081

Assets: $77.8 billion

Rank in Own Industry
Banking: 3

Top Three Stockholders
Chase Manhattan
Rockefeller Family Interests
Bankers Trust New York

The third largest U.S. bank and a large shareholder in many of the biggest transnationals, Chase Manhattan specializes in helping transnationals, particularly oil companies, move their money around the world to get the best from fluctuations in currency markets. The company has exercised its influence over foreign policy through the leadership of its former chair David Rockefeller in such groups as the Trilateral Commission, the Council of Foreign Relations, and the Americas Society.

CITICORP

309 Park Avenue
New York, NY 10043

Assets: $119 billion

Rank in Own Industry
Banking: 2

Brand Names
Citibank

Top Three Stockholders
J.P. Morgan & Company
First Boston
Rowe Price & Associates

One of the leading private creditors in Central America, Citicorp is the largest U.S. lender to South Africa. Citicorp holds over 4% of all money on deposit with U.S. banks. The company was the first U.S. national bank to open a foreign branch when they established a branch in Buenos Aires in 1914. The bulk of the company's deposits are overseas, where loans are usually large ones made to governments and transnational companies.

COCA-COLA

310 North Avenue
Atlanta, GA 30313

Sales: $6.1 billion

National Rank: 58

Rank in Own Industry
Soft drinks: 1
Citrus drinks: 1
Wine: 5

Top Three Stockholders
Woodruff Family Interests
Trust Company of Georgia
J.P. Morgan & Company

Brand Names
Coca-Cola
TAB
Sprite
Fanta
Mr. Pibb
Mello Yello
Fresca
Minute Maid
Hi-C
Snow Crop
Maryland Club
Taylor Wines

Coke is sold in 135 countries; sales outside the U.S. accounted for 46% of revenues and 61% of profits in 1978. The company buys 10% of all the sugar sold in the U.S. to make their product, which is 99.8% sugar. Each 12 ounce can of Coke contains 65 milligrams of caffeine. In 1978, the average consumption of soft drinks was 36 gallons, while the average consumption of milk was only 25 gallons. Working for Coca-Cola is probably as much a hazard to one's health as drinking it. Union leaders at Coca-Cola's plant in Guatemala were assassinated in the late 1970s by death squads.

COLGATE-PALMOLIVE

300 Park Avenue
New York, NY 10022

Sales: $5.3 billion

National Rank: 72

Rank in Own Industry
Rice: 1
Soap and detergent: 2
Toothpaste: 2
Adhesive bandages: 2
Shaving cream: 2

Top Three Stockholders
Helena Rubinstein Family Interests
Citicorp
Charles A. Collis

Brand Names
Colgate toothpaste and dental products
Ultra-Brite toothpaste
Hand-i-Wipes
Curity first-aid products
Curad first-aid products
Helena Rubinstein cosmetics
Irish Spring soap
Palmolive soap
Fab laundry detergent
Dynamo laundry detergent
Ajax cleanser
Water Maid rice products
Etonic golf and running shoes

Colgate owns and leases 31.7 million square feet of manufacturing, distribution, research, and office facilities around the world. It markets in 58 countries and exports to 70 more countries. The company does more than half its business overseas, with the foreign sales generating three-quarters of the profits.

EXXON

1251 Avenue of the Americas
New York, NY 10020

Sales: $108.1 billion

National Rank: 1

Rank in Own Industry
Oil: 1
Retail gasoline sales: 1
Natural gas: 1
Shipping: 1

Top Three Stockholders
Exxon
Rockefeller Family Interests
Chase Manhattan

Brand Names
Exxon
Esso (outside the U.S.)
Uniflo motor oil
Vydec text-editing system
Zilog microcomputers
Qyx typewriters
Qwip telephone facsimile devices

Exxon's annual sales roughly match the Gross National Products of countries like Mexico, Sweden, and Iran. Exxon brings in $10 million in sales an *hour*. Its 65,600 gas stations (known as Esso outside the U.S.) around the world sell gas to six million customers every day. The Rockefeller family dominates the Exxon empire. In a 1968 tour of Latin America, Nelson Rockefeller was driven out by crowds angered by the Rockefellers' extensive economic control of the region.

GOODYEAR

1144 E. Market Street
Akron, OH 44316

Sales: $9.2 billion

National Rank: 38

Rank in Own Industry
Tires: 1

Top Three Stockholders
Batterymarch Financial Management
Capital Group
TIAA-CREF

Brand Names
Goodyear tires
Kelly-Springfield tires
Lee tires

Called "The Brute" by other rubber companies because of its high-powered marketing strategies, Goodyear is the top seller of tires in the U.S. Goodyear operates on the "runaway shop" premise, having closed its factory in Akron, Ohio, to avoid union demands and headed south for cheaper wages. In 1977, the Securities and Exchange Commission accused Goodyear of using slush funds for foreign pay-offs and illegal political contributions. One such fund was in Guatemala, where a Goodyear subsidiary had a $50,000 fund that wasn't recorded on its books for use in payments to government officials in Guatemala, Nicaragua, and El Salvador.

NABISCO BRANDS

East Hanover, NJ 07936

Sales: $5.8 billion

National Rank: 60

Rank in Own Industry
Cookies: 1
Crackers: 1
Margarine: 1
Nuts: 1
Yeast: 1
Baking: 2

Top Three Stockholders
Horizon Bancorp
Rosenhaus, Matthew B. Family
  & Associates
Wisconsin Investment Board

Brand Names
Oreo cookies
Fig Newton cookies
Chips Ahoy cookies
Nabisco Shredded Wheat cereal
Premium Saltines
Wheat Thin crackers
Mister Salty pretzels
Junior Mints
Milk-Bone dog biscuits
Geritol vitamins
Sominex sleep aid
Acu-Test in-home pregnancy test kit
Rose Milk skin-care products
Aqua Velva men's toiletries

Nabisco's ten U.S. plants turn out one billion pounds of cookies and crackers a year. In July 1981, Nabisco merged with Standard Brands, which does a third of its business outside the U.S. and owns substantial interests in the liquor industry.

PEPSICO

New York, NY 10577

Sales: $7.0 billion

National Rank: 49

Rank in Own Industry
Snack foods: 1
Sporting goods: 1
Soft drinks: 2
Fast foods: 4

Top Three Stockholders
Sarofim (Fayez) & Company
Rowe Price & Associates
Wisconsin Investment Board

Brand Names
Pepsi-Cola
Mountain Dew
Fritos
Chee-tos
Doritos
Lay's
Taco Bell
Pizza Hut
North American Van Lines
Wilson sporting goods
Pro Staff golf balls
Chris Evert Autograph tennis rackets

There's more to the Pepsi Challenge than a brand of sugar water. Pepsi not only is the second largest soft drink manufacturer but also is the largest maker of sporting goods and ranks as the fourth largest fast-food server. As for beverages, Pepsi has cut down Coca-Cola's lead from 20 to one in overseas markets to two to one in twenty years. In 1980, workers at a PepsiCo trucking firm charged that of 820 long-distance drivers employed, only five were Black and eight Hispanic. Pepsi settled the law suit with a payment of $2.7 million in damages to 82 blacks denied jobs.

R.J. REYNOLDS

Reynolds Boulevard
Winston-Salem, NC 27102

Sales: $9.8 billion

National Rank: 32

Rank in Own Industry
Cigarettes: 1
Container shipping: 1
Canned fruits and vegetables: 1

Top Three Stockholders
Wachovia
Dupont Family Interests
Mercantile Bankshares

Brand Names
Winston cigarettes
Camel cigarettes
Vantage cigarettes
Prince Albert tobacco
Del Monte products
Hawaiian Punch drink
Chun King chinese food
Patio mexican food

In and out of tangles with the Securities Exchange Commission, R.J. Reynolds has been involved with illegal political contributions and objectionable corporate payments. Its subsidiary Del Monte, purchased in 1979, had an equally dubious reputation before it joined the Reynolds flock. In 1975, the *Wall Street Journal* reported a $500,000 payment to a Guatemalan "business consultant" who negotiated a deal with the Guatemalan government that allowed Del Monte to acquire a 55,000 acre banana plantation despite initial government opposition. Del Monte produces one out of every six cans of fruit and vegetables that pass through the supermarket checkstands of the U.S.

STANDARD OIL COMPANY OF CALIFORNIA

225 Bush Street
San Francisco, CA 94104

Sales: $44.2 billion

National Rank: 5

Rank in Own Industry
Oil: 3
Retail gas sales: 7

Top Three Stockholders
Midland Bank Group
Rockefeller Family Interests
Sarofim (Fayez) & Company

Brand Names
Chevron
Standard
Ortho chemicals

Standard Oil of California sells gasoline at 14,000 filling stations in the U.S., Canada, Central America, Puerto Rico, and Tahiti. Chairman Harold J. Haynes is one of the top ten highest paid executives in the U.S. While Haynes complains of often being accused and maligned, critics say that the company's reputation is well-deserved, pointing to 147 violations of federal drilling regulations in 1970 and $156 million in unpaid taxes in 1977.

TEXACO

2000 Westchester Avenue
White Plains, NY 10650

Sales: $57.6 billion

National Rank: 4

Rank in Own Industry
Oil: 2

Top Three Stockholders	**Brand Names**
Manufacturers Hanover	Fire Chief
TIAA-CREF	Sky Chief
Union National Bank of Pittsburgh	Havoline

Texaco's rude treatment of the Honduran government over its oil refinery is just one action in a long tradition of rotten deeds. Texaco sold $6 million worth of oil on credit to Spanish dictator Franco in violation of the neutrality act. The company shipped oil to Germany after the outbreak of World War II, and the company president became a courier for Hitler's regime. Texaco is disliked even among its own. "If I were dying in a Texaco filling station," a Shell executive said, "I'd ask to be dragged across the road."

UNITED BRANDS

1217 Avenue of the Americas
New York, NY 10020

Sales: $4.1 billion

National Rank: 92

Rank in Own Industry
Bananas: 2
Meat packing: 3
Food processing: 7

Top Three Stockholders	**Brand Names**
	Chiquita bananas
Lindner Family Group-American Financial	E-Z Beef
Milstein, Seymour & Paul Family Interests	Full-O-Life plants
Fisher, Max M. Family & Associates	A & W restaurant & rootbeer

United Brands has helped shape the history of the Central American countries where it is the largest private landowner. In addition to assisting in coups, using bribes to lower taxes, and attempting to destabilize governments it disfavors, United Fruit gained a reputation for its unusual advertising campaigns. In the 1950s, Miss Chiquita Banana had a popular song in the hit parade and regularly danced with a banana United Fruit described as "a good eight inches along the outer curve, at least 1¼ inches across the middle, with the peel fitting tightly... sleek and firm." In the same era, United Fruit produced a promotional film called "Why the Kremlin Loves Bananas." In the early 1960s, United Brands furthered its anti-communist campaign by supplying two of its ships for the Bay of Pigs invasion.

INDEX

LATIN AMERICAN TITLES FROM ZED PRESS

POLITICAL ECONOMY

DONALD HODGES AND ROSS GANDY
Mexico 1910–1982:
Reform or Revolution?
(New, updated edition)
Hb and Pb

GEORGE BECKFORD AND MICHAEL WITTER
Small Garden, Bitter Weed:
Struggle and Change in Jamaica
Hb and Pb

LIISA NORTH
Bitter Grounds:
Roots of Revolt in El Salvador
Pb

CONTEMPORARY HISTORY/REVOLUTIONARY STRUGGLES

GEORGE BLACK
Triumph of the People:
The Sandinista Revolution in Nicaragua
Hb and Pb

WOMEN

LATIN AMERICAN AND CARIBBEAN WOMEN'S COLLECTIVE
Slaves of Slaves:
The Challenge of Latin American Women
Hb and Pb

MIRANDA DAVIES
Third World — Second Sex:
Women's Struggles and National Liberation
Hb and Pb

MARGARET RANDALL
Sandino's Daughters:
Testimonies of Nicaraguan Women in Struggle
Pb

BONNIE MASS
Population Target:
The Political Economy of Population Control in Latin America
Pb

JUNE NASH AND HELEN ICKEN SAFA (EDITORS)
Sex and Class in Latin America:
Women's Perspectives on Politics, Economics and the Family in the Third
World
Pb

INTERNATIONAL RELATIONS/IMPERIALISM

DAVID STOLL
Fishers of Men or Founders of Empire:
The Wycliffe Bible Translators in Latin America
Hb and Pb

JAMES PETRAS ET AL
Class, State and Power in the Third World
With Case Studies of Class Conflict in Latin America
Hb

Zed press titles cover Africa, Asia, Latin America and the Middle East, as well as general issues affecting the Third World's relations with the rest of the world. Our Series embrace: Imperialism, Women, Political Economy, History, Labour, Voices of Struggle, Human Rights and other areas pertinent to the Third World.

You can order Zed titles direct from Zed Press, 57 Caledonian Road, London, N1 9DN, U.K.